HI...

Idukki Di...

0   6·25 Kms.   12·9 Kms.

E V I C O L A M   T A L U K

2

Village

...lai

= To Udumalpet

Nachivayal Village

= To Kanthallur

PAMBUMALLAY

Kanthallur
Village

Kottakombu Village

GUNDUMALLAY

CHUNDAVURRAI

Vattavada
Village

KUNDALY

E.P.Puram

CHITTAVURRAI

To Kodaikanal

YELLAPATTY

Tea Station

...ro Project

ARIVIKAD

Kottagudi   Village

UTHAMAPALAYAM
TALUK

Misappuli Malai
▲ 2640

M A D U R A I
D I S T R I C T

TIGUDI

SILENT VALLEY

CHIKULAM

Chinnakanal Village

...nad Malai

PERIAKANAL

T A L U K

To Kumali, Madurai etc.

M B A N S H O L A

Reference

Tata-Finlay Estates.........	
Other Estates...............	
Government Lands.........	
Factory...................	

A TIGER'S WEDDING

my childhood in exile

by
Isla Blair

JULIAN CALDER PUBLISHING

First published in 2011
by Julian Calder Publishing
7 Nepean Street
London SW15 5DW

Text and photographs © Isla Blair 2011

© Designed and produced by Julian Calder Publishing Ltd

Printed and bound by Butler Tanner & Dennis Ltd

ISBN 78-0-9553253-2-8

www.juliancalderpublishing.com

TO FIONA

What an older sister doesn't know
is that she has a fan for life.

Acknowledgements

There are many people who have helped me with this book to whom I owe thanks.

Geoffrey Palmer for encouraging me to write it. My literary agent, Gordon Wise, for his persistence, patience and belief in me and the book. My editor, Gillian Stern who inspired, cajoled and encouraged me with unaccountable optimism. Jacquetta Pease for her patient work through several drafts. Bill and Jean Henderson, Paddy and Alice Lappin, Drew Cameron, Bruce Duncan, Susanna Rook and Juliet Clough for their Indian stories. Duncan Gilmour of James Finlay Ltd for his co-operation. Clare Paterson and James Finlay and Co Ltd at Glasgow University of Glasgow Archive Services for their permissions.

I am grateful to the Enitharmon Press for permission to use a quote from *Walking Away* by C. Day Lewis (*Selected Poems*, Enitharmon Press 2004).

My publishers Julian Calder and Clare Harington for their attention to detail, their stylish, artistic eye. Ali Muirden and Lorelei King for their professionalism, enthusiasm and confidence. Sasha Behar for her cogent questions.

And then my family: Julian and Jamie Glover for their constructive criticism, encouragement, support and belief. And, of course, my parents whose company I miss always, and my sister Fiona, whose memories, while her own, coincide with mine and whose friendship has sustained me all my life.

Some names in this book have been changed.

Contents

exile – *[eg–zahyl, ek–sahyl]* – an unwilling separation from home

ONE

Telling the Bees

I banged my sandals together to shake out any cockroaches or scorpions, the gesture an automatic reflex, like saying "bless you" when someone sneezed. I pulled them on and ran after Fiona, my older sister, who I knew had started the day's little rituals and routines without me. I followed her like a shadow.

I was still in my cotton pyjamas, rolling up the legs as I scrambled down the steps of the verandah and out to the bees. There was a little wooden hive for them with a gently sloping roof painted white, the brittle paint coming off in my fingers when I picked at it. Fiona was already there, in her pyjamas and white plimsolls, stretching out her hands for any of the stray buzzing creatures to land on her. Neither of us were afraid of bees; they only stung when alarmed and besides they held our secrets – the big ones and the little ones. Our mother had told us that the bees had to know all the significant things that happened in our lives, otherwise they'd feel insulted and fly away – like when Fiona was born and when Mummy was expecting me, or when the Boy's fifth child, a little girl, had simply not woken up from sleep one day. I had told them how desolate and lonely I felt when Fiona had been sent away to school, how the pain in my chest had become like a solid rock that threatened to rise up into my throat and choke me.

I was born in Bangalore, South India, where my father was stationed during the war in the last, dying days of the Raj.

He was a tea planter in Kerala, as was his father before him, and I lived there with him and my sister, Fiona – three and a half years older than me – my mother and our beloved ayah. In fact, our Raj days were very much alive, golden, secure, full of sunshine and laughter with the scent of the pine and eucalyptus in the air and the ever present tea and far away, the trumpeting of elephants.

There was a bubbly feeling inside me, part excitement, part apprehension – because I knew things were about to change. We had been telling the bees for days now that we were "Going Home." They were probably heartily sick of hearing about it, but we told them again anyway. We always started our days with a visit to the bees, not in the monsoon, of course; the leeches put us off, as we knew they would be lying in wait for us, creeping over our socks and into our shoes. The monsoon and the dry season governed and set out our days…days that had a routine to them, punctured only by little unexpected happenings.

There had recently been a large, unexpected happening in the shape of a seven foot perria pamba – python – thankfully dead, which we had seen carried between two poles by a group of six excitedly chattering men. Daddy came out as the creature was deposited on the steps of the verandah. He thanked the men, paid them what was expected, and remarked on the python's beautiful markings. It didn't look very beautiful to me – I thought it looked horrible, all fat and grey brown, and it had this strange musky powdery, earthy smell, sour and dusty. If I had wondered what Daddy was going to do with it, I didn't have to wonder long; it was taken to the tanner in Munnar town where it was immortalised into a wallet for him and shoes and a handbag that Mummy wore reluctantly. Fiona and I were appalled. Dry, the python's skin felt scaly and rough and the markings looked ugly and snaky. We implored our mother to give them away.

One day, when I was very little, we were out walking, my sister, my mother, Ayah and me. I think I was about three years old and my sandaled feet stood on the head of a small, surprised snake that curled itself round my leg. Panic gave voice to shrieks and shouts from Mummy, Ayah and Fiona, filled with alarm and concern – for the snake, although small, was the exceedingly poisonous one, called a krait. It didn't bite me, but the reaction of my three loved and trusted companions filled me with proper fear. I was unable for days to be put on the floor – I had to be carried, rigid, everywhere. I couldn't trust my feet to be on the ground. Snakes? I don't like them; I fear them. I don't like the way they move, how they seek out dark corners; I don't like their eyes, the fact that they don't blink; I don't like their tongues. I don't like snakes at all. Even a picture of a snake in a book makes me shudder.

Each morning we would get out of bed, bang our shoes together and, blinking hard to get used to the brightness of the light, we would run through the red canna lilies to the swing that hung from the lime tree. We'd visit the bees and the hen house and laugh as the cockerel strutted amongst his wives and cock-a-doodled. Then we would go in with Ayah to wash our faces and brush our hair before breakfast on the verandah. We always had the green and white checked table cloth and napkins on the verandah: a yellow and blue sort of tartan-y one when we had breakfast in the dining room. In the evening, the cloth was changed to a white one. There was always a jug of water with slices of lime in it (the water, of course, had been boiled), covered by a white lace mat that had little beads or shells hanging from it. This was to keep out the flies. We would have pineapples and plantains and sometimes stewed fruit – prunes and apricots and slices of softened dried pear shipped out from England. We usually had toast, but one morning there was a packet of Vitawheat on the table, wheat biscuits with dimples in them. I opened the packet and – oh horror! – lots of little creatures that looked like small silver fish scuttled out into the light. I dropped the packet. "What are they? Hundreds of tiny silver poochis. I don't like it." Daddy laughed. "They are weevils, Isla." Weevils seemed to live in most things. "Just bang on the biscuit and they will fall off." I did, and they did, but I was still reluctant to put the biscuit in my mouth. Weevils or not, it tasted like cardboard. We were supposed to drink a glass of boiled milk, but it made me gag. Mummy felt the same about boiled milk, so she didn't force me.

After breakfast, we would brush our teeth and go out and look for Sunduraj, our chokra (in England he would have been called a valet). Sunduraj would let us jump up on his shoulders and he'd run round the garden with us. Sometimes he would bring out the box of bricks onto the verandah and build towers and bridges. Ayah would join us and she would bring the dolls out and the doll's tea set and we'd picnic on a rug under the lime tree with pretend tea and cakes. Once she found an old mirror and surrounded it with moss and leaves and flowers and it became a magical glade with a small mirror pond in the middle. We'd try to make things out of papier–mâché – water and newspaper. Fiona managed to make shapes and one creature she made had distinct arms. Mine nearly always remained blobs like fat sausages. We played shopkeepers and bought pretend things and put them in our pretend basket and we'd end each encounter with "Thank you very much. Good morning." Ayah was usually the shopkeeper.

Ayah was small and though she wasn't fat, she was quite round and felt soft. She always wore a white sari with a white blouse under it and they never seemed to get dirty, despite our sticky hands clutching at her. She wore a gold cross around her neck and two gold bangles on her left arm that chinked when she moved. She always wore her hair in a bun after she had combed coconut oil into it. She smelt nice as she put me on her lap to undress me. She smelt of her coconut hair oil, of course, and curry and rice starch, which she used on her white muslin saris – and sometimes she would have a blossom of jasmine tucked into her tight white bodice. She had soft brown eyes that looked as if they were made of velvet and always seemed to be smiling, even when she got cross with us, which wasn't often. If I was tired, or hurt, or a bit sad, she would cuddle me and rock me on her chest and sing soothing songs, or just tell me I was her Missy Baba Isla and I was a good girl and everything would be alright. Ayah's soothing crooning, combined with her gentle stroking of my back, calmed my childish fears and cajoled me into slumber.

At the time of year when the jasmine was out, she would make a chain of the flowers and wear them round her wrist and make me a wreath for my hair. It smelt lovely. She'd do the same thing with the orange blossom or the frangipani; I felt the most fragrant girl in all India. And on special occasions, she made garlands out of orange marigolds and hung them round our necks.

Ayah's name was A J Alyama, but I never knew what the A or the J stood for. She was just Ayah, our ayah, the best ayah in the world. She never struck us, or raised her voice to us. She would sometimes look upset and wring her hands and say, "Eye-yo, Eye-yo," and say, "Missy Isla, No." When I had done something after she had repeatedly asked me not to, or when

Fiona, Ayah and Isla on day
of departure from Munnar

I had hurt her feelings by saying something unkind or rude, she would leave the room and go and sit quietly on the sewing room floor, or she would sit on the steps of the verandah and not look at or speak to me. I would almost immediately ask her forgiveness, but Ayah's forgiveness was not always readily won. She would sit looking straight ahead of her as if I was not in the room. I'd say tearfully, "I'm very sorry, Ayah. I won't do it again. I'm very sorry I hurt your feelings and I wish I hadn't." And Ayah's velvet eyes would turn on me and soften, as she held out her arms and I'd fall into them sobbing with real regret and shame.

Ayah was a Catholic and would go often to church – on Sundays she seemed to spend most of the day there and so we were in Mummy's sole charge. It wasn't often that we, as a family, went to the Presbyterian church in Munnar town, certainly not every Sunday as Ayah did, just for weddings and christenings and at Christmas and Easter. Sunday was the only day we would have lunch with our parents; I liked Sundays.

Often on Sundays, our parents would give tennis and lunchtime cocktail parties. Fiona and I would scuttle into the drawing room and, before the servants came in to clear up, we would down all the "heel taps" – all the dregs of the gin and tonics and whiskies left in the glasses, even though we didn't like them very much. We guessed from the colour of the lipstick on the rim of the glass which lady had had what. "This one is bright red – it must have been Grace Brent's." We liked Grace Brent; she spoke the same way to us as she spoke to our parents. Only once did Ayah catch us draining the dregs, but she never told our parents, even when we were sick. Some ayahs put opium on their little finger and let their charge suck it to send them to sleep. Our Ayah never did that. Well, I don't think she did.

On weekdays, we would lunch in the nursery with Ayah and sometimes Mummy would come in and talk with us. After lunch we were supposed to have a "rest". The curtains were pulled shut and we lay on top of our beds with a light counterpane over us. Ayah would stroke our backs and murmur shooshing sounds. I felt this was such a waste of the day, but usually my eyes closed and I nodded off. On waking, it was walk time – rain or shine. Even in the monsoon, we'd set off, sou'westers on our heads and Wellington boots on our feet. Poor Ayah only had her "chupplis" (flip flops) and carried a big umbrella. Mummy had bought Ayah a pair of Wellington boots and a large pair of woollen socks but after wearing them only once she told my mother she couldn't walk in them and went back to her chupplis. She wore a large green waterproof poncho type garment that exposed her arms when she held up the umbrella, but she said it was better than the cumbli that some of the other servants wore. When we returned from these watery walks, we would look inside our Wellington boots to make sure there were no leeches.

We never went far, just up the road and through the tea. Occasionally our mother would come too, but she was usually busy in the house, so it would only be the three of us. If it was the hot season, we would wear our sun hats and if it was very hot (though it never got really, really hot in the High Range, not like in the low country where the air got so thick you felt you couldn't breathe), Ayah would make us walk in the shade of the same huge umbrella.

Interesting things often happened on our walks. Once, we saw some baby snakes come out of eggs and squiggle together and then head off in a line. I didn't much like the look of them and Ayah called us away saying the mother or father was probably nearby and it was best to move on.

On occasion, Ayah would meet someone she knew. She would stand and chat, but she wasn't very good at Tamil, a she was a Malayalam, and the languages were quite different – so they'd end up speaking in English. Once we met the watchman from the factory, a really tall man with blue eyes. I thought he was beautiful. We salaamed him and walked on. I asked Ayah why he had such startling blue eyes, when all the other Indians I knew had brown eyes. She said "He's a Pathan, Missy Isla, he comes from the North. He is only working here and will go back home soon." I still wanted to know why his eyes were blue. Being a Pathan didn't seem a good enough answer. Did all Pathans have blue eyes? Ayah said most Tamils were small and dark skinned, the Pathans tall and lighter skinned, and Parsees fair skinned. Malayalams, like her, were somewhere in the middle. "But his blue eyes...?" Ayah changed the subject.

We were on our ordinary walk on one ordinary afternoon, when Ayah suddenly stopped. She held us both and whispered to us "Missy stand still, very still, no moving." We stood still. Some one hundred yards ahead was a large black cat the size of a calf. "Pulli, Missy. Look at the ground, make no contact with eyes, don't look Missy." We stood very still, looking at the ground, holding our breath. We knew panthers were dangerous, but they usually came out at night and this was the middle of the afternoon. Perhaps that was why Ayah was so nervous. When animals behaved unusually – especially wild animals – there was often something wrong. I'd heard about rogue arni and man-eating perria pulli – elephants and tigers. I'd only ever seen a tiger once and that was on the Periyar Lake when it was swimming – very unusual indeed, for a tiger.

The panther looked like a giant version of Mingo, my black cat. Ayah said we could look up now, but to go on keeping very still. The panther must have got bored, because it walked off into the tea without a backward glance. "We go home now, Misses." Ayah told us that if we had we moved or run away, the panther would have been sure to chase us, but we could run home now to tell Mummy of our adventure.

Usually after our walk we would wash our hands and have tea in the nursery, sometimes on the verandah – tea was made up of bread and honey and biscuits and a cake baked by Boy. Mummy would have a cup of tea with us and soon we would get ready for our special time with her. We would go into the cool drawing room – there were blue and white ginger jars on the floor in corners and there was always a small bowl of flowers – hibiscus or lilies or a tiny vase of English daisies. Before our tea and time with our mother, Fiona and I – when we remembered – would go to the farthest back part of the garden, where the waterfall had become a trickle and slid over bits of slimy moss, and we'd pick the tiny wild orchids that grew there, nestling under the ferns. We'd take them into Mummy, who thanked us and kissed us. The orchids never lasted. They had gone brown and droopy by the next morning and the chokra would throw them out. They were so pretty where they grew, with little splashes of water on them; it was hugely disappointing that, when you picked them, they almost immediately died. Mummy said it was the same with wild bluebells that grew in Scotland; it was best to admire them and leave them alone.

In the drawing room, we would sit on the sofa, one either side of Mummy, and listen to the radio. She would have her arms around us when we'd hear the tales of Mr Mayor, Larry the Lamb, Dennis the Dachshund, and Mr Grouser. This was Children's Hour on the World Service and Uncle Mac really did seem like our uncle, we knew him so well. There was much interference as we strained to listen, but we didn't mind. I put my thumb in my mouth and twiddled my hair, I felt utterly content; this was our world and we were safe and happy and nothing could change it.

After playing in the garden, riding our bikes and doing gymnastics, the shadows in the garden lengthened and we knew it would soon be bath time. Ayah prepared us for our baths by rubbing us all over with almond oil. "Good for the skin Missy." During these bath time preparations and rituals with Ayah and the almond oil and us running around, behind the bathroom door that led off from our bedroom, the Goosle Man would come from the kitchen with huge pans of hot water to fill the tin bath for us. He would boil up the pans on a charcoal burning stove until they were bubbling hot – and he had to make several journeys to our bath to fill it up. We knew he was there and what he was doing, but as he was never there when we were about to get into the bath, we never thanked him. I'm not sure it occurred to us to thank him. I wish we had though, for the pans must have been heavy.

Mummy would come in and wash us with duck shaped soaps, which were really Imperial Leather – I love the smell of Imperial Leather soap – and squishy big rubber sponges and face flannels that we would wet and put over our faces and breathe in and out and suck the soapy water through the cloth. When baths were over, Mummy would pull us out, slippery and pink, and she would towel us dry, but first she would cover up our heads and make us disappear and call our names and kiss our faces when she saw us again. We laughed and laughed. She would comb my hair and didn't seem to mind that it was bolt straight, unlike Fiona's, which curled softly and prettily. "But your hair is shiny like a great big chestnut. You are my baby Saluki."

And she would tell me what a chestnut was, and a Saluki, and that I was the baby kind, with shining silky hair – and I felt nice. I'd put my thumb in my mouth as I nestled into her and smelt her sweet lily of the valley fragrance. And she would tell me things. She didn't mind my thumb in my mouth or that I curled my hair with my fingers. It was just something I did. I was Isla and it was my habit. Then we would run around some more in our pyjamas, but not so much as to get over-excited. We would slick our wet hair down, like Brylcreemed boys, and get into our pyjamas. We knew that Daddy would soon be home.

It wasn't long before we heard him. "Hello, Vi dear, hello girls" and we would rush to him. Fiona was too big to scoop up, but I wasn't – and he'd hold me against his shoulder and I marveled at the smell of him: sunshiny, horsey, wood smoky, tea – of course – pipe smoke and, inexplicably, crushed limes. I'd kiss his neck and it tasted salty on my lips. He took Fiona by the hand and carried me into the drawing room. The chokra didn't need to be told that a whisky and soda would be welcome and in a breath it appeared on a small silver tray which was put down on the table beside the chair Daddy usually occupied, with Fiona perched on its arm and me on his lap. "So what has been happening today?" We would chatter on about our day until the news came on the World Service. He'd tell us to shush and he'd sit with his ear right up to the radio as it crackled and whistled and he kept twirling the little dial "...to get a better reception." Sometimes he would give up and we'd go back to his chair and he'd tell us what things he'd been doing.

Very soon it was bedtime and one or other of our parents,

but usually Mummy, would come in and read to us. We liked the "Just-So Stories" best. How the elephant got its trunk, for example. They seemed to be part of our world here at our real home in India. I liked Jemima Puddleduck and Peter Rabbit too, but they seemed foreign – I had never seen a fox, or a rabbit for that matter, or foxgloves or radishes. Crocodiles and elephants and tigers and panthers were real to me. The jackals were certainly real. They started crying at night, howling – a sickening sound, like a small baby screaming as if it were being hurt. The sound scared me and made me want to cry.

Mummy or Daddy, or sometimes both of them, would kiss us good night and tell us to sleep tight, not let the bugs bite and tip-toe out to have their baths and their drinks and change for dinner.

Those were the days when I felt happy and loved and surrounded by all my favourite people.

* * * * *

Fiona, Beverly and Jane Beaumont and Isla at Cananoor

But this was a special day – the day before we were going Home. Fiona and I kept saying to each other, "This is the last time we will...". Everything became the "last time".

There had been so much rushing about and conversations over the black steel trunks that were lined up in the hall. They all had labels on them and there were several that said "Not wanted on voyage," some that said, "For voyage, cabin trunk." All had the name "Blair-Hill" written on them in white paint and a number, so Fiona said, as she picked up the labels, "Look, Isla, this one says 'Misses F. and I. Blair-Hill – for voyage'. That's us." We had packed our small brown leather suitcases, achingly heavy even when empty. Getting ready for Home overpowered any thoughts of goodbye. We both sensed on this day that something momentous was about to happen. Fiona looked sad sometimes as she touched the bedside table or smoothed down the counterpane on the bed. I wondered if she was feeling the little stirring of panic that I felt. I didn't say anything, for maybe she was only happy and excited – besides, voicing the fear that I felt, that I may never come back, would make it solid somehow and I was nervous, too, in case Fiona shared my apprehension and that would make it greater.

There seemed to be lists everywhere: lists of things to pack, things to do, lists for the servants of their duties while our parents were at Home in the UK. I couldn't read them, but Fiona said she'd never seen *so many lists*.

We ran from the bees to the bottom of the garden just before it sloped away down the hill and looked out over the valley and the Munnar River to Grahamsland Estate on the other side. Everywhere was tea, clipped neatly and symmetrically so it looked like the lawns at the manager's bungalow, Ladbroke House. From where I stood at the edge of our garden at Ailsa

Craig, I could look down at the tea, the brightest greenest green you could imagine, brighter than the green grass in story books or the frog with the bulging eyes we had in our bath each night. If there was a breeze, you could smell it, impossible to describe – not mown grass, or parched earth suddenly rained on, it had its own scent, just tea. "Oh! Girls, smell the tea," Mummy would say. I always had an urge to be able to fly over it, brushing the bright green leaves with my feet, it looked so soft, satiny and shiny. On this special day, there was no breeze. It was still, but not silent. Buzzing and twittering and croaking, cooing and cawing made up the morning sounds. I loved this time of day when, wherever you looked, things were sharp and clear and clean, without the blurry haze of midday or the soft peachy glow of late afternoon before the sun slipped behind the Anamudi Hill. Now, soon after dawn, it was as if everything had been washed and this was the slice of the day that held all the secret promise of the unfolding morning.

Usually we would have breakfast on the verandah, but today we were in the dining room when Daddy came in. He had been up since dawn doing his final "muster", giving instructions about what jobs were to be done that day and the duties that were to be carried out by his assistant in his absence of four months. We had papaya, a special treat, but I didn't like to tell Mummy that I thought papaya – or as Daddy called it, "paw-paw" – tasted like sick and I was always rather alarmed by the black, shiny seeds that looked slippery and sticky with tendrils of orange flesh hanging from them. My mother saw me looking at the slice of papaya in "that way" and said, "Isla, don't be silly now, give it to me and I will slice away the seeds and cut the papaya into little cubes." I'd said nothing about the sinister black seeds, but she seemed to know. "I didn't like the seeds either, when I was a little girl." I'd almost forgotten that she had lived here in India since she was thirteen.

I looked at my parents and felt so lucky that they were mine. I thought they were both beautiful. My mother was slender, with small hands and nails kept clean and not too long. Sometimes though she painted them red and I didn't like that. I thought it made her look like the horrible queen in Snow White. She had high cheek bones and eyebrows that arched over her blue eyes. I thought her eyes were the loveliest I'd ever seen. I'd sometimes look at my own eyes in the mirror and see, reflected back, green/tawny/brown eyes that were called "hazel". I wondered if they would grow to be blue like hers as I got older. The most noticeable thing about my mother was her hair. She was a natural blonde, very blonde, and it was gently wavy, framing her face like a halo – like all the saints in Fiona's book from Kodaikanal Convent School.

Last month she had visited a friend's house on a neighbouring estate and they decided they would give each other a perm. She came home with a tight frizz that looked like wool. I shall never forget the look on my father's face. He looked at her for a long time and then said "Oh Vi, dear, what have you done?" "I know," she said, "A mistake, but it will grow out." She never permed it again.

I loved her hair, which she sometimes wore in a snood – which I thought was such a funny word – but usually it was just left to blow about in the breeze. Sometimes she would let me brush it for her. It was soft and looked like spun gold. She was endlessly patient and let me put combs in it, but drew the line when I suggested bows and ribbons. Fiona had bows and ribbons in hers, which looked nice because it was curly. But I wasn't allowed bows, as my hair was too straight and slippery and anyway, I "wasn't the type for bows."

Only last week, at the High Range Club, I was in the lavatory in the Ladies' powder room when I heard two of my mother's friends, Dulcie Mann and Myrtle McCall, talking about Fiona and me. "Fiona is such a pretty little girl isn't she?" There was agreement and then a silence. "Funny how the two girls are so different." I sat on the lavatory with my pants round my ankles and I felt I had been slapped around the face. I couldn't come out of the cubicle, because the two women were still there and maybe some others who had heard them. I felt anguished but also that I'd let my family down. My father was tall and handsome; my mother was beautiful – everyone said so – and Fiona, with her way of looking up at you with her head bowed by shyness, was pretty. How was it that I was so different from them? Where had I come from? My father, my mother, my sister had hair that curled. Mine lay in sheets beside my face. Mother's eyes were blue, Daddy's and Fiona's green – mine were this tawny, greeny mix. I wasn't like any of them. Was I part of them? Was I a baby found under a bush, whose real mother didn't want her? Maybe I wasn't a Blair-Hill at all. A bubble of panic rose in my throat. What if I didn't belong anywhere, to anyone? The powder room became silent. I still sat there and wanted so badly to cry. If I wasn't pretty, I would have to be good at something else, because I'd noticed that people, on the whole, responded to prettiness.

Fiona was calling me. "Isla, Isla, where ARE you?"

"I'm in here."

"Why are you still in there, are you alright?"

"I don't know if I'm alright, because I'm not pretty".

"Isla, come out."

I did.

"What is this?"

"Well I heard them say it, that I was not pretty like you."

"Who said it?"

"Mrs McColl and Mrs Mann."

"What rot, you look alright to me."

"Yes, but I'm the only one of us with straight hair and my eyes are not any sort of colour, but a mixture of everything. And I can't wear bows or frills because I'm not the type."

"I don't know about any of that, but I think you are being a goose. Come on, all the ayahs in the children's room have started a game of blind man's bluff and Alice Souter is IT."

I joined the game.

This incident, small in itself, has stayed with me all my life. For a long time I felt as if it was not possible for me to measure up – not just to Fiona, but to anyone. I'm sure the two overheard women didn't mean to damn me by saying I wasn't as pretty as Fiona. I suspect they were commenting on our different personalities, but it felt like a slap and I still feel the sting of it. I have never believed people when, as an adult, they have complimented me on my appearance, as that little voice in the dark corner of my head spreads the virus of doubt. Daddy would say, "Looks are not everything; if you believe that prettiness is of such consequence, you'll believe that's all you really are and you can be so much more than merely decorative. Other things about people are far more important." He, who was married to the most beautiful woman in the High Range. I imagine, like most children, I needed to be reassured about these seemingly trivial things and I was to learn that soon there would be no-one there to supply the reassurance I coveted and so the doubt persisted, locked up, growing solid and impenetrable. But I also learned as I grew older that he was right – again – that the complexities of

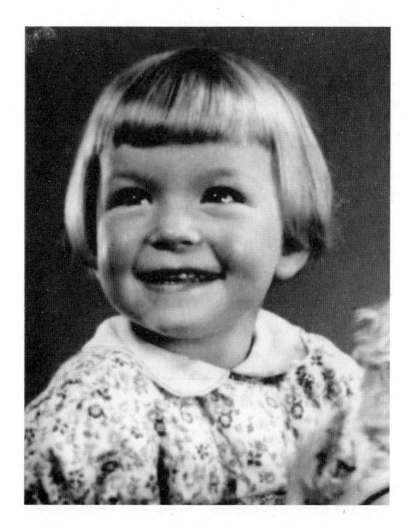

Isla aged 2

the human spirit were worth far more than a pretty pout and prominent cheekbones.

* * * * *

Soon the evening was upon us and it wouldn't be long before morning came, and our journey Home.

Daddy came in to say good night and read us a story called "Grey Friars Bobby", about a little dog in Edinburgh who was so faithful to its master, he never left him, even when he was dead; he just sat on his grave. The story made me feel rather sad and then the jackals started howling. Daddy said "Well, you won't hear any jackals in Scotland." He kissed our foreheads and told us to sleep tight.

Ayah slept not very far away from us, but not in the same room. After Daddy had left us, she crept in to our bedroom and sat on our beds and stroked our backs.

"Sleep now, Missy."

I threw my arms around her. "I wish you were coming Home with us, Ayah. Please, please come with us."

Ayah said nothing. The jackals started again. "I don't like them, Ayah, I don't like the jackals."

"I know, Missy, Ayah will put a shoe upside down on the window ledge outside and the jackals will not come near. They will see the shoe and run away."

I don't know if they did, but the howling stopped and I slept.

TWO

Not Wanted on Voyage

I arose on the day of departure, excited, a bit apprehensive and confused by the rush of activity in the house when, in a blink, it was time to go. We said goodbye to Boy and to Matey and to some of the Boy's children and we tried to find Fiona's cat, Samson, but he was nowhere to be seen.

Fiona was inside putting on her sandals, when Ayah called me to her. She put into my hand a little round box wrapped up in see-through tissue paper. You opened it by pressing a little button on the front; inside, it was a goldy colour and there was a mirror on the inner lid, but the outside lid was the special thing. It was the brightest, bluest blue: iridescent, luminous, almost metallic. Ayah said it was made from a butterfly's wing. Against the blue was the black silhouette of a man and a woman in old fashioned clothes, she with piled up hair and wearing a wide dress and he with buckled shoes and hair tied low on his neck with a ribbon. Above them was a branch of a tree filigreed against the sky with leaves and soft round apples. I was enchanted.

But I was filled with regret that I had no present to give Ayah. I took off my silver bangle, the one with a Scottie dog on the clasp, and asked her to wear it – which was silly, of course, as it didn't fit her. "I want you to keep it anyway, Ayah. We can think of each other when we take out our presents and then we won't seem so far away."

31

She kissed my eyelids; my chin went all prickly and tight as I kissed her cheeks and her coconut-oil hair and hugged her so tight that Daddy had to peel me off her. I didn't cry though, nor did Ayah.

Daddy called for Fiona to "juldi, juldi" – hurry up; she still couldn't find Samson. Ayah stood between us when Daddy took a photograph of the three of us – the sun was very bright. Then Ayah gave us all garlands of orange marigolds, one for each of us. They smelt of crushed up sunshine and the red earth after rain and a bit curry-ish. Then she pulled the bottom marigold off Fiona's garland and one off mine and folded our fingers round the flowers. "For luck, Missy Fiona. For luck, Missy Baba Isla." Then she was gone. I put my marigold into the butterfly-wing box.

The servants lined up on the verandah in their crisp white dhotis and their turbans and salaamed us goodbye. And we salaamed them back. Saying goodbye to these loved people, so far as I was concerned, was like saying goodnight and I half expected to see them all again when I next woke up.

The little black car bumped down the red road, through the tea and Munnar town and out towards Pullivasal Estate and down the winding ghat. We went through the coffee and the cardamom groves and the fragrant lemon-scented grass wafted its delicious scent through our car windows on the breeze, along with the smell of burning eucalyptus and pines. Pye-dogs barked and tried to chase the car, snapping at the wheels. Fiona's face had gone all still and stiff and she sat silently looking out of the window. I wondered if she was trying to imprint these scenes on her memory, as I had done. Her hands lay in her lap clasped but unmoving, and she kept swallowing. I didn't say anything to her in case she cried.

Michael, Boy and Matey outside our bungalow

Soon the little car brought us towards the low country, passing the chattering monkeys and the brightly coloured birds. We stopped to have a picnic of boiled eggs and Bovril sandwiches and bananas and I laughed as the sandwiches were whisked from my hands by a tiny monkey. Our parents pretended exasperation with much "shooing", but they found it funny too and soon we were coaxing the nimble little creatures to eat from our hands, until our father decided we should finish our lunch in the car. It wasn't long before the coffee bushes and the blue High Range Hills were far behind us and we were passing the water buffalo as they slowly moved up and down the fields yoked together and looking doleful. We passed the flooded paddy fields and the banana palms and went through the noisy, colourful little towns on the way to Cochin.

The gulls told us we were near the sea and soon we smelled it and the oil of the big ships in the harbour. We also smelled the cloves and the cinnamon and the spices that told us we couldn't be anywhere but Cochin. We passed the thousand year old Chinese fishing nets and the stately Arabian dhows and drove up the Bougainvillea-bordered drive to the Malabar Hotel, a house with dark wooden floors and mosquito nets shrouding our beds; the corridors were cool and smelt of damp books, floor polish and citronella oil.

Cochin is famous for mosquitoes, which sometimes carry malaria, as well as the dreaded elephantiasis or dropsy, where people's legs swell to huge proportions, making them heavy and painful. My father and I seemed to attract the mosquitoes, while Fiona and my mother were left in relative peace. So he and I sat having our evening drinks, with our legs in pillow cases, sloshed and sprayed in Dettol (it was thought this would keep them at bay, but actually it didn't; it just made us smell of hospitals), watching the fishing boats come back with their catch, hovered over by the ever present swooping gulls and we waited for the sun to go down, suddenly, like a light going out, as if the horizon had swallowed it with one gulp.

The next day we went on a boat round the backwaters, to little lagoons fringed with coconut palms, banana and cashew trees and climbing pepper vines. We saw people braid their hair, scold their children and feed their chickens; the air was heady with the scent of cloves, ginger, cardamoms and pepper. Daddy said the houses were painted according to the religion of the occupants – Muslims preferred green houses, Hindus blue, orange, yellow and pink, while the Christians houses were painted white. They were all jumbled up together and side by side. He said that families had been living like this for hundreds of years and, just for a moment, I wished I lived like that too, shaking the coconut trees, fetching pails of water and carrying them on my head. The children all seemed to be smiling.

We swapped the mosquito nets and the cool sheets of the Malabar hotel for the hot and stuffy berth on the ferry that would take us on the long journey to Columbo. We listened to the cries of the vendors of all kinds as they passed us on the harbour quay, with delicious smelling sweet things and spicy curries and fruit. I put my head in Mummy's lap as she and Daddy told us things about Scotland and soon it was time for the next stage of our adventure – the big ship.

The ship's siren had sounded so loudly, it seemed to reverberate through my whole body. There was something exciting about it though. It heralded a beginning and a certainty that we were on our way. I wasn't sad leaving the bustling quay–side, with the mass of moving people in their white dhotis and shirts, the seagulls competing with the crows, the loud chatter of the crowds on the pier, the droning cry of the beggars, the tinkling bicycle bells, the car horns, the wail of crying children. The whole scene seemed so frenetic and here I was high up on the deck watching them all below me. Traders with trays of mangoes or bananas on their heads, the water wallah with his cask and lots of little tin mugs, goats and pye-dogs darting in and out of the crowd. People were waving handkerchiefs and some were crying. I stood beside my mother and father and Fiona and we waved too. The siren sounded again and Fiona and I laughed as we cupped our hands over our ears and felt the boat slowly pull away. I didn't feel sad, because it didn't feel like goodbye, not like the end of something. We shouted out above the rushing of the waves as the ship knifed through them, we shouted above all the quayside noises, "Goodbye, Columbo Harbour, goodbye India, goodbye Ayah and Boy and Matey and Sunderaj, goodbye Samson and Mingo and tigers and elephants and the club and the wobbly bridge and Munnar and The High Range Tiger – goodbye, goodbye, goodbye...."

We were now in a different world; on board ship life assumed a different pattern, disciplined, ordered. There were certain rules on board that we children had to adhere to. I think we were expected to be seen and not heard and there were certainly places where we were not allowed, such as the ballroom and the grown-up dining room. There were appointed children's times for the pool. Fiona and I had never learnt to swim and so we sat stiffly on the edge with our legs dangling into the water, embarrassed by our nylon costumes that looked like blue eiderdowns and our inability to jump into the water like most of the other children. Our father saw our reluctance about getting into the water as we watched the little boys and girls from Australia dive and splash and generally have a good time. We weren't having any fun and Daddy said, "You girls must have swimming lessons; you must not feel left out of things. We must put that on the list of extras required at the school."

Eventually we were persuaded to go into the water with rubber rings and although we were self-conscious to begin with, we soon started splashing about and when the children's hostess lowered the water in the pool, we started to do a rough sort of doggy-paddle. There was a young Australian boy who had lots of warts on his hands, but who could swim like an eel; I was fascinated by him and he was equally fascinated – not by me, but by my feet. On my left foot are two toes, the ones next to the big toe, that are half joined together.

"Webbed, feet, webbed feet, you've got webbed feet like a duck. You should be a brilliant swimmer and you can't swim at all. Webbed feet, webbed feet, squishy squashy webbed duck." It had never occurred to me that they were odd. Mummy said they were special and when we played "This little piggy went to market," she kissed them for being nice. So I thought they were interesting and unusual toes and that I was lucky to have them. I didn't realise that they were yucky or the subject for mockery.

Each day after breakfast (we had to have all our meals separately from our parents, although Mummy was allowed to sit with us when we had ours), we were shepherded by the children's hostess to the pool. I hung back as I saw the freckle-nosed Australian boy with warts all over his hands diving and swimming like a dolphin. I was scared of him in case he shouted at me and started chanting. He did.

"Hey, Squishy–Squashy Duck – you don't need flippers, you've got them already!" I shrank back a bit more; I felt hurt and embarrassed and as if I was going to cry. The children's hostess, in her white dress and white shoes, tried to pull me towards the pool, but I refused to move, so she picked me up and carried me to the edge of the pool, but I kicked and lashed out at her with my fists. She said I was a silly girl and she could do nothing with me and went to find my parents. Mummy was having her hair done and sat under a dome-shaped dryer, so Daddy came.

He saw my rebellion, but also my distress. "What is it Isla? Why do you not want to splash in the pool? Is it because you can't swim?"

"No, it's because of my feet, they are all wrong. The big toes are too big and those ones," I said, pointing, "are webbed, like a duck. Ducks swim and I can't and all the children are laughing at me and want to touch my webbed toes and when they do, they run away going 'Eeah, ugh ,Yuk, Yuk, yuk.' And I've got this pain here," I patted my breast bone, "and I never, never want to go in the pool, not ever."

Daddy put his arms around me. "Uncle Roy has got two toes like that. It must run in families." I wasn't comforted. "There is nothing really strange about webbed toes; lots of people have them. That little boy hasn't seen any, that's all."

"He's got warts on his hands."

"Well there you are, then. As a matter of fact, your toes are two of the things Mummy and I and Fiona love most about you."

"And Ayah," I said.

"And Ayah."

That night as I sat on the bottom bunk (Fiona had the top bunk as she was the oldest), I looked at my offending toes and wondered if I could cut them up the middle.

The sea view on the *Orion* was a pretty permanent fixture for some three weeks. The days were broken up by meals and formalised games, parties, and sing-songs.

After breakfast and after our swim, we were supposed to do some lessons, then there would be a break – adults had beef tea (probably Bovril or consommé – whatever the weather) and we children had orange squash and sometimes delicious Italian ice cream stuck between two wafers.

There were fancy dress parties and a headdress competition where everyone won a prize. Fiona's was a blue and white rabbit with springs in its legs to make it bounce. She declared it was too babyish for her and gave it to me. My prize was a dark brown hare with a blue stomach and long, lollopy ears that fell over his face. I was enchanted. The best things about him were his eyes; they were tiny light bulbs that lit up every time you pressed his tummy. I pressed his tummy a lot.

There was an entertainment committee, which was formed from the ship's officers and some of the passengers. It must have been quite daunting trying to fill each hour of each day; no wonder there were endless meals that were served all day and most of the night. There was Scottish dancing, choir practice, "Housey-Housey" – this was Bingo and seemed to be played somewhere most evenings. There was the ship's orchestra, of course, and people would dance in the evenings and listen to "light music" in the afternoons. Sometimes the passengers performed for each other, by invitation of the professional singers and dancers on board. On one occasion, in the afternoon, the Master of Ceremonies at a concert said, "Is there anyone here who would like to sing for us?"

I put my hand up. "I would."

The MC looked surprised and said, "This little girl with a fringe. And what would you like to sing dear?"

"I would like to sing 'The Girl that I Marry'." There was a nod to the pianist and I started. I'd worked out all the gestures to the song back in India and I loved singing it. The ship's tannoy was turned on and my parents and Fiona heard my voice blaring out – interrupting their game of deck quoits.

Family history relates that Fiona said, "Oh my God, it's Isla. Stop her, Daddy, you must stop her."

But it was too late. I rather liked the applause and the fact that lots of people were putting their heads round the door to listen.

"That was very good. What's your name little girl?"

"Isla.".

"Well, Isla, would you like to sing another song?"

"I would."

And I started into "If I knew you were coming, I'd have baked a cake."

I don't think I was showing off; I just liked singing. My mother and father looked embarrassed, surprised and a bit proud as the applause swelled. Daddy said, quietly, "Very good, Isla, but that's enough now," and I knew he didn't want me to get above myself. But I never forgot that first-time feeling of holding the audience and making them go quiet. It was as if I had somehow hypnotised them, for they didn't laugh as they had when I was a pixie in the High Range concert; they were silent and seemed to be holding their breath. It was an intoxicating feeling and one that stayed with me for a long time; in truth it never left me. It didn't matter that maybe they were just relieved that I got through the song without stumbling; small children singing in public was much less common then than now.

The ship progressed westward and soon we were in the Red

Sea and the days and nights got hotter. We were witness to the most spectacular sunsets – blood red skies and golden clouds, like a miracle each evening. We would stand by the rails on deck with our parents holding onto us tightly as we watched flying fishes jump and dive. Sometimes porpoises and dolphins swam alongside the ship; they jumped and dived too, in greeting and just for sheer pleasure – lovely, smiling creatures.

A tradition that goes back years when in the tropics is "Crossing the Line" or "Crossing the Equator". King Neptune arrives at this ceremony with his court, including his beautiful queen, Amphitrite, and his first assistant, Davy Jones. It was an initiation ceremony for those sailors who had not crossed the equator before and I thought it was quite frightening and watched with horror as the drama unfolded.

Neptune appeared in a long red beard, and hair that seemed to be made out of seaweed. He had a painted face and sat with a large trident in his hand and said in his boomy voice that he wanted his "victim". The Queen was also a man, with long yellow hair and a bra made out of coconut shells. There was a "doctor" and a "barber" and the former would hand out "medicine" to anyone who felt a little seasick. I cowered behind my Mother when he came near me. A young sailor who had not crossed the line before was made to kiss a smelly kipper at the feet of Neptune, kiss Neptune's ring and then, amidst much cheering, he was thrown in the swimming pool. He was ducked three times and then fished out to kiss Neptune's ring again, after which he was handed a certificate to show that he had Crossed The Line.

Everyone cheered and drinks were handed round, even for us children, and we had fruit punch with bits of orange and squares of pineapple and little leaves of mint in it.

I wondered where the line was. If we had crossed the equator, crossed the line – where was it?

"Where is the line, Daddy? The line we've crossed, the equator line."

Daddy said you couldn't see it. I ran with Fiona to the ship's rails and Daddy shouted at us to "Stop! Wait for me, girls!"

He took our hands and said we were never to go near the rails on our own, in case we fell into the sea. "The ship is going so fast we wouldn't be able to stop for you."

"But where is the line? Where does it come from? What colour is it? Is it blue or red and where does it go?"

Daddy scratched his head in the way that he had. "Well, it's a sort of belt around the earth. You know there's a northern hemisphere and a southern hemisphere and the equator is what separates them."

"What sort of belt?"

Daddy said, "Why don't we go back and get some more fruit punch?"

It wasn't long before we were sailing through the Suez Canal and met the famous Gully-Gully men and saw all sorts of sights and wonders. Traders stood with their wares along the quay and you could buy almost anything, but you had to be wary. Daddy told us about one gullible young man on his way out to India through the Suez Canal, who had bought a pair of green canaries that he kept on the deck. He wondered why they didn't sing the way he expected them to; the reason became clear when, in a tropical downpour, the canaries revealed themselves to be little brown sparrows.

There were scarves and trinkets, bangles and necklaces, pots and lanterns, tables and rugs; the list just gets too long. We were allowed off the ship and visited the famous Simon

Artz store where Daddy, as a young man on his way out to India, bought his tropical gear, topees and shorts and boots – all things necessary, apparently, for his new Indian life.

The Gully-Gully men were remarkable, incredibly clever. They came on board in their galabias and one of them wore a red fez hat. They made baby chicks come from the most amazing places, from inside their mouths, behind your ear, inside your shirt; the chicks were so sweet, tiny and yellow and "cheep-cheeping". Sometimes people would stand by the quay holding out the skirts of their galabias and people threw coins into them; little boys not much older than me would dive into the water beside the boat to retrieve the coins people threw. It must have been hideously dangerous and Daddy kept repeating, "Poor little buggers, poor little buggers." Mummy told him off for saying that in front of us. He felt it was awful that children had to do this, but he threw them some coins all the same.

We left the shouts and the smells and the Gully-Gully men and the small boys behind as we glided out of the Suez Canal and headed towards the Mediterranean. We docked at Marseilles and Daddy bought a beautiful oil painting of the quay at Capri; I was more fascinated by the lines of washing that hung from windows on either side of the streets, rows and rows of them flapping away above our heads and the women would shout at each other across the towels and shirts and pillow cases. Daddy said it seemed more like Italy than France.

It was dark and Fiona and I were fast asleep when our parents came in with much excitement and said to put on our dressing gowns and slippers as the volcano Stromboli was erupting and it was the most amazing sight that we just had to see. Indeed, it was – rivers of hot red lava poured down the side of the mountain and there was a rumbling, hissing sort of noise. People took out binoculars, others took photos, but I had something much more important to concern myself with. My brown hare with a blue tummy and lollopy ears had gone blind. His eyes failed to light up however hard I pressed his tummy. It was dreadful. A blind hare who would never see Stromboli or me ever again. I still liked him though and took him back to bed to comfort him.

The nights got cooler and the days grew longer and soon we were steaming our sedate way into Tilbury Docks. This, then, was "Home".

THREE

A Postie in Auchtermuchty

It seemed strange and all wrong somehow. The sounds and the smells were alien; there were no turbaned heads and betel nut smiles. There were no limes or marigolds, no mangoes, no crows caw-cawing; it was noisy though on the quayside, full of men in collarless shirts and black waistcoats, with flat caps on their heads. Some wore brown overalls and shouted a lot. So this "Home" so talked about, so planned, so packed for, argued and dreamt about – I did not understand it at all; it was grey and wet and smelt of cigarettes, but not the familiar beedees, and damp raincoats, towels that hadn't been dried properly and a smoky smell that wasn't wood – but, according to Daddy, was coal.

All the big black steel trunks that were "not wanted on voyage" were being sent straight up to Scotland where they would be stored by my mother's parents until we were ready for them. We made our way down the gangplank with our suitcases, my mother's hat boxes and beauty case, coats, over our arms and made our way to the train that would take us to London and the promised "marshmallow" beds of the Cumberland Hotel in Marble Arch.

We spent four or five days in London, going to see all the things strangers to London should see: Trafalgar Square, Buckingham Palace, the Tower of London with its forbidding traitor's gate and beady-eyed ravens. The crown jewels didn't impress me as much as they ought – the jewels certainly sparkled, but I thought the crown was spoilt by the wodge of purple velvet in the middle of it. We walked up the Mall and into St. James's Park. We walked to the Albert Memorial and saw Peter Pan's statue in Kensington Gardens.

By far the most exciting thing we did was to visit a real theatre – the Theatre Royal in Drury Lane; *Kiss Me Kate* was playing and this was my first time in a theatre. It was hard to take in the enormity of the auditorium. Its huge chandeliers sparkled as they hung from the painted ceiling and all the way round there were boxes with people holding opera glasses, chatting and laughing, just as excited as we were. The seats were made of velvet; Daddy rolled up his raincoat for me to sit on, to make me taller.

The orchestra played all jangle-y music and my mother said this was "tuning up." Then the lights went down and the orchestra played properly for a bit and slowly – very, very slowly – the velvet curtain was raised and I gasped with the wonder of it, as people in beautiful costumes sang and danced and seemed to be doing it all just for me. I think I metaphorically held my breath throughout the whole performance and my parents said I didn't move at all. I declared on the way back to the hotel that I was going to do that. I was going to sing and dance and bang cups on the table and sing "I Hate Men." I asked if I could go and see it all over again the next day, but apparently there were other plans.

The drizzle of London tired me out more than the heat of Cochin. It was like looking at everything through a veil that wet my fringe and eyelashes. Standing on the red road outside our bungalow in the High Range in a monsoon downpour was like standing under a waterfall. Here in London the drizzle was

46

like being spat at by my cat Mingo. Ah! Mingo. I wondered where she was. Padding her sleek black way through the jungle; I wished I was with her.

We hired a small Austin car and drove north to Scotland, being saluted on the way by AA men when they saw the badge on the front of our car. On our way to Blairgowrie, where Daddy's mother Granny Sara lived, we visited Edinburgh and we saw the Castle, the Flower Clock and soldiers marching to bagpipes and drums at the famous Edinburgh Tattoo.

The Tattoo was spectacular. We sat with rugs over our laps and sticks of Edinburgh rock and the chilly East wind ruffled our hair. There was lots of marching, but my favourite bit was when a man appeared at the top of the castle all on his own in a spotlight and played a sad lament that echoed across the parade ground. It was very quiet, apart from the piper, and the sound pricked my eyes and gave me an ache in my throat.

Going north the Forth Bridge was rather a disappointment; I hadn't expected it to be a sort of rusty brown.

We got our uniforms from Forsyths, everything a little bit too big so we would grow into them. We put our kilts on (my tartan was Stewart, Fiona's – I think – was Gordon) and we had to kneel on the floor to get the measurements right. I rather liked our gym slips and skirts and blouses and jumpers, but the pants or bloomers made Fiona and me laugh, for they were huge, like those Tudor pants men wore in Fiona's book about Elizabeth I. I didn't understand why we needed Liberty Bodices with their rubber buttons. Mummy said we'd understand when the winter came. Winter was a concept neither Fiona nor I could grasp.

For a while we stayed at Loon Brae the house our father's mother, Granny Sara, shared with her sister Ann. It was nice being tucked up by our parents under slippery eiderdowns (we never had those in India – just starched sheets and thick cotton covers and in the monsoon months we'd have a blanket). They would read us stories and I would twiddle my hair and suck my thumb.

I had a hollow feeling inside me though, because I wanted Ayah so much – but I didn't say so, in case Mummy thought she wasn't enough. I wanted Ayah to stroke my back and call me her Missy Baba Isla; I wanted her to kiss my eyelids to make me go to sleep and I wanted to smell her coconut hair oil. I knew she was not coming "home" with us, but next morning I decided to speak to Daddy.

"I know that Ayah is staying behind in India, but I think she'd like to be with us – so will you send for her? I need her to be here and so does Fiona." Mummy was, after all our mother and we didn't love her less because we loved Ayah, we just loved Ayah too.

Daddy sat me on his lap and looked straight into my eyes like he did when he had something important to say.

"Isla, you and Fiona are big girls now and you don't need Ayah anymore. You are going to school here in Scotland and Ayah wouldn't like it here. Besides, she has gone to a new family."

"But she's ours! She's our Ayah. How can she have gone to another family? Which family? She belongs to OUR family."

"She's gone to Nicholas and Catherine Cook, you remember them, and their new baby boy."

Nicholas Cook had eyes so bulgy I thought they would fall out of his head one day. I'd never noticed the new baby, only that it was small and purplish with a fuzz of ginger hair. I felt a surge of jealousy for this child.

"I'm sorry Isla, I thought you knew. We can visit her next time you come out to India."

"Yes, but she'll have forgotten all about me. She'll be too busy with her ginger baby."

I got off his knee and went to the bedroom I shared with Fiona. I took out my butterfly wing box. Inside the marigold was going a bit brown and it smelt a bit funny. I closed the lid and looked at the man and woman silhouetted against the blue. I had a pain in my chest from missing Ayah and it was made worse by the feeling, however unjust, that she had somehow betrayed me, us. I know she had said she wasn't coming but I wondered, in that self-oriented way children have, how could she possibly exist without us; her world would end. Instead, my world had changed – it was an empty, Ayah-less world.

I went to find Fiona and she told me that she knew that Ayah had gone to the Cooks. So everyone had known but me – I felt shut out because I wasn't old enough to be trusted with the truth. They thought I'd be upset and angry and... Well, they were right. I was angry and upset, so they knew more about me than I did. I felt as if I couldn't breathe. I wanted to push away the walls and run from the garden. I didn't though. I walked around it some more, kicking at the leaves when, through the kitchen window, I heard Granny Sara talking to her cat in a straight, conversational sort of way, as if he were a person. "And where are you off to today my darling? Don't get shut in the summer house again. I will see you later. Perhaps we can have a nap together after lunch; we'll draw the curtains." I liked the way she spoke to him. He was called Watson and he had a silver moustache.

I sought her out. She was in the kitchen making fudge, or "tablet" as they called it in Scotland. She said I could stir the pan very slowly but I had to be careful – if any of it splashed on me, it was so hot and sticky that it wouldn't come off and would burn right down to my bones. The skin on Granny Sara's arm was so thin I could see the little blue veins and the pulse in her wrist go beat, beat, beat, almost popping out. I asked if I could put my hand over her beating pulse. It felt like a tiny fluttering bird trying to escape. I swiftly took my hand away.

"Yes darling. When that stops, I stop."

"What is it?"

"It's where my heart beat sort of echoes in my wrist, that's all. My heart beating. Let's find yours." She put her hand over my wrist and neither of us could feel the beat.

"I think it's stopped. Perhaps I'm going to die."

"Don't be so dramatic, Isla. Of course you're not. It's here somewhere. Ah, yes. Here it is, put your fingers here."

I liked Granny Sara. She was quiet and would move slowly in a calm sort of a way. And she had a lovely laugh, not a polite way of laughing but laughing as if she really found things funny. At tea time she would bring in a tray and a three-tiered cake stand with little cakes set in paper cups; my favourites were the cornflakes in chocolate. I was a little afraid of Aunt Ann, Granny Sara's sister. She wasn't pretty like Granny Sara and she was always telling us to sit up straight, in a cross sounding voice.

One evening Granny asked me to take up some tea to Aunt Ann without spilling it. I knocked on her door and when I was told to come in I found Aunt Ann wrapped in a shawl sitting in a chair with her teeth in a glass beside her. She had a jug of wine on the floor with a hot poker sticking out of it. She said the wine was "to keep the cold out." She sounded slurry when she said it, perhaps because she was toothless. I put the teacup and saucer on the table and made for the door.

"Thank you, dear," said Aunt Ann. I turned to look at her and she had put her teeth back in.

We woke up to a watery sun and very soft rain that Daddy called Scotch mist. It was so fine you could hardly see it and, although it wet your hair and your clothes, you couldn't open your mouth and swallow it like you could with the monsoon rain.

At the back of the house and up a steep path in the garden was a small summer house where Aunt Ann would nap in the afternoons. There was a folded up rug on the long chair and a lantern that I suppose she used to read by. The little room smelt of paraffin and peppermints and of damp, as if the rain had slid in under the door and sogged into the wooden floor boards. But it was a nice room, warm and cosy. Outside there was half a coconut shell and little strips of bacon on a string; this was what Granny Sara fed the birds, birds we had never seen before – blue tits who ate upside down on the coconut shell and sparrows, speckled thrushes that sang so sweetly

Loon Brae

and, our favourites, the robins who sometimes came and sat right beside you and looked you straight in the eye.

"Girls, I am going to walk you down to Aunt Mina's house where you will have lunch. After lunch your parents will come to collect you."

Aunt Mina was Granny Sara's other sister and so different from Aunt Ann. She was round and always seemed to be smiling. She was full of stories about herself as a little girl. She was my father's aunt, married to a rather posh but taciturn vet who had been made a Sir for his services to veterinary science. The house smelled of chloroform and metaldehyde. I loved saying these words, as no-one really knew what they meant and they sounded grown up – "Metaldehyde and Chloroform." This house was a source of delight to Fiona and to me.

But not the Chinese room, that was all black and gold lacquer and Chinesey – birds with hooked beaks and ivory carvings of men with wide hats crossing bridges with poles in their hands and lizard-y things with black eyes and spiky claws. There were tall vases of grasses that were dusty and full of cobwebs and there were screens and shawls that hung from them. Aunt Mina was very proud of this room and because she was nice and kind to us and really quite old I didn't let on that I thought it was the ugliest and most suffocating room I'd ever been in. It was like being in one of my own bad dreams, frightening and dark with horrible images everywhere you looked. She kept the blinds down to keep the sun from fading the carpet and the silk screen with a dragon on it that had an open mouth and bulging eyes like a Pekinese dog.

Jessie was Aunt Mina's maid and Fiona and I liked her. She had a round, red face with purplish veins on it and stiff swollen hands. She walked with difficulty when she carried in the tray, but she winked at us and smiled and slipped a marshmallow chocolate biscuit into our pockets. We sensed that she liked us and we liked her back. She and Aunt Mina were very good friends. You knew this because they scolded each other a lot and laughed together.

We were in the garden when our parents came for us. We said goodbye to Aunt Mina and "Thank you for having me."

"We are going to the golf course girls," said Daddy.

We loved the visits to the golf course. Our task (Fiona's and mine) was to find as many golf balls as we could. It became an exciting game. We would periodically shout out "found one" and we would hold out our skirts with a growing pile of golf balls, some in pristine condition and others with their rubbery guts spilling out. We would stumble over and through the heather as it scratched at our legs and delight at the sight of a white golf ball nestling in the bracken like the egg of a ground-nesting bird and we'd laugh and be pleased because Daddy was pleased. He put all the balls into his large pockets and we would all hold hands and go to the Clubhouse and give the man there the balls and he put them (the good ones) in a big jar and said golfers could buy them for tuppence each.

The first afternoon was to set the tone; we found lots of balls and under a clump of bracken we found two baby hedgehogs. After we had delivered the golf balls to the man at the club we were to have a special treat. We were going to drive to the river Isla – "Your river, Isla!" – and have our high tea as a picnic.

I felt proud that this fierce little river was mine. We took our picnic out and spread everything on a tartan rug; boiled eggs with little twists of salt wrapped in grease-proof paper, and ham sandwiches, and we had fizzy Irn-Bru to drink although our parents had tea from a flask, the milk was separate in

Isla, Ian and Fiona – Blairgowrie golf course

a little bottle. There were mutton pies which I didn't like so Daddy had mine. And we had apples and a slice of lemon cake and Fiona and I shared a wagon wheel biscuit and we pretended not to mind about the midges or be surprised that Daddy really hated the wasps. I sat on Daddy's lap and held open his hands so I could pretend to read his fortune in his palm like the old lady had done in the bazaar. I didn't know what I was looking for, of course, but I liked looking at his hands, which were square with long fingers and a ring on the little finger of his left hand which had a thistle on it and a snow plough and the name "BALLO" (I asked him what it meant but he didn't know). He let me put it on my little finger and it felt heavy as it slid on and off. He told me that one day I would have my own ring, on my twenty-first birthday.

In the evening we went down to the field beyond Loon Brae and gave the horse there with the name of "Dobbin" ("How original," said Mummy; I think she was being sarcastic), some apples and some peppermints and we walked back through the clouds of midges down by the river and played "Poo Sticks" on the bridge, running from side to side as we watched the little twigs whirl away in the rushing, slightly foaming brown, peaty water. We laughed with delight and it didn't really matter who won.

That night both our parents came to our bedroom and took it in turns to read us stories; Daddy kissed us goodnight and said he'd see Mummy downstairs. Mummy stroked my hair and whispered "Baby Saluki, Baby Saluki," over and over again. I half sat up and took her face in both my hands; it felt soft and smelt of flowers and the heather and I smoothed her hair away from her forehead and looked at her properly. "My Mummy, my own mummy." I saw her face go sad and her eyes

Isla, Violet and Fiona – Blairgowrie golf course

filled up with tears. "It's alright Mummy, it will be alright."

She kissed me again and pulled my quilt up to my face. "Sleep tight darlings." She went to kiss Fiona again and switched off the light and closed the door behind her.

We lay in silence for a bit but then I said "Fi, are you awake?"

"Yes."

"I think Mummy was starting to cry."

I know." She was quiet a bit more.

"Go to sleep now Isla."

We drove into Prestwick on the west coast of Scotland in the late afternoon and settled into my mother's parents Granny and Grandfather Patterson's small bungalow. Slowly the atmosphere in our family seemed to change. We would go shopping with our mother and I would sometimes be allowed to hold the shopping list and Fiona the basket. But Mummy seemed distracted, as if she wanted to get back to the house, even though she was in the middle of the High Street, with lots more shops to visit. Daddy became quieter and sucked a lot more on his pipe. Granny and Grandad didn't talk much to us. Sometimes Granny would show us how to put clothes through a mangle, to squeeze all the water out (you had to be careful not to get your fingers caught) and how to set the fire and pour coal on it from the long nosed coal-scuttle. But there were long silences that somehow were filled with spikes.

The greatest change was in Fiona. At night there'd be choking sounds from her bed, which she'd try to muffle with her pillow and when I asked her if she was crying, she always said no. But she was – a gulping sort of crying. I remember once I climbed into her bed and squeezed myself hard against her back to protect her from her crying self, to hug her away from the sad place she'd gone to and I'd feel those deep shuddering sobs, like the ones babies make, almost like hiccups. She didn't want to worry or upset me, so she said there was nothing wrong – but I knew there was. Sometimes she would turn over and cuddle me, because I was her little sister and she'd hold me to her to protect me, but I'd still feel her thudding heart and her occasional hiccupping breath. She'd say, "It's alright now," and it was meant for me, to quiet me and send me to sleep. Then I'd go back to my own bed and the soft shuddering sobs would begin again. I'd notice her muffle them with her pillow and I'd stay silent and pretend to be asleep. If I spoke, she somehow felt that she'd failed in her sisterly duty to comfort and protect me. Yet it was she who needed the comfort. In the morning she would help me to dress if I was being slow, buckling my shoes and doing up the buttons of my cardigan. And I'd notice little white salty lines around her eyes and down her cheek and I'd realise they were dried-on tears. She would wash them away and get into her clothes, but I knew in the evening that followed, her tears would build up and spill into her pillow with the hiccupping sounds that she'd try to hide. They were a give-away and they broke my heart.

The reason, of course, was that everyone knew that the summer was coming to an end and we would have to go to school and our parents would go back to India, leaving us behind. Mummy's mouth would tighten with little lines round it and she seemed to hold her breath a lot. Sometimes Fiona would cry during the day too, and so would Mummy, and Fiona would ask our parents, "Why, why have you got to go back to India? Stay here with us".

And my father replied, "It's difficult to get a job here now dear. There aren't many jobs so soon after the war and I don't really have any qualifications. The job in India is a good one and I need money to give you and Isla things and Mummy and for your school and everything. If I stayed here, the only job I would get would be as a postie in Auchtermuchty."

This was meant to make her laugh, but it gave her the chance to put in her plea. "But I want you to be the postie in Auchtermuchty; I want you to be here with us. I don't want you to go away. I can make the lunch; I can do lots of things. I can sew and sweep the house and make supper and everything." And Daddy looked sad and said,

"You have to be a brave girl, Fiona, none of us want to be parted from each other, but that is the way things have to be. We all have to be brave. Besides, we are trusting you to look after Isla."

And so Fiona's responsibility for me was laid on her as a sort of oath; she was handed a torch and she took it very seriously.

Each day she would try to recover from her fear of the night before and for a while she would succeed and then the day and the thought of it ending would overwhelm her and her heart would beat and the panic would set in and she would breathe so much she would get dizzy and it would start all over again.

The anticipation of our parents' departure was more agonizing than the event when it arrived. My anxiety took the form of defiance. I didn't cry, I became fierce and difficult to control. One day I was sent to my room for being horrible to Mummy. I can't remember how our quarrel started but I ended by saying, "How would you know? You're not Ayah. You're just my mother."

Mummy made a gasping sound and put her hands to her face. Daddy said, "Isla, that was a really nasty thing to say. You know it was cruel and hurtful. Go to your room and think about how you have hurt Mummy's feelings and then you can come back and say sorry."

I was too hot and angry to be sorry, so I went to Fiona's and my bedroom and slammed the door.

Still in a fury, I pulled the stiff window up, climbed out of it and thumped my way down the very busy main Ayr road. It was several minutes before my father checked on me in the bedroom to see if my tantrum had abated and I was ready to apologise, only to find the window open and the white net curtains blowing in the breeze – but I was nowhere to be seen. My father rushed out of the door and I was almost, but not quite, out of sight. He ran to catch up with me and after hugging me to him, he unleashed his relieved wrath on me. Daddy's anger was always quiet; he would tell us off more in sorrow than in anger. He'd say how disappointed he was in us, which had the effect of quelling us; his disappointment was far more terrible than his anger. He rarely raised his voice, but on this occasion he did, telling me I was a naughty, naughty girl and he picked me up – kicking angry legs and screaming loudly– and carried me home.

Later, he explained to me why he was so angry. Not only had I been hurtful to Mummy, but the road was full of cars and one could have knocked me over, or I could have got lost somewhere in Prestwick and he wouldn't know where to find me. He said all this in his quiet, reasoned voice and I felt rotten that I'd given him such a fright. Even Fiona told me off for being thoughtless and impulsive and I felt chastened. I went to find Mummy, who was in the sitting room blowing her nose on a handkerchief. I rushed to her. "I'm very, very sorry Mummy. I didn't mean it. Mummy, Mummy…" I started that hiccupping crying that Fiona did. She hugged me and said we were friends again and that everything was alright.

The car was loaded up with our black trunks that had our names written on them in white gloss paint. We put on our stiff new school uniforms of maroon and blue with the St Maray's badge on the gym slip and on the beret. Granny Jessie pulled the beret on for me and said, "This child needs her hair cutting." She had a way of talking about me as if I weren't there. She kissed me goodbye and then gave me a big hug, I think she was trying not to cry. She saw Mummy start to cry and her mouth tightened as if to hold her tears in. Then it was Grandad's turn. He brushed my cheek with his cheek; he smelt of hair oil and cigarettes. Granny bustled us into the car and gave us a small paper bag with barley sugar to share on the journey to prevent car-sickness. Sweets were still rationed at that time.

Fiona waved out of the window and I knelt up on the back seat and watched them, still waving, becoming smaller and smaller, until the car rounded a corner.

* * * * *

The September day was sunny, a bit hazy with the ever present midges dancing in the air above the scattered sheep in the fields that bordered the long drive that led to Kilbryde Castle, St Maray's School.

All the way there I sat behind Mummy with my arms about her neck, inhaling her scent and feeling her warmth against my cheek. I had a pain in my stomach from all the butterflies that flew about in a tumult there and my heart was beating so fast it made me feel sick. Mummy held my arms in her hands that trembled and all the time Fiona sat behind Daddy, looking straight ahead of her. Her mouth was tight and her eyes were dry and dark.

Fiona and Isla "Going Out Day" St Maray's

The castle loomed in front of us through the trees, from a distance rather forbidding, dark red stone with towers and turrets and crenellations. Daddy said, "Here we are, girls."

And here it was. The moment that we had hoped would never come. We got out of the car and pulled up our blue socks, already escaping from the bands of elastic that held them up. Fiona took my hand, we stood still for a second and then, in our too-big school uniforms, we walked up the front steps of our new school.

FOUR

Love Walked In

As Fiona and I walked forward into our new lives, our parents had to turn away and walk back to theirs. It was a good one, the Indian life. There were servants, polo matches, tennis and cocktail parties, the climate was clement – not the soggy heat of the plains, or the bitter cold of Scottish winters. The privileged life they led as a middle class couple was that led by Edwardian aristocracy, but it came at a price. What did my mother feel as she climbed back into the car? She told me later that she had become adept at holding on to her tears, but that she let them flow that day as she and my father drove away from Kilbryde Castle down the rhododendron drive, back through the midges and past the sheep, my father listening helplessly to her shuddering sobs. Fiona and I were too young to take on the burden of their apprehension and grief; at the time, we were too busy with our own. Can you ever be completely happy separated from those you hold most dear and are responsible for – especially when they seem so small and defenseless with round, frightened eyes and tight, brave smiles? You continue aching for their presence, their nearness, for weeks, months after parting. Or am I projecting my feelings onto them? And, after all, they did have each other. If they weren't wholly complete without their daughters, they were deeply content as a couple.

Nearly half a century earlier, my father's parents, Andrew

and Sara Blair-Hill, had suffered the same anguished partings and separations which were part of the assumption of the Raj. It was something everyone accepted – sending your children "home" was a duty you owed to them and to the Empire. We cannot conceive of it now. People, especially in continental Europe, find the notion of sending children to boarding school bewildering, even barbaric, but it would be fruitless and foolish to impose modern day expectations of parenting on the past.

Andrew Blair-Hill arrived in the High Range in 1894, but it wasn't until eleven years later that he returned on furlough to Blairgowrie to collect his young bride Sara and bring her on the long and hazardous journey to the hills he had made his home. It took courage and fortitude to face the unknown as Sara did. Her life, she knew, would not only be rigorous and spartan, but very different from the cosy, comfortable world of Blairgowrie.

There was no running water, of course, nor electricity; there were few of the comforts of home and she spent her time "making do". There was no doctor in the district and certainly no antibiotics. She had to learn at least the basics of the local language; she had to learn to ride a horse, the only means of transport. Her horse, Lustre, was given to her as a wedding present and she grew to depend on him for her independence and for companionship.

In 1907 she gave birth to her first born boy, Roy. A local midwife administered to her and for a time was concerned that Sara was losing too much blood. She was urged to drink a brackish brew of roots and herbs and quite soon the bleeding stopped. Sara never knew what was in this mixture, or if the bleeding would have stopped anyway. It was indelicate to discuss childbirth or "women's matters". She engaged an ayah

Andrew, with Sara on Lustre, and the syce

to help her care for the small mewling creature that tugged at her heart.

The sunlit days were spent in playing with him, singing, rocking him, protecting him from the ever-present Indian hazards: infections of every kind, scorpions, snakes and bandicoots (rats the size of small dogs, intelligent and fierce). She held him close in the monsoon months, making sure his blankets were dry, that the damp did not penetrate his clothes; she held him aloft from the leeches and sang to him over the howls of the jackals and the far away bugling of elephants.

James Finlay's company records are kept in Glasgow University – letters between the manager in India and the Head office in Glasgow in the early years of the twentieth century. There are comments, sometimes very personal ones, about my grandparents, where they complain of them being profligate by wanting an advance for trips home (always denied). And a complaint about my grandfather being, "Too much married, with one child coming fast upon the others' heels."

Sara, as a young bride, kept a journal – not detailed, just jottings of daily happenings, but through it you can hear her wonder at my father's birth, fourteen months after Roy, on November 18th 1909, and her love for both her boys. She wrote of dresses to be mended or altered by the tailor, fetes to be arranged at the club, dinner dances and Masonic meetings, lists of duties for the servants. She pressed flowers, kept little notes and calling cards and baby curls wrapped in muslin at the back of her journal and I suspect it was for no eyes but hers. On her death, it was found by my uncle Roy's wife Doris and it became a family treasure, not of any real value, of course, but precious to us because it let us have a glimpse of this stoical woman's life. On Aunt Doris's death, it vanished.

Chokra, Ian, Roy, Sara and Andrew

My father, Ian Baxter, was born in the same bungalow at Top Station where Roy had been delivered, with the same attendant midwife, this time with little fuss and a mercifully short labour. Sara related in her diary that, to her, her sleeping son looked perfect. He was creamy pale with tiny ears and a cupid mouth – he looked like "a small cherub that has just climbed out of a painting." The two little boys soon became inseparable. They were carried in dhoolis by doting servants, they ran in and out of the canna lilies, they chased dragon flies and tried to teach a myna bird to talk. They wore large topees in the sun and long rubber coats in the monsoon rain – they were her babies. Roy was five and Ian just three and a half when she had to give them up.

"But why? Why? Wait until they are a little older. I cannot be parted from them now."

The rows ensued each evening while the little boys slept in the bedroom at the back of the bungalow.

"Sara, dear, I will not get furlough for another five years. By that time Roy will be ten and Ian eight and a half. Do you think it is fair to them to deprive them of an education, of being members of British society? They are British boys."

"Then why did we come here? Why have my boys at all, if they are to be pulled away from me. I cannot be without them. Supposing it is years and years before we see them again? My own children will be strangers to me. No, no, I cannot do this."

But she did. Money was saved for all four of them to travel Home, where the boys were left with Aunt Ann

I watch my granddaughter Edie, aged three and a half, and see her feeling hurt and her lip tremble when someone pushes her away, or she is excluded from a game. My heart aches for her when she runs after "big girls" who cannot be bothered with her; but when she falls, someone picks her up, kisses the hurt forehead or knee and brushes away her tears, distracts her from her distress. Who, I wonder, did Sara's little boys run to when sad, frightened or lonely? Of course, I was not there to hear her conversations, nor was I privy to her thoughts, so I have imagined them in a voice I do not believe was too different from hers.

Sara and Andrew made the desolate return journey to the High Range, up the rocky road to their bungalow at Top Station.

The silence hit her with a force. No whoops of childish delight, no squabbling little brothers that she needed to separate. They were gone; the joy of her heart, the light that shone in her life was thousands of miles away. But Sara did not give way to self-pity. She pushed her fervent yearning deep down inside her and tried to live the life expected of a Memsahib. She became involved with the activities of the Club.

The High Range Club was an institution that combined

the Munnar Club and the Gymkhana Club and was started in 1909. In 1913, Andrew was in charge of catering and my grandmother Sara seems to have been the first of many wives who served as honourable manageress. Before she left for Scotland she had written a letter to the chairman of the club, Mr Cole:

'Dear Mr Cole

'I believe there is a meeting of the Club Committee this afternoon. I would like to take an interest in the Club when we return from home. I will be quite willing to take up the work thoroughly and do all I can to make things comfortable, keep things nice at the Club.

'If you care to mention this at the meeting this afternoon you might do so.

Yours sincerely,

Sara Blair–Hill'

Nothing unusual in the letter, but it touches me profoundly – because that was just before she was to deliver her two baby boys Home. No wonder she wanted to fill her time with club duties.

Andrew became a mason and joined Lodge Heather. There were meetings once a month and an annual Masonic dinner. He enjoyed the masculine company in this man's world. He missed his boys, but the tea estate kept him busy with little time for regret or to feel much sense of loss. It was Sara who had to fill the long lonely days. Her horse Lustre, though ageing, was her friend and confidante. She would lean on his neck, her pent up tears flowing and whisper her longing to him, "Oh my boys, I miss my boys, Lustre," and he would whinny in reply and she felt comforted. She made no mention of her sadness to

Andrew. What would be the point? "You knew that this was the way of it when you married me Sara."

They sat on the verandah in the evening just before night snuffed out the day, he with his whisky and soda, Sara with her gin and lime and the boys' absence sat between them.

Letters were sent home every week taking about three weeks to arrive in Blairgowrie, where they would be read aloud by Aunt Ann to Roy and Ian, who sat with wide eyes remembering their parents. But gradually the faces faded and they just became names, Mamma and Papa.

After the first year of separation, Ian asked his older brother, "Roy, who are Mamma and Papa?"

"They are our parents, you remember. Papa smoked cigars and Mamma smelt of roses, remember?"

Ian wanted to remember, wanted to cling to the fading shadow of them but very soon they were gone. Roy would tell us this tale with a smile. "Wasn't your father a funny boy?"

He did not seem funny to me, just a sad, lonely, bewildered little boy and the vision of him haunts me still. Life must have been so strange for him, so young, so vulnerable in the care of the formidable Aunt Ann.

Miss Ann Stewart, my grandmother Sara's spinster sister, was round and of quite astonishingly unprepossessing aspect. In fact she was, to put it bluntly, very ugly. I remarked on it once and was reprimanded with a strong, "Shush!"

Her ugliness must have caused her great anguish, for she grew a shell of bitterness that caused her, on occasion, to act with a savagery that was startling. She never had a suitor; no beau called for Ann Stewart at Loonbrae in Blairgowerie to ask her to a dance, to tea, to walk. During World War I, she claimed, like countless others in her situation, that her fiancé had been killed.

It was her shameful secret that no fiancé had ever existed. Did she know, I wonder, that her secret was common knowledge in Blairgowerie? "Poor Ann," they would say.

Poor Ann sealed up her ears and hardened her heart. Men were shallow, faithless creatures anyway. In her eyes, all boys would grow into men and therefore were not to be trusted. Indeed, they were to be punished just for their gender before they grew into the enemy.

Little Ian was a ravishingly beautiful child, with blond curls and a sensitive, sweet nature. His beauty and his sweetness provoked Aunt Ann's ire, so that punishment of him was a daily occurrence: punishment, it seemed, just for existing. His hands were strapped and caned if his eyes cast the wrong look. It was common at that time for boys' hands to be put into splints to prevent thumb sucking and nail biting. He had a ruler pushed down his shirt to make him sit up straight; he was shut in a cupboard in the dark until he "learned to behave."

On one occasion, in a sweet shop in Blairgowrie he went to buy sherbet dabs and gob stoppers with his pocket money, when he was overwhelmed by the need to pee. His bladder opened involuntarily. He was mortified and didn't know how to make amends.He handed over his treasured penny to the shopkeeper. "I am sorry, Sir, I will give you a penny if you wipe it up." The outraged shopkeeper gave him a thrashing and the news of this shameful incident soon reached Aunt Ann.

"You wicked, dirty boy, how could you shame this house?"

He was beaten again and sent to bed with no supper. He lay in the dark and wondered where his mother was, his father – what had become of him? And his ayah, his beloved ayah, where was she? Ian was three years and seven months old. These tales of my father's childhood, so part of our family history, provoked from my mother murmurs of "Poor wee boy," but Ian just laughed. "It was fine. I got over it. It made me stronger."

Aunt Ann was perverse though. For it was she who took him to a studio in Dundee, brushed his hair and made him pose, with a clay pipe, as a representation of Millais' "Bubbles" – the image was later used to advertise Pears soap. Fiona still has the picture, which hangs in an Edwardian ebony frame in her house. It was Aunt Ann who was to be my father's tutor at Miss Ann Stewart's School until he went to the local school, aged five, and thence onto the parish school, Hamilton Academy. Roy was sent, aged eleven, to the public school, Glenalmond.

* * * * *

Ian spent his teenage years living in Uddingston with his aunt and uncle, Sir William and Nell Marshall, and, when he was not away at school, his brother and friend Roy joined him there during the holidays. He grew to love and respect these surrogate parents who treated him with kindness and affection and allowed him to find his own way through the thorny path of his adolescence. He remained thin and wiry, his brown hair, with the hated curls, Brylcreemed and brushed daily. He supported Uddingston Football team and learned to play cricket and tennis – he wasn't very accomplished at either, but his enthusiasm made up for his lack of prowess. He and Roy were given a dog to share, to love and to care for – he was called Roy-dog, a rough-haired, smiley-faced mongrel, who followed them through heath and heather, into rivers and ponds, chased balls and butterflies and lay panting between them after the exertions that boyhood brings.

Ian pretended not to notice when young girls with sleek hair and dimpled cheeks smiled at his good looks. He was too shy to approach them and anyway, fishing for tiddlers was safer and more pleasurable than going to a dance in the stuffy village hall, a hall that smelt of sweat and fruit sweeties and illicit Woodbines. He never dared imagine that one of these slender creatures would honour him with a dance. What would they talk about if she did? Would he have to take her home? What then?

Ian had his first cigarette aged 9. He was caught by Uncle Will Marshall, who hoped to put him off the habit by insisting he smoke two full cigarettes right to the end. He was, not unnaturally, sick. But it didn't put him off tobacco. He and Roy would pick up discarded Weights and Woodbines, only half smoked, and save them up to smoke away from the house, down by the river or behind the cricket pavilion, clichéd as it was. By 14, he was regularly buying packets of five cigarettes or singles; by 15, he was spending his pocket money on packets of ten.

In the summer months he and Roy would hitchhike through the soft Scotch mist to Pitlochry to the Highland Games and down to Blairgowrie, now no longer their home, where they earned a small wage for picking the raspberries and sweet loganberries that were turned into jam in Dundee.

One summer they took a ferry to the Isle of Man for the TT races. They took Roy-dog with them and the three of them stayed in a small boarding house in Port Erin where dogs were allowed. They rolled up their trousers and paddled in the sea with Roy-dog splashing beside them. They ate silky thick ice cream between two wafers from the Italian/Scottish man in his van, had Manx kippers for breakfast and fish and chips doused in vinegar and wrapped in newspaper for their suppers, sitting on the edge of the short pier, their legs dangling over the side. They watched girls parade along the promenade in floaty little skirts and seamed stockings and strappy shoes, white net gloves and pulled-on little cloches that prevented their curls from blowing free in the sea breeze. Roy took much pleasure in relating these anecdotes and we took much pleasure in listening to them.

Ian was pleased to leave school. He had worked hard at his lessons, but he didn't shine in any subject and, unlike Roy, he was not a natural sportsman and, while he enjoyed music, he could not play an instrument. His diffidence, shyness and sensitivity made him a target for bullying, especially when things marked him out as different from the other boys: that he didn't have a proper kilt jacket to go with his kilt, or the right knee high prickly green wool socks or a dirk to put in them. He didn't have brown or black brogue shoes, but plain school ones that he wore every day and which were constantly being re-soled and heeled. Andrew and Sara, his parents, were always short of money (the reason they were unable to visit their children), so sent home enough to cover the children's board with the Marshalls, but not enough for clothes or extras. Both boys outgrew their short trousers and shirts, jumpers and shoes and there are many photographs of them both with knobby wrists protruding from too-short shirts and jackets.

William Marshall bought the boys new clothes and ensured that Ian was engaged as a junior clerk with W. M. Marshall, Ross, Munroe, solicitors in Motherwell (his own firm) and shortly after as an audit clerk with Messrs. Fraser & Ferguson, Chartered Accountants in Glasgow. He was exchanging weekly letters with his stranger–father who put the idea to him that a life in India might be an agreeable one for a lad "without many accomplishments." In fact, Ian was a bright boy – and diligent. People just expected so little of him, that he never expected much of himself.

Parting from Roy was harder than he had imagined. Despite their different educations, public school/local academy, they remained close. Roy had become a clerk in a bank and laughed with Ian that it was "Dull, old boy, but I'll play rugger at the weekends and maybe some golf and I'll be fine." He saw his brother off at Central Station in Glasgow and Ian long remembered his wavy, sticky-up hair, his red cheeks and the warm clasp on his shoulder as he smiled his too tight smile of goodbye. "Dear chap, I'll miss you, but you'll be too busy to think of me. We'll write. Make sure you do!"

He stood on the platform in his bank clerk suit and his dark Glenalmond Old Boys tie and waved Ian away to the sun and a life he admitted he could not imagine. He ran with the grey muzzled Roy–dog down the platform as the train, puffing smoke and steam, chuffed its way forward, carrying Ian to his new life, as Roy waved him away with all the goodwill from his generous, brotherly heart. They were not to meet again for ten years.

On the 25th October 1930, Ian sailed on the *SS Orford* for India, where he spent the next 29 years.

* * * * *

People said that each child born of the Raj felt that they were in some way superior to the natives of the country their fathers' ruled; that being British gave them permission to look down on anyone who wasn't. This was not true of Ian. I am not sure what his parents taught him – they were, after all, absent during his childhood and were themselves children of the Empire – but he brought Fiona and me up to believe that all men and women were equal. The chance of birth could mean that their lives were very different, but he knew that each life was as valuable as anyone else's, not just in the eyes of God, but in his eyes too. The caste system in India was complicated and unfair, but so too was the class system in England.

SS Orford arrived at Columbo where he was met by his father, Andrew, and they proceeded to Cochin and thence up the winding ghat to Munnar, the strange and beautiful place that was to be his new home. My father told me they were shy of each other and the first meal they shared at the Malabar Club House in Cochin was strained and awkward, with frequent pauses – only to be broken with both of them speaking at once. Ian had the impression that his father was already disappointed in him. This probably was not true, but he was so anxious to be approved of by the man who had been the distant hero of his boyhood, a fantasy father that he felt unable to measure up to in any way.

He had no physical contact with his parents in the intervening years; James Finlay's records show the company constantly turning down Andrew's requests for an advance of his salary to visit his boys in Scotland. The pain this must have caused Sara can only be imagined. In Ian's breast pocket was a photograph of Andrew on a horse playing polo and another one, sepia and crumpled, of both his parents on horses, his mother seated side-saddle and being led by an Indian syce. He had gazed at it secretly and with longing through the lonely years without them – and now here was his father, broad-chested and sun-tanned, with white crinkles around his eyes; a man who laughed easily and loudly, but who became silent and embarrassed by the admiration and hero-worship in his young son's eyes. They shook hands as they bid each other good night. "We'll make any early start in the morning. We'll go first to the High Range Club and I'll introduce you to some of the chaps. Mr Pinches the General Manager will be there; he is boss to all of us. But Mr Davison is the manager of Letchmi Estate. You will be answerable to him."

Munnar, seen from the High Range Club House in the early morning light, resembled nothing so much as the soft hills of Perthshire – only the heather was missing; not like one's image of India at all. A slow moving river cut through the middle of this grassy punchbowl and beside it grew reeds and rushes, and willows wept just as they did beside the river Ericht as it ambled its way through Blairgowrie and the undulating fields and peaty moors.

Generations of planters had made it an enviable sports ground. Tennis courts, cricket nets and a nine hole golf course. And about two or three miles away, the High Range race course, where my grandfather rode with some success. Polo was played with great enthusiasm; indeed I still have the silver cup won by my grandfather, "Andrew Blair-Hill on Euclid in 1906."

Letchmi estate had the highest rainfall of anywhere in the High Range, closely followed by Kalaar. Averaging 225 inches in the monsoon months, it could be much more; one July in 1924, 171.20 inches fell in that month alone. With the rainfall came the leeches and Letchmi and Kalaar estates had an abundance of them.

The assistant's bungalow was small and white–washed with a corrugated iron roof. Inside, it smelt of kerosene, stale tobacco and citronella oil; the floors were dark brown wood, the furniture was practical but drab – heavy brown chests and

Tea and the High Range Hills

cupboards and wicker chairs. There was not much in the way of crockery or cutlery and not much in the way of adornment, either. A picture of George V and another of a hunting scene hung from the wall. There was a single bed in the bedroom, a small bedside table with a kerosene oil lamp and a carafe and a glass and a copy of the Bible. The bathroom too, was small. It had a "thunderbox", a large latrine encased in dark brown wood, emptied each day by the sweeper, and a small tin bathtub with a large tin cup used for "dunking". There was a china basin with a large jug in it, with a small mirror above, suspended from a hook on the wall by a piece of string. The mirror was slightly cracked in one corner and Ian, who was superstitious, hoped it didn't mean bad luck.

He met his cook and his young chokra and learned to salaam them both, putting his hands together and bowing his head. He prepared for his first night alone in his new home by unpacking his topee and his shorts and shirts, bought at Simon

Artz shop in Port Said. His mother had stayed at the High Range Club in order to meet him and spend a few days with him before she and Andrew left for the Plains, where Andrew was transport manager for the company in Trichinopoly. It seemed odd to come all this way to see his parents again, only to be parted after such a short spell in their company.

So this, then, was his new world. Arriving in India just as the nights were drawing in in Scotland, he was to enjoy the delicate air of the hills and witness each day dawn with a soft sunrise and a sun shining on his head until it slid behind the Anamudi Mountain in the west.

He had been obliged to sign a contract with his employers, James Finlay & Co., before he set out from Glasgow on his long journey to the unfamiliar east. Young planters were to be given a period of six months trial or probation and they were paid a basic salary of 200 rupees a month (roughly £15) and they were not encouraged to take home leaves or "furloughs". It was part of your contract that you would not marry for the first five years. The young men were required to have Tamil classes, the least easy to master of all the Indian languages, and until he acquired the necessary standard of fluency, Ian was not allowed any leave at all. This would take at least three years. You got 250 rupees (£19.25) if you passed your oral exam and 1,000 rupees (£77.00) if you passed the Tamil reading and writing exam, so there was incentive. You were allowed two failures, but if you failed a third time, you were on the boat home. The company decreed: "Managers and Assistants proceeding on furlough pay their own expenses from the estate to England, but will receive the sum of 500 rupees towards the cost of their return journey."

In those early days he rode round the estate on horseback.

Indeed, some of the young men would arrange to meet up at "Cigarette Point", a crossroads where they would have a smoke and exchange news, or just chat for a few minutes. In this isolated area, the need for conversation was not often met; sometimes the only conversation you had in English was in the Club at the weekends. The nights must have seemed long; oil lamps to read by after supper, but then what else to do but go to bed. Besides, the dawn would soon press its pink fingers against the blinds.

The day started early with the "mustering" of the labour at 5.30. The pocket check roll and other records were the assistant manager's responsibility and, like the workers, he had to carry his "tiffin" (lunch) out to the field. The working day lasted until 6.30 or 7.00 pm, seven days a week, and as most estates had three or four assistants, they were allowed one day off in the week in rotation.

Despite the fact that his bungalow was provided, it is hard to imagine how he was able to pay for all his needs: servants, food, clothes, his horse and his (admittedly meager) bar bill, let alone save any money in case, when his five years enforced bachelorhood was up, he chose to marry. To be fair, the company did give you allowances: 175 rupees for a horse, 150 rupees for a wife. And 100 rupees a month for the servants.

In the 1920s, the tea pluckers were paid about 12 annas for a ten hour day, the equivalent of a shilling (the 1920s wage of an English private soldier). Pretty poor wages, but there were perks and benefits; they had a rice allowance (instigated by Andrew, my grandfather) and their children were given a somewhat rudimentary primary education, and the medical care, whilst primitive, was the same for everyone who worked for the company, planters and pluckers alike.

There were the hazards of snakes and scorpions – Ian was not afraid of either, but was respectful of both. There were the pests of cockroaches and rats and mosquitoes, although in the High Range malaria was rare. Water had to be boiled at all times and ice was never taken in drinks, for fear of typhus, typhoid and cholera. In 1930, when Ian first arrived in India, there were no antibiotics; if you had an injury that turned septic, it was only patient good nursing that pulled you through. Hygiene was very important. You washed your hands at every opportunity and he was taught the rule about food: "Peel it, boil it, cook it, or forget it."

You never went barefoot for fear of the dreaded hookworm. The larvae of these ghastly little creatures entered the body through the skin (usually the soles of the feet) and they travelled through your blood, up into the lungs (which sounds hard work), through the bronchi and trachea and then would get swallowed, but their journey was only half way through. They would then pass into the digestive tract, attach themselves to the wall of the small intestine, where they would mature into adult worms and live happily for about ten years. Your skin would itch and irritate from a rash, you would get asthma–type symptoms or pneumonia, abdominal pain, diarrhoea, weight loss and excessive farting, anaemia – due to the little buggers feeding on your blood – weakness and heart problems, even heart failure. Wearing a pair of slippers or shoes at all times seemed a good habit to get into.

The assistant (senadori) was expected to know his place and his dignity took its fair share of dents. One of my father's friends, who rode neither a horse nor a motorbike was obliged, on his first chukka (round) of the estate, to maintain a gentle trot on foot beside his mounted manager (periadori).

The young assistants rarely had cars, and being given a lift back from the club one night, my father's friend was dropped off at the estate office and had to walk through the monsoon rain and the leeches, some four miles to his bungalow without a torch or light, drenched of course, and fearful of meeting some dangerous wildlife on his way. In turn, the assistants got up to some scallywaggish behaviour, constantly scheming and conniving to outwit their managers. One trick was to lie in bed after a late and often excessive night and send their syce appropriately attired in solar topee and field clothes around the estate on the horse, occasionally passing the manager at a strategic distance offering a business-like wave. Another ruse was to keep one's hat and raincoat soaking wet on a peg in the porch to prove that one had "just that moment" returned from the field. The manager was seldom duped.

Prior to the Munnar/Cochin road being opened up, there was a ropeway that ran from top station to bottom station, Kottagudi in the foothills near Bodinayakanur, and tea was sent down to be transported by rail to Tuticorin and shipped from there to the UK. Rice and assorted goods would, in turn, come up. It was the most heinous offence to be caught riding on it. The punishment was instant dismissal. Fear of injury or death and subsequent costs to the company was the main reason for the rule. When asked about insurance and personal injury, there was no question of payment to individuals. The management and staff were insured so that the company could claim the compensation to cover the loss of service of any of their employees.

My father and two friends dared each other to travel from top station to bottom station, hideously dangerous – it was utter madness. They arrived, shaken and in one piece, but had to make the return journey (this time by car); the date was

1931, when my father was a foolhardy 23 years old. He was never found out.

Assistants were required to fulfil any request their manager made of them, however childish or unreasonable. Indeed, one night three young assistants (including Ian) were summoned to their manager's bungalow and were there required to arm themselves with topees, an umbrella, a walking stick and a shooting stick respectively, and to enact the Changing of the Guard at Buckingham Palace for the manager's small daughter, instead of a bedtime story. They felt foolish, and the warm sweet sherry proffered by the manager's wife didn't make up for their humiliation, but they had to do it. It was a strange feudal existence.

Socially, and in sport, assistants had to turn out regardless of transport problems and return to their estates the same night. Cricket, tennis, squash, fishing and golf were the High Range sporting attractions and shikaar (shooting), which my father always hated. Rugby, though, was the top High Range sport and good rugby players were bought drinks, slapped on the back and generally thought of as "good eggs" and "top men".

Ian's brother, Roy, was a very good rugby player indeed. He played for Uddingston back in Scotland and stories of his sporting prowess spread to the High Range club through the newspapers and gossip and my grandfather's proud boasts in the men's bar at the Club. When Ian – shy, skinny and, frankly, hopeless at rugby – arrived in the district, the men shook his hand with real admiration and bought him pints of beer in the men's bar. "Of course you'll go immediately into the team, Ian. No trials for you." My father's protests were not heeded and his cry of, "No, that's my brother Roy," was not believed. People just accused him of being over-modest. His ineptitude was soon discovered on the first Saturday of the rugby season, which found his spindly legs not fast or nimble, sprawled almost constantly in the mud, with the opposing team trampling him into the hole he wished would open up for him. It took a long time in this macho world for him to recover any sort of dignity. However, his kind, gentle nature and his self-deprecating humour won round even the coldest shoulder, but it took time.

Loneliness for Ian and his colleagues became routine. Their lives consisted of estate work, organising the labour, bookkeeping and accounts, riding around several hectares of tea, inspecting for blight or any other damage or infestation, Tamil classes, Tamil homework, Tamil exams and housekeeping discussions with "the Boy". Breaks in routine were jaunts to the Club, Masonic meetings, gymkhanas, the odd game of Polo and very occasionally a dance or ball with visitors from another district.

One day in October, there was one such visit from planters and their families from Peermade, a hill station further down the Western Ghats. As my father had his bath with a tin jug to scoosh over him (no sponges as they were a lurking place for scorpions), shaved and Brylcreemed his hair, little did he know that his life would change forever, as a blonde young woman with the bluest of blue eyes looked at herself in the mirror and wondered if she'd "do".

* * * * *

Beside the French windows that led from the ballroom to the verandah of the High Range Club, stood this young woman with the palest gold hair, paler than a field of corn, as pale as moonlight. Her eyes were round and that blue that is commonly seen in babies, but usually fades with adulthood.

Violet

Her cheekbones were high, her wrists and ankles delicate and she was slim as a branch of willow.

Ian caught his breath. Where had this vision sprung from? Was he dreaming? Who was she? She seemed to belong more to the world he saw on the silver screen on the third Friday of every month in the small cinema in Munnar town. But she looked artless; she had a shy way of casting down her eyes when someone addressed her, her small hands held together, lightly clasped, as if she had been told not to fidget. She wore a light coral lipstick, but no other makeup, and her dress was a cream coloured silk with English flowers on it – poppies, daisies, cornflowers – and caught in the middle by a small belt, accentuating her tiny waist.

This was Violet Barbara Jamieson Skeoch, but she was known as Violet Patterson; her stepfather's name was bestowed on her without her ever being asked if she approved and she became one of the Patterson Girls, along with her sister Ailsa, 13 months her junior. A small part of her minded that her real father, the handsome, blond young man, brutally injured in mind and body in 1918 just before the War to end all Wars came to an end, had been airbrushed from her life. His death had been long and lingering and Violet's memory of him was contained only in a small sepia photograph taken in a stuffy studio in Ayr. She would look at it in secret; it was deemed impolite and ungrateful that she should have thoughts of her real father when her new stepfather had given her a home and security and a new life in India, as he swept his new bride, Jessie, my grandmother, away from the drab greyness of her life in Prestwick, where she'd been trying to support her two small girls. Because her first husband lived, gibbering and in pain and in nearly every respect dead, except that his heart still beat it's pitiful beat, she received no pension of any kind.

Violet's loyalty to her mother made her swallow the distaste she felt at losing her real name Skeoch, which was, after all, a more interesting name than Patterson. But she was introduced as Violet Patterson and given the initials VP. It was a secret pleasure when she looked at her passport, "Violet Skeoch", hanging on secretly to that identity, that part of herself that was Charles Skeoch's daughter, the father she so very much resembled, but never knew.

As Ian watched her, Violet's eyes were cast down as she fiddled with the clasp of her watch, given to her as a 21st birthday present. Her blonde hair framed her head like a halo. Something caught in his throat; he seemed unable to move. On enquiring who she was, the reply, "One of the Patterson Girls. Hands off, old man – one of them is engaged to Patrick Leahy and he is 6' 5" and a rugby player."

Ian was dashed. Here was the loveliest woman he had ever seen and she belonged to someone else. Of course she did. No one as beautiful could still be free. Men would be falling over themselves to sit at her feet. Anyway, what hope could he have? He wasn't good at much, not sport (memories of the dreadful rugby day flashed before him), he wasn't rich or clever. What on earth could he offer such a prize? What he had, of course, was gentleness, warmth, humour, kindness and a quiet strength. Violet's eyes had taken him in already; this slim, dark haired, good looking young man, with eyes that looked at her steadily and never really left her. It was unsettling to be so regarded and his gaze pulled her eyes to him in response. Of course, she didn't know of the muddle about it being supposed she was the one engaged to Patrick.

He asked her to dance and once she had consulted her

dance programme, she agreed gladly with a shy smile. I loved to hear my father relate the story of their meeting and that first dance which he told with a secret smile and a faraway look in his eyes. I made him tell it again and again and it became my favourite fairy tale. He said, "She felt tiny and fragile. It was as if I held a shaft of sunlight in my arms. The band was playing Gershwin's 'Love Walked In' and it became our own special song." He'd draw on his pipe, look embarrassed, cough and laugh. Theirs was an instant falling in love, although Violet pretended to be cooler than she felt. It was part of the rules, the ritual of courtship. But Ian proposed and Violet accepted. He brought a choice of diamond rings for her to choose from as an engagement ring and with an unerring eye she chose the most expensive – a large solitaire on a bridge of little diamonds. Ian's diet became even more frugal and treats to himself became non-existent.

Violet and Ian were married on 10th May 1940 at Peermade Church. Violet wore a heavy silk dress, long, cut on the bias and with a train, and a seemingly endless veil with a headdress of pearls to keep it in place. Theirs was probably one of the happiest unions I've known.

Nearly ten years were spent in the sun and in the monsoon rain content in each other's company, watching with joy and pride as their girls grew into their own separate and unique personalities. They didn't look too far into the future, but of course the future soon pulled them into an unsettling and sorrowful present; the inevitable parting from their children as they handed them into the care of strangers. This is what was expected – it was the price you paid for the Indian life.

I can imagine my father holding his wife when the pain of parting from their daughters was too much to bear alone. He

Violet and Ian on the day of their engagement 1939

understood and shared her grief; they were part of each other, but they felt things, of course, in their different ways. As the P&O Chusan pulled out of Tilbury Docks, Violet wept as Ian's arm encircled her shoulders. There was no one to wave to on the quay, no handkerchiefs fluttering goodbye, but every movement of the ship took her further from us, her babies.

She ate the smoked salmon and gazed at the stars, watched the flying fish and listened to the band with a heart inside her chest that seemed to have gone numb. She was lucky, she knew, to be travelling in a first class cabin with all the attendant luxury but she kept wondering what her daughters were doing, how they were feeling, if they were hurting. Her lip got stiffer and she tightened her mouth to hold in any escaping sighs, for she knew she must endure this heartache, as it was what was expected of her; she was a daughter of the Raj, after all.

And so on up the winding ghat road, back through the pepper vines, the lemon-scented grass, through the tea and to the bungalow – our bungalow. It was empty now of children; the silence fell on her ears and her heart and she clenched her fists against the pain of it. Ayah had moved on to the Cook family, so she no longer smelt the familiar coconut hair oil or jasmine.

She went into the bedroom Fiona and I had shared. The servants had put abandoned toys on our counterpaned beds and she saw one brown leather sandal. Whose? Too small for Fiona – it was mine. As she picked it up, she saw the imprint of toe marks, with the big toe longer than the others – yes, it was mine. She steeled herself to win through this grief, much like my grandmother Sara had years before. She stood up, pulled her shoulders back, ran a hand through her hair and went to find Boy, to go through the housekeeping list and restock the larder.

FIVE

A Tiger's Wedding

The lights from the candles filled the room, blotting out any other light. They were reflected in the long windows, shining off the polished shutters; there seemed to be a hundred cakes with six candles on each of them – six hundred candles and voices raised, singing for ME. "Happy birthday, dear Isla – happy birthday to you." My chin felt tight and painful and my throat was swollen as if I couldn't get enough air, my eyes pricked. But I didn't cry. Not crying was my brave boast now, for weeks and weeks.

I hadn't cried when my parents rounded the corner in their little Austin car, engulfed, shrouded from sight by rhododendron bushes, only a little puff of dust, the last view of them. I hadn't cried when Alexandra showed me my bed and said I was allowed to put a bear or a doll on top of the counterpane. "You need your own sheets, blankets, eiderdown – have you got them? Have they got name tapes on them?" They had. But my name stitched in red looked a bit silly now. Just a week ago, I was so pleased and proud – Isla Blair-Hill seemed a good name, important, and now it just looked as if I'd made it up.

But it was my birthday. I was six and I was no longer a little girl. I was a big girl who did not cry. Other people would be hurt by my tears and so I learned not to spill them. I seemed to taste them in my mouth instead, salty, a little bitter, accompanied by that slight pain, as if my tongue had been paralysed and my jaw and chin just ached and ached.

People were clapping and laughing and I was being urged to cut the cake. More applause. Then, it was announced that everyone should make a wish for me with their first mouthful and then they could make a wish for themselves. Only with hindsight did I notice people gulp the first bite of rather squishy sponge and jam with too much icing, move on swiftly to the second mouthful which they relished, eyes closed – wishing and wishing.

We all sat down and as the cake was cut up, Maureen Cameron, a big girl who was on the point of her exams and leaving, started singing. She had a sweet, clear voice, "Westering home with a song in the air," and she ended the chorus with, "Isla, my heart, my own one." She was *singing* to me about *me*. I didn't know anyone else called Isla, so who could it be? Perhaps this dark, cold, rather forbidding place was not so bad after all, if someone who didn't know me loved me enough to sing about me and call me her "own one". I didn't know that the "Islay" she was singing about was an island. I wanted so much to be noticed and liked and here was someone who did both; Maureen Cameron became the focus of all my longings and missings. I kept hoping she smelt of lilies of the valley. But she didn't and she never looked at me again.

And this *was* a strange place. It seemed so dark and so cold and you seemed to get told off for things you didn't know were wrong – and punished without explanation. It was all so different from Munnar. Ayah would scold you, but she told you why. "No, Missy, don't put the pencil in the light socket. It will frizzle you all up and then you'll *die*."

I stopped doing it, because I didn't want to die – and Sunderaj would tell me not to prod the ants' nest, because they would get cross and bite me. There was a reason. But Munnar was sunny and smelled of warm, sunshiny things – limes, crushed marigolds, wood smoke and pine trees. The garden was tall with canna lilies and poppies and brightly coloured flowers and bright green birds that made a lot of noise and swooped and darted in and out of the trees. Even the crows sounded warm and friendly in my memory. Of course, there were the monsoon days, but I didn't think of those, not now in this dark place called Scotland. The best days were those of a "tiger's wedding" – sunshine and showers and great big arching rainbows. You felt you could just stretch out your hands and pull the colours out of the sky, wash your face in them, taste them and paint them all over your body.

In Munnar Ayah would rub me all over with almond oil before our nightly goosle and she would say, "Run around Missy, run around." And we did, naked and giggling, unselfconscious, warm in the sunny evening light.

But now, in Scotland, we had to have our baths with Matron soaping us. She couldn't really see us, as the windows were painted black inside and out, so she would pour water over our heads and didn't know when we got soap in our eyes and noses and were choking. No one explained about the blackened windows, but later I realised it was so we couldn't see each other or ourselves. We were Presbyterians and someone called John Knox said that we were the source of sin. But why were we the source of sin? What had we done?

Equally bewildering was dressing and undressing in bed. Why? I found it hard and I was slow, as I kept putting my legs through my vest or my liberty bodice. I'd only just learnt how to button shirts and now I had to do it without looking. I wasn't the only girl to turn up to morning assembly with things done up all wrong. And ties? Well, it took me ages to learn about ties. Once I learnt, of course, I couldn't stop and put ties on everything: teddy bears, bottles, vases, even the anthracite scuttle in Form I. I didn't understand why we just couldn't get out of bed and put our clothes on and no-one explained.

I began to notice what I'd not known before – COLD. In India there was often heat and even in the monsoon months when the Cardamom Hills were shrouded in mist or sheets of rain, it was not cold. Sometimes your books, clothes and toys would grow a delicate bluish skin of mould from the damp – but there were log fires and hot baths and warm towels. It wasn't cold.

Here in Dunblane, the cold ate into your bones and held you fast. My fingers and toes swelled into red chilblains. We wore fingerless gloves in prep and watched as our breath crystallised into little splinters on the air. Bedtime was worst. There was one hot water bottle that was passed around the dormitory and it was just your bad luck if your turn came last when the bottle was cold.

Because I was newest at school and the youngest I was usually last. But I didn't mind, really. I put my face on it in the dark and it wobbled a bit. It felt like lying on Ayah's soft chest when she told me one of her stories about Jesus or the goddess Letchmi, or just called me her Missy Baba; I imagined that her soft arms were round me huggling me and her kisses brushed my hair as she smoothed it back from my face. I wanted Ayah so much, I got a pain in my chest from wanting her and tears started leaking from my eyes onto the rubbery hot water bottle that of course wasn't Ayah at all. I remembered my promise not to cry and I brushed the salty drops away with my pyjama sleeve. The hot water bottle was quite cold now anyway and I pushed it away onto the floor.

There were wood- and coal-burning stoves in the classrooms, but no heating in the bedrooms; our little tumblers of water by our beds would be frozen solid when the dark dawns summoned us from slumber. Liberty bodices were novel and strange – thick woollen over-vests with rubber buttons down the front and even my slight 6 year old frame was bulked by them. Woollen socks to the knee held up with bits of elastic, Viyella woollen blue blouse, gym slip of maroon, and a maroon and blue striped tie, this was the uniform and was worn every day. We had underpants and over-pants (sort of big bloomers), but the cold fastened you in its hard grasp that no amount of clothes could slacken – overcoats indoors, scarves, gloves, jumpers, nothing kept the cold out – rather they seemed to seal it in.

After a breakfast of usually porridge, we would go upstairs and we "little ones" had to sit on rows of humiliating potties until we had performed. Embarrassment joined humiliation and a growing bubble of fury. Why did we have to do this? We had to dress in bed, have our baths in the dark, but this most private and personal thing, defecating, we were expected to do in public – with the big girls rushing by, others cleaning teeth and joining the dreaded queues for Virol or Cod Liver Oil. It was not long before I became totally constipated. To begin with, I didn't want to perform like this in public – but then I couldn't.

So the daily spoonful of Virol (a rather thick and petrolly looking malt) usually had a spoonful of syrup of figs with it. Eventually I was allowed into the big girls' loo, but wasn't

96

allowed to lock the door. The only thing to stop anybody walking in was a slightly peevish "Somebody's in" as I sat there with my knickers round my ankles. That got a good score on the humiliation board, but it was a hundred-fold better than "Potty Row".

Virol was supposed to be full of vitamins and things that would make little girls big girls. It made me gag. I don't know if our diet was balanced or not, but I remember the things I didn't like. In India there were mangoes and pineapples, papaya and gooseberries, lychees and passion fruit and delicious cinnamon sticks to chew on; there were cashew nuts and oranges, sugary pistachio-puddings. Here, in Scotland, there was "White Pudding" – sticky sausages made of oats, I think – and even more disgusting, "Black Pudding", which was a sort of white pudding soaked in blood – well, that's how Janet Glendenning described it – and I had trouble swallowing a mouthful. Herring, or some hateful fish full of bones, dipped in more oats. Sardines squashed up on bread, horrid smelly fish with their eyes still in, and mashed turnips – orange in colour with a taste of rained-on hay and something that had been buried in the earth for a long time. The mash had horrid spiky bits in it that felt like wooden splinters; the girls called them toenails. That was a thought to put me off too. But worst, oh worst by a long way, worse even than liver with veins in it and blood coming out, was TRIPE. Oh tripe, tripe, tripe. Just the smell of the tripe at Friday lunch times would cause a silence in the dining hall followed by repressed moans, the odd gulp and smothered sobs. Tripe is the most – yes, almost certainly – the most loathsome of things that people put in their mouths.

Tripe is not possible. Its odour is unbelched belches and it looks blubbery and porous, with wavy bits like flapping seaweed, only white; a sort of white, grey-green – like a giant's tongue that has been cut up and stored in a dark cellar for 100 years. It is everything that is uneatable – I'd rather eat a fox.

The onion sauce the tripe sat in was floury and tasted of nothing at all, not even onions. It was sort of viscous, like jelly fish – Irene Lamb said it was like afterbirth. It sort of lay there, glutinously surrounding this lining of some bovine beast's stomach. And we were expected to eat this. The notion of eating it grew more monstrous, the more I looked at it on the plate. I looked, and looked. I could not swallow at all.

One of the rules was "Everything on your plate must be eaten – everything. If you do not like something hold your breath and swallow it, for eat it you will. If, by the end of the meal you have not eaten it, you will sit there until you do. You will forego your next meal until you have eaten this one." But tripe was not possible. One of the reasons I never learnt to sew is because sewing class followed tripe on Fridays and I missed the class. I'd be sitting in the dining room, usually alone, with tears blinked back by pride and defiance. I became something of a cause celebre. "Isla's not here, Miss, she's in the dining room; it's Friday." It wasn't a celebrity I liked.

The powers that be (headmistress, form mistress, matron) decided that lessons must be learned; an example had to be set. Not only would class be missed, but I would have the same meal (tripe) served at each meal – supper, breakfast and so on – To be fair, 24 hours or so later, as soon as I did stretch my fork towards this repulsive thing, with hunger beating the battle over defiance, they removed the plate and gave me what the other girls were eating. It was a strange breaking of the spirit, like people used to do with horses sometimes in India – I hated watching it; so did Daddy. "That's not the way," he'd say.

I was utterly bewildered by the punishments. Very often I hadn't known what it was I'd done wrong. In India, when I was naughty I would be summoned to the drawing room where Mummy would look sad and Daddy would speak to me in his quiet voice – telling me of his disappointment in me and explaining exactly what I had done and how it was unacceptable. I was never struck or shouted at, but asked to go to my room to think about things – and I'd creep away, defiance evaporating, replaced by the lump in the throat that made it hard to speak or swallow. For I usually did know what was wrong, what was rude, what was unkind, boastful, cruel, or silly. And thinking about it in my bedroom would bring the punishment – shame. I was always forgiven.

But now my hands would be hit for being over-eager with a wrong answer, for being late; I stood in the corner for longer than I attended classes for answering back, or giving a wrong look, for pulling someone's hair or talking after lights out. Although I found this surprising – these little thwacks didn't bother me; my hands stung for a bit (longer if there were chilblains), but this didn't last long – the really horrible punishments were the ones that went on and on.

We were all sent to school with wooden "tuck boxes", little trunks that held fruit and biscuits and chocolates, cake and Turkish Delight and favourite treats. At tea time we were allowed one piece of fruit and one chocolate biscuit or cake with our tea. Our parents had arranged for tuck parcels to be sent from Stewarts in Blairgowrie (the shop had been owned by our great grandfather). Oh, the excitement when they arrived! We had one each. "Isla Blair-Hill, parcel for you. Fiona Blair-Hill, parcel for you." The tearing of paper revealed shortbread and chocolate and fudge and all sorts of delicious things.

Some misdemeanour on my part led to the elongated punishment of all my tuck being shared out daily amongst the other girls until the end of term – and I would get nothing. It was wounding and seemed unfair that Peffy Shanks should get my Wagon Wheel and Janice McClure my Blue Riband wafer. This punishment just seemed spiteful.

Being sent to bed in the middle of the day as a punishment – without food, without a book, without any work – would often, through boredom, lead to further bad behaviour. I remember once catching sight of the collection of glass animals owned by the senior girl in our dormitory. She was several years older than us and it was her duty to keep us in check. Gwen Kelly was her name and her glass animals were kept – dusted, loved by her – on the mantelpiece of the dormitory. They were her pride, her treasures and I became enchanted by them on this boring bedtime punishment day. Little green seahorses with yellow eyes, a black and white penguin with a baby by its side. Stripey tigers, white sheep with rough coats and black faces, horses with blonde swishy tails – I got up to look closer. We were all forbidden to touch these precious little pieces of art. But I found myself reaching for the seahorse and – oh horror! The cuff of my pyjama jacket caught the horse's tail and it smashed to the floor, taking with it a grey mother rabbit and her three babies. I was mortified. I scurried back to bed with thumping heart, awaiting the discovery of my disobedience and misplaced curiosity.

It didn't take long. Gwen was in anguished tears as I explained how a huge gust of wind had entered the dormitory and swept the animals off the mantelpiece. I watched as everyone's accusing eyes took in the unruffled beds and curtains, dolls in their places on smoothed counterpanes. I felt ashamed and stricken and genuinely upset for Gwen, but I can't remember the punishment that followed. I doubtless thought that I deserved it.

Fiona was always being sent to bed. She missed birthday parties, Halloween parties, all sorts of happy occasions – she almost took herself to bed before the pronounced punishment as soon as she had done something that was a bit out of order. She often misbehaved, but her behaviour was not disruptive or malicious; she was just naughty sometimes. For example, tying Mrs Cock's gown to her chair (Fiona said Mrs Cock's name was rude and she and Janet Gordon giggled about it), or arranging midnight feasts and getting caught. She was as naughty as any of the other girls; she even led the odd uprising.

The midnight feast – a phenomenon discussed with relish in girls' novels like "What Katy Did at School", was never really enjoyed much by any of us who took part in them, but you'd rather die than admit such a thing. Well, imagine it. Being woken at 1.00 a.m. by a sleepy girl in charge of the alarm clock and forcing your feet into slippers, yourself into your woolly dressing gown, having pulled yourself from the (at last!) warmth of your bed. Crouching in torch light and pulling from underneath the loose floor board curled up pieces of bread and jam saved from tea, Penguin biscuits and Wagon Wheels, jelly babies and sherbet lemons; all of them coated in a sprinkling of dust and bits of fluff, despite their brown paper bag wrapping; an abundant hoard for any mouse or rat that lurked or scurried – or whatever mice and rats do.

And so you would sit, shivering with cold in the unheated dormitory, pretending enjoyment with sleepy "ummmms" and "yummmms" until it was time to pack up the debris and deposit it under the easily lifted floorboard and go back to bed, only to find that sleep had fled and you were awake and ready for the day, but had to lie in the dark in your now-cold bed, shaped like a canoe, the mattress having such a dip in the middle, and you'd feel a bit sick with bits of jelly baby in your teeth while thinking longingly of the lime trees and the sunshine and the canna lilies and mother's lily of the valley perfume and Daddy's pipe and slow smile.

"Going to Coventry" was the worst punishment of all. You were sent to a room, where your meals were brought up to you, your schoolwork and so on, but no-one was allowed to speak to you – staff or pupils. It was only for twenty-four hours, but they were the loneliest twenty-four hours imaginable, and frightening; you felt as if you were living at the bottom of a dark well, with light and life, laughter and chatter seen and heard, but out of reach. You would beg not to be sent to Coventry.

I came out of the "Coventry Room" blinking, as if I had been in the dark for a long time. The room, in fact, was quite light, with a long window that reached nearly to the ground, but it was so narrow that you couldn't really see out of it. I was blinking a lot: so much so that people mentioned it, Alexandra Kelly and Pamela Murdoch. "What's the matter with your eyes, Isla? You keep blinking."

Matron Howisman noticed I was blinking as I had my Virol in the morning. "We'll have to cut your fringe, Missy. That's the problem, your fringe is too long." But she didn't say "Missy" like Ayah said it, as if it was my name and I was her "Missy Baba"– she said it as if I had done something wrong and blinking was something that was bad and I would get sent to Coventry again. I so did not want to be sent to Coventry again.

I was told that I had to go to the Infirmary at tea time; Matron was there with a pair of scissors. I'd seen her use these to cut up pillowcases into squares for dusters. "Sit down, Missy," she breathed with a wheezing sound – and I don't think she could remember my name, so she just said "Missy" in that frightening way, as if she were going to punish me. She put a towel around my neck, sat me on a stool and told me to close my eyes. I felt the scissors slide over the scar on my forehead that was sensitive if anyone touched it and I heard a slow "clip, clip" and it was over. The towel was pulled off and wiped across my face.

"You can go now." So I went. I saw myself later in the darkened window of the dancing room before they closed the shutters and my fringe had become a frill on my forehead about an inch long. I hate short, heavy fringes; why have a fringe at all? Actually why did I have a fringe? Mummy and Ayah said it framed my face, as they clipped it slowly with little snip, snips and showed me myself in a little hand mirror and so I didn't mind it. It felt nice, but I hated this. I felt like a sheep when they cut off its wool, or a plucked chicken. I felt reduced and that I was no longer a Saluki and Mummy would not like my slippery inch of hair and she would say "It's a shame."

I went on blinking.

I forgot about my fringe, because I never saw it again, there were no mirrors, of course, and I soon stopped touching it, but I went on blinking and blinking and annoyed everyone, but didn't know I was doing it, so it was hard to stop. This lasted some months.

It was soon to be Halloween and we all had to have costumes. I had been in "Coventry" when it was decided what we were to be – so all the best parts had gone, the witches, ghosts, vampires and black cats, the bats and wrapped up Egyptian mummies. I was to be an apple blossom fairy. What on earth had a spring-time apple blossom fairy to do with darkness and spooks and hook-nosed, warty, scary people? "That's all the crepe paper that's left, pink and green, so Miss Rae says you can cut it out and be an apple blossom fairy with petals. You have to make a skirt," Janet Glendenning said.

I had no idea how to make a skirt from cut out crepe paper petals. Miss Rae drew petal shaped pieces on the pink and green crepe paper. They were long and looked like the lozenges that Ayah sucked when she had a cold, but bigger of course. It was enough to make a sort of crepe paper petal-y skirt. She said I was to cut round the drawn in lines – but I couldn't. The scissors were blunt at the ends and the blades didn't seem to meet, so when I tried to cut the paper it just skewed off and made a bend in the crepe. I got tearful with frustration and Miss Rae had to cut it out for me. I had to glue the top bits together so that it could be wrapped over a piece of elastic that would go round my waist to make my apple blossom fairy skirt. The glue got everywhere, globs of it fell onto the bit of the petals that were supposed to look nice, and it got on my hands so that there were marks on the crinkly crepe with stretchy tendrils of glue all over it. It looked horrible. I felt humiliated and ashamed that I was so hopeless and I knew I'd look awful as an apple blossom fairy, when everyone else had long black dresses and pokey-up hats as witches and wizards, and Pamela Murdoch (a day girl) had got her father to make a skeleton suit; she was all in black apart from white painted on bones that bent and moved as she walked.

I was trying to stick my petals together, when Fiona came into our form room during "recreation time".

"Isla, Isla come, come now. Come quickly."

"What is it?"

She led me by the hand up to the dormitory at the top of the school. "Come here. Look out of the window, over there to the left, do you see? A tiger's wedding." It was a rainbow arching over the brown coloured moor and above it, another rainbow, just as bright and stretching right up, right over and right down to the ground where it disappeared.

"Do you remember what Mummy said? Her bit of the rainbow, can you say the colours?"

"Red, orange, yellow, blue, green, indigo, violet."

"Yes, blue, green, indigo, violet – do you see the last colour, her colour? Do you remember she said if we saw a rainbow, the last colour was her colour, her name, Violet. If we saw that, we were to know she was there with us, that she was thinking of us."

I looked at the wonder above me and the last colour that was vibrant and then bleached into the sky – Violet. Mummy. Her colour.

I inhaled deeply, as if to invoke the colour from the rainbow into me to pull my mother into my lungs.

The rainbow faded, Miss Rae called me back to my petals and Fiona sat down beside me to glue them into place. She made me my apple blossom skirt.

During my first few days at school, an incident occurred that has stayed with me; the shame of it never goes away.

I sucked my thumb. I was six years old and Matron thought it was time the habit was broken. I've no doubt she was right, but it was a comfort that no one had named "bad" before. So all us thumb-suckers were singled out and we had to have little lint bags put over our hands at night and our hands tied behind our backs – so that we couldn't reach them. It was hard to sleep, thumb-less and uncomfortable. I wanted to go to the loo in the night, but wasn't allowed to talk to anyone in my dormitory and I couldn't pull my pyjama bottoms down. Perhaps I didn't really want to go? I could hold on until morning? And it was very dark and very cold. I went back to bed where I dreamt I was weeing and woke up and – horrors – found that I had. I was not a bed-wetter. I had never done it before and there was an explanation for it. But no one asked me. Matron's lips puckered into a prune of disapproval. She took me to the bathroom, removed my pyjamas and washed me down, all without a word. My bed had been stripped when I returned to the dormitory and it was time for breakfast. Fiona, in the bigger girls' dormitory, had heard what had happened. She told me not to worry as I hadn't done it before and I wouldn't do it again. She stopped the tears before they came by telling me it would all be alright and giving me her bear, Wampus, to hold.

It wasn't alright. At morning assembly, we came to the end of the first hymn. Suddenly my name was called.

"Isla Blair-Hill, come out here please. We don't like dirty girls at this school." And with that I had to go to the laundry room with the wet sheet in my arms. Still tears did not come. They seemed to grow solid and become a hard ball of humiliation in my throat; my jaw ached with it and my heart hurt and the bubble of anger rose up as I tried hard to swallow. Unkindness caused anger to flare, further unkindness could not extinguish it – it just made it harder and colder. I felt very alone as there was no–one to take my side, no one to tell, no one to report to, "I'll tell my Mum on you" – but my Mum was not there to speak up for me. There was no one except Fiona and she was as powerless as I was.

In the quiet and darkness of the night, when I was feeling hollow and sad, I'd reach for my mother's handkerchief that

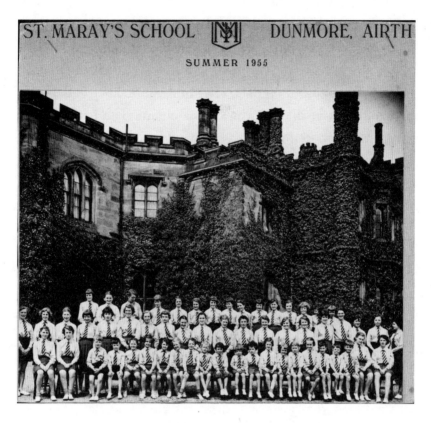

ST. MARAY'S SCHOOL DUNMORE, AIRTH

SUMMER 1955

St Maray's School, Dunmore Park

I kept under my pillow. It was soft linen, with a small V embroidered in white thread in one corner. It held the scent of her; it had little stiff bits that held her salty tears and, in one corner, a smudge of her lipstick. I would hold the hankie over my face, filling my nostrils with her essence, memories of her – her blonde hair, the little white fleck on her nail, the tiny mole by her eyebrow. I would put my mouth to the lipstick stain where her mouth had been on the corner of the little linen square, the pinky coral a lasting imprint of her breath. The handkerchief stayed with me, in my drawer, taken out at night to gently nudge me into slumber. She was here, she was with me, all was well.

But gradually, well no, not gradually at all – quite quickly, the scent became fainter, almost not there at all. Only my willing it to be there made the smallest whiff remain, but it was gone really. The hankie was crumpled, the embroidered V had gone a bit creamy coloured and, like a splodge of tea, the smudge of Indian Coral lipstick had oddly darkened into a henna-ish blur.

So she really was gone, my mother. She was no longer with me under the pillow. I did not soak my pillow with tears of homesickness as the other girls did. My eyes remained dry, but my throat ached.

I couldn't remember my mother's voice, her face was out of focus in my mind and now her smell, her very essence, was gone. This was a panicky grief, this loss. There was now nothing of her left. Just photos. She always smiled too much in photos, so she never looked like herself. Her eyes were too crinkled up so they never had that blue steady gaze that told me I was her special Saluki.

My mother was gone and my father and Ayah, but I still had Fiona. In the morning I would see Fiona and that made me feel safe.

SIX

My Protector

In our new Scottish world Fiona took the blame for me, comforted and protected me – drinking half my obligatory third of a pint of gag–making milk at break-time, even though it provoked in her the same reaction. When I was punished, she would come to find me, take my hand in hers and remind me of Ayah and Sunderaj and Mingo and sunshine and I would be transported back to a place where we both belonged.

In India, when Fiona was nearly six she was sent to the local nursery to learn her tables and her ABC from Hannah Tewson and Mrs Souter, our friend Alice Souter's mother and wife to the general manager, George Souter. Each morning off she would go with her sunhat and a little case filled with pencils and crayons and her lunch – sandwiches and an orange and a banana. No apples in India. I was left behind. That abandonment I felt keenly. Each day I would lay out my small case beside hers with a banana and an orange and each day Ayah would say, "No, missy. Missy Fiona go; Missy Isla too small."

I hated being too small. Where Fiona went, I went as well; being left behind was not any part of my comprehension. Each day this ritual persisted. Fiona's case with orange and banana sat by the front door. Each day I put my case with my orange and banana beside it and I'd put my sunhat on top of them all as a sort of claim. Each day Fiona went alone and I'd watch as the little black car took her down the road, leaving behind a cloud of dust. Each time there was the same tight feeling in my chest and throat – the feeling with which I was to become so familiar. My chin felt all wrinkly and tight and a sort of choking feeling came upon me, as if I'd just swallowed a red gundamalley bead and it had lodged itself in my throat. Here was a little grief, a tiny bereavement. I learnt early what a suffocating pain it was. I was what? Two and a half? But the dull ache stayed with me until Fiona returned at teatime. Then we would sit together on the red earth amongst the canna lilies and she would tell me of her day and what she had learnt. Everything in the world was right, now that Fiona was beside me.

Everyone was surprised when she suddenly became ill. She had a very high temperature and complained of pains in her legs. I think she was actually sick, I mean vomited. She was showing signs of malaria, according to "Uncle Doc", a large ageing highlander, with a gentle bedside manner and sweeties for the children. Doc said no one had had malaria in the High Range for years – in the temperate climate, the mosquitoes did not flourish – but after blood tests, it was confirmed that yes, Fiona had it and she was very ill indeed. She would sweat and fret and moan and then, within minutes, her teeth would chatter and she would shiver with cold, unable to speak as she huddled herself into a ball. Quinine became a force-fed imperative for her, no tablets, just liquid. This bitter brew was forced between her lips and gradually, very gradually, she got better. But malaria returns.

Much later at school in Scotland, when Fiona got sickly, I took the responsibility of telling people about it. "She's had malaria you know."

I'd get a pat on the head for this information. "Yes, dear."

But I would insist, "No, she really has had malaria, and sometimes it comes back."

This, to Scottish doctors who had hardly ever heard of the illness. They would be nonplussed by this condition and were glad to know that there was an explanation for these inexplicable and unusual symptoms. I felt grown up that I could take responsibility for Fiona's malaise, her medication and recovery. Sometimes she would know it was coming on. She would talk about her "malaria legs", an ache that later spread to the rest of her. It was like being able to forecast a thunder storm; her malaria legs heralded a serious bout of sweating and delirium alternating with shivers and much teeth chattering, the bed piled high with blankets and eiderdowns. The bouts lessened the older she got, but they chased her well into adulthood.

* * * * *

We shared a small Scottie dog, Lassie by name; she was Fiona's dog really and, like me, she became her shadow. She came with us on walks and was always rushing into the tea and occasionally she'd come out with a small snake that she would toss into the air like a circus juggler. We were afraid she would get bitten, but she survived to scamper in front of us or pad behind Fiona along the red tiled corridors, her nailed feet tap-tapping as she went. She was a sweet creature with her comical square face and mischievous eyes and Fiona and I could swear, on occasion, she was smiling.

One day Lassie disappeared. We called and called for her, but we couldn't find her anywhere. All day we called and Fiona was starting to get distraught. Day turned into late afternoon and soon it would be night. No dusky twilight, just the snap into darkness, like a light being turned off. Seeing Fiona's distress, Matey was prevailed upon to go with one of the labourers into the fringes of the jungle carrying a hurricane lamp and a stick. It wasn't long before he heard Lassie's barking and found her in a wild boar trap, frightened but unhurt. He carried her back to the bungalow in a towel and placed her into the arms of a sobbingly grateful Fiona. Had Lassie stayed there, tethered, she would have been like a gift for a passing tiger or panther, a nice present of supper. She certainly would not have survived the night.

My mother's black cocker spaniel, Hodge, wasn't so lucky. My mother was fifteen and her sister Ailsa was fourteen when, calling for Hodge everywhere, they came across his black spaniel ears by the river bank, which was all that was left of him. Poor Hodge; no wonder the jungle was forbidden to us children.

We had a cat each; Samson was Fiona's – Mingo was mine. They were black and semi-wild with no manners at all.

Mingo was pregnant. I watched her little black belly swell and was so excited I couldn't stop picking her up to tell her so and say how much I was looking forward to her kittens. Mingo didn't like it very much and occasionally struck out at me.

"Missy Isla, no. Mingo has kittens, if they are born dead it will be Missy Isla's fault." Every one of Mingo's kittens was born dead and she carried them round in her mouth and meowed a lot, making such a sad sound that I was stricken that I had been their executioner. I was the murderer of Mingo's babies. She disappeared after that. My crime and ensuing remorse cut me to the quick. I would go round seeking her everywhere. There was no sleeping Mingo on the window ledge outside the kitchen, no Mingo sitting on the porch, tail swishing as she watched the quarrelsome crows fighting in the garden. I was inconsolable, although Sunderaj tried to console me.

"Missy Isla, not your fault, Mingo belongs to the jungle, she is happier there. Do not be sad. We all belong somewhere. I belong here, you and Missy Fiona belong in UK and one day you will return there, as Mingo has gone back to the jungle."

All this was said with Sunderaj's nodding head and white smile (made whiter by the betel nut that stained his gums red). I was bewildered. I belonged here. Home was here not that other place they called "home", the place I'd not seen. I belonged with the canna lilies and the jackals crying at night, and the swirr of the fan above my head and the plantains for breakfast and the mangoes eaten greedily in the bath, their juice dripping down our chins and arms – plopping into the water. Here was home.

One day I went to look for Sunderaj to tell him about some particularly large ants that were marching across the verandah carrying huge leaves and bits of bark like an army waving banners – Burnham Wood coming to Dunsinane. Fiona told me to hurry, as the ants might go before I got back, and I called for Sunderaj all the way. But Sunderaj was nowhere to be found. I called and called for him, and then Boy heard me and called me to the kitchen. "Missy Isla – Sunderaj has gone."

"Gone? But this is his home, he told me."

"No, Missy, Sunderaj has gone."

I ran back to tell Fiona, who was as bewildered as I was, but even more crestfallen. I liked Sunderaj a lot, but he was Fiona's special friend. He heard her tables and listened to her read and threaded marigold garlands and made eggs and coins and matchboxes disappear and appear again. We sought an explanation from our parents who sat us down and told us that Sunderaj had become ill and had to go to his family in the plains for them to look after him. It transpired that Sunderaj had syphilis (incurable in those days) and had made the decision himself to leave my father's employ. My father paid him a severance sum and found him a post in Trivandrum until he got too ill to fill it. So Sunderaj was gone, leaving two disconsolate little girls behind him.

At Christmas time Fiona and I would sit in the lime tree, heavy with hard little green limes, and watch the procession of people come up the road to give my father and mother Christmas wishes and "the compliments of the season." They would present my father with bottles of whisky and little bags of coins, my mother with cashmere scarves, fine enough to loop through a wedding ring, and gold bangles and earrings. My father, with grace and courtesy, refused all these gifts. He never, ever accepted any of them, as they were always bribes, and my father would have no truck with bribery. But he was polite, so that the present giver would not be offended. He did, however, accept small baskets of mangoes or oranges and sprays of orchids and gold tinseled garlands, but that was all – and he would always look at the bottom of the basket or box of fruit to see if there had been anything discreetly left there. Indeed, one Christmas at the bottom of a basket of oranges was a beautiful gold watch. My father at once got the chokra to run after the giver and ask him respectfully to take the watch back – he would keep the oranges, but would not accept the watch. My father stuck rigidly to this rule all his twenty-nine years in India.

The day came when Fiona was to go to "Big School" – Presentation Covent in Kodaikanal. This meant a whole term away from me. My life became aimless. It wasn't fun chasing dragonflies on your own, or opening your mouth when it rained and swallowing as much rainwater as you could, giggling and spluttering. It wasn't much fun being covered in almond oil by Ayah and running around at bath time (goosle kawasti) on your own, or looking at the long shadows on the nursery walls, the dressing gown on the back of the door transformed into a scary hooded man. Fiona and I would giggle in mock fear; without her, the fear was real. The sound of the jackals calling, a chilling sound at the best of times, in the dark lonely room all on my own froze my girlish blood.

Time passed and so miserable was I without Fiona, my parents agreed to send me to Kodai school too – just for one term. I was five years old and I was delighted to be going to "Big School". I was proud of my uniform, even though the beret sat on my head like some huge flying saucer and everything was much too big. I felt grown up and I was going to join Fiona. It hadn't occurred to me that it could be quite a responsibility for her to have this volatile little limpet clinging to her, a persistent little duckling strutting in her wake – and a responsibility I was. Fiona was a shy child, sensitive, and didn't want to upset authority, break any rules or draw attention to herself in any way. Walking into a room of strangers was a trial for her, as she was convinced each eye was upon her. She had learnt already at Kodai that breaking the rules was not an option; you just did what you were told.

Being a Catholic school, fish was served on Fridays. I hadn't had much fish before and I didn't like it. I hated the little bendy bones and the fishy taste displeased my palate. I told the nuns I wasn't allowed to eat meen, (fish) as it made me sick. It wasn't true, but the lie worked and I got off the obligatory Friday menu. That seemed easy enough. I was fascinated by everything. The nuns' wimples and how they kept them on, the little phials of Holy water at the entrance to the Church and the big ballroom; lining up for classes, washing at the long line of basins with freezing cold water, making sure to use your soap from your sponge bag with your name on it and drying yourself with your name-taped towel. I was fascinated by the rows of little desks, each with their own pot of ink in the right hand corner.

I liked the look of the ink and the way it stained my finger and seeped its way under my nail. The taste was sweet and bitter at the same time. I thought I would try it properly and picked it up and drank it. My blue stained lips evoked squeals of horror. Fiona was summoned. Schooled in the knowledge that prayer to Jesus and the blessed Virgin cured all ills, she had all the children in my class on their knees with their rosaries out pleading with our Blessed Lady that her stupid little sister may not be poisoned and only a few minutes away from death. Sister St John appeared and asked, "Whatever is going on here?"

"It's Isla Blair-Hill, Sister. She has drunk ink and she is going to die. Any minute now she will die."

"Stop this at once. Isla Blair-Hill, come this way with me."

And I followed her to the Sick Bay where I was prevailed upon to drink a glass of salty water. Within minutes I was heartily sick. Not the sick that looked like vegetable soup, but what looked like the ink from an octopus that had been turned inside out by some business-like fisherman. There were no ill effects, just my notoriety and Fiona's shame.

Above all, Fiona was nice. She seemed to have time for people, especially me, and showed me how to tie up my shoe laces, how to polish my brown shoes. "Polish on, rub it round and round, now the polishing off brush, brush, brush, brush until the shoes are shiny. Now wipe them all over with the cloth."

She became not only my sister, but a surrogate mother and protector. And protect me she did – fiercely.

She kept things neatly and all in order, not all scrumpled and chaotic like me. Fiona let me play with her dolls, even with the knowledge that they would be returned to her with an arm missing or an eyeball stuck inside its plastic head with the somewhat disconcerting vision of straight, bristling eyelashes protruding from the eye socket. She would sigh in a very grown up way, she would even tell me off, she would weep with frustration but she always forgave me. Fiona has remained my confidante and closest friend and, on my sixtieth birthday, she gave me a glass bowl engraved with all the significant milestones in my life. Badges, names, quotes – and she gave me too a photograph of us together, aged ten and six, standing in our new school uniform of maroon and blue about to go to St Maray's School in Dunblane. On this photo she has written, "Even at 60 you are still 6 to your sister."

So here we were in Scotland, where the sun rarely shone, where instead of bright canna lilies, there was an abundance of rhododendron bushes and fir trees that looked different to the ones at the golf course in Munnar. The colours in India were bright, the women's saris, the birds, the fruit, and the flowers; even the food was brightly coloured – turmeric and chilies, green "Ladies' Fingers", pineapples and mangoes. Here in Scotland, things seemed diluted or bleached out; the food: grey porridge, white pudding, grey tripe and onions, the white bread that stuck to the roof of your mouth – not like the charcoal baked chapattis, or the bread full of little seeds baked by the Boy. And it was dark most of the time. In Munnar I woke up to light that cut its way through our linen curtains, sunbeams with dust motes floating, suspended, and I would long to be up – legs out of bed, bang shoes together, put them on and call for Ayah, "Ayah, Ayah, where ARE you? I'm up."

And I went to bed sometimes – well usually, really – when it was still light, before the jackals started howling.

But here in Scotland, it was dark most of the time. I got up when Matron turned the lights on and clapped her hands. "Up now all of you, time to get up."

It was dark, certainly gloomy all day long, and when the white strip lights were put on, they gave me a headache and made everyone look a bit green, as if they were about to be sick. It was dark going to bed. After prayers in our beds, the light was snapped out and that was it. No moon, no chatting to Fiona, no good night. It always took me a while to go to sleep.

It was strange that although Fiona and I were here together, we saw so little of each other. We slept in different dormitories, sat at different tables at mealtimes, had different classrooms, of course – even at break time, Fiona had her own group of friends and I had mine. Except that they weren't my friends yet. I felt that Fiona and I spoke a different language from the other girls and in truth we did. I came out with words that made no sense to them and they laughed in bewilderment – sometimes in mockery. Tapal (post), goosle (bath), lili (bed), cutcha (haphazard), pyti (mad). I spoke of my ayah, which made me sound like a posh girl when I tried to explain who she was and what she did. "Oh, you mean a nanny? Isla has a nanny. Did she make your bed and put your clothes on for you? Did she run your bath and get you ready for meals?" When I replied that yes she did, they were incredulous and started calling me "Lady Isla". That I spoke English in what I later learnt was an RP accent, compounded this theory that I was from an aristocratic family that had fallen on hard times. This could not have been further from the truth. I was very un-posh indeed and there was nothing at all grand about being a tea planter's daughter, but because they didn't know anyone else whose father was not a bank manager, or a sweet shop owner, or a hotel manager, a doctor or a teacher, it made him, and therefore me, a bit exotic and odd. I very soon learned the Glasgow accent that was more acceptable and drew me closer to my contemporaries.

Part of me wanted to be like them so that they wouldn't laugh at me, but another part wanted to keep the Indian side of me. I didn't want to lose that thread that bound me to my memories of Sundaraj and Boy and Ayah and the sun and our chupplis and sand shoes, the silly topees we wore that felt heavy and wobbled. My parents were part of that Indian-Isla side and sometimes I felt that without that and them, I would stop being me. It was as if I was acting this Scottish school girl with scratchy socks and too-short hair and a fat liberty bodice and baggy pants and as if I'd left behind the lean, laughing me under the lime tree in our garden.

Every Monday morning a letter came to each of us from our mother and every Thursday we both got a blue air-letter card from Daddy. Fiona and I would arrange to meet outside the linen cupboard on the first floor landing at break time, just before prep, as there was no one around then and she would read the letters to me. I liked the sound of her voice. I memorised the words by heart. "Read that bit again, Fi," and she would indulge me and I engraved the sentences in my memory.

I've always learned lines by hearing them. I am a quick study in that way. I can usually learn lines at rehearsal, but if not, I will record them, listen and learn them. Looking at a page of script means nothing to me unless I hear it too.

On Sundays, we were to write letters on an airmail letter-card home. Fiona would help me. Sometimes I'd copy her words. Often, because I was slow, she'd write them for me. They were just "all is well" kind of letters. We were told not to send grievances or moans home. "You don't want to worry your parents when they are so far away. Besides when they get your letter, your problems will have resolved themselves" – which was probably true. So they never heard of my heartache when the one friend I had made, Linda Roselle, stopped being my friend. I had sought her out, only to find that she was avoiding me. What had happened? "I can't be your friend any more, Isla. I am Peffy Shanks' best friend now, and we have paired up in lots of things, so you will have to find someone else to walk in croc with, and everything." Peffy Shanks had ginger hair and couldn't pronounce her "Rs". She came from Nottingham and Linda came, not just from America, but CALIFORNIA – the land of dreams and movie stars. With her accent alone, Linda held up a mirror of what I thought I wanted my future to be.

It was my first "dumping", my first rejection and I felt rebuffed and hurt – but never a word of this was sent home. It seemed a bit trivial to write it down – besides, Fiona would say, "Do you really want to say that, Isla? It might worry them." So I said I didn't and she didn't write it down.

I was good at signing my name. I'd write in block capitals ISLA JEAN SALUKI. I hoped it would make my mother smile.

What we knew to be true was that children had been sent away from their parents at home as evacuees during the war. Some of them were well looked after, some of them had a horrible time and others learned patience and acceptance and knew that one day the war would be over. We were like them and we learnt to just get on with it. There was a frightening moment when Fiona was told that the school was for orphans and we thought our parents were dead, but the moment passed; it was just a tease. We had to grow into ourselves faster because we were alone. There was no one to turn to, or ask, or hug, so we had to learn to ponder things, puzzle them out, be self-reliant. It wasn't a bad thing.

St. Maray's became Fiona's security; her friends became her family, not at my expense – she always had time for me – but sometimes she was stricter with me. "Isla, you must be good." "Be quiet, Isla." "Isla, don't."

She was fearful that something would happen that would provoke the school into sending me (us) away and where would we go? There was no home to be sent home to; she was the one who had to be responsible for me.

She rebelled sometimes, too. She was naughty, as all children are, but she was not defiant. We both became aware that my hot temper, my looks of fury or disdain with a newly-perfected raised eyebrow, were maddening for those in charge of me. I was not sulky, but I looked at some of the staff with dumb insolence and was sent to stand in corners or got sent to bed more often than was comfortable and this caused Fiona anxiety. For me, it was a way of hanging on to who I was. Fiona was growing up fast; she was learning to be independent, but she was aware that I was dependent on her.

It was the same with the guardians my parents found for us in the holidays. Fiona was afraid that I would do something that they would disapprove of and we would be told to leave, with nowhere to go. Fiona would take me to one side and say," Isla, we have to be good, we have to behave," and I'd say, "I know," but I didn't know that I wasn't being good, so I didn't know how to be different. I was not naughty on purpose.

Even if people were kind to us – and they usually were – however well we were treated, we couldn't lose the feeling that we were paying guests in their houses and because each home we went to was not ours, there was nowhere to put our "things", somewhere that was our very own special place. Not that there was anything secret to hide; there was just nowhere to keep anything private. So your treasures, a bracelet with a four–leaf clover on it from Aunt Doris, the lace handkerchief of my mother's, Ayah's pressed marigold in the butterfly wing box, my scrapbook of film stars with pictures of pools and palm trees and smiling long-haired women and men with very short hair and very white teeth that I'd cut out from my film star magazines, my Debbie Reynolds doll that I could fit different dresses on – all these had to be carried backwards and forwards to school and holiday home, or they would have to be abandoned or thrown away every time I went to a new place.

That was always the question I dreaded. "Where is your home, Isla? Where do you come from?" I didn't know. I'd say "India" and watch the look of surprise, disbelief or pity wash over their faces. It felt somehow shameful that I didn't have a home. I'd hear songs of "homeland" – but where was mine? Was it India, or was it here in Scotland? "Going home" became a phrase I'd hear so often, but where was it? On "Going home days" at the end of term, most of the girls were lined up with their trunks and suitcases to be taken to the Glasgow Escort, the train that would deliver them to Glasgow's Central Station, where their joyous parents would rush forward and scoop them into their arms and the girls would whoop with delight as their hats fell off in the tumble of hugs and kisses and they would walk off arm in arm with their mothers, as their fathers ruffled their hair and picked up the luggage.

Fiona and I would stand watching them go and once I saw Fiona looking stricken that there was no one to meet us, before she picked up the suitcase and asked a porter which platform we needed for the train to Prestwick, when we stayed the short time with our grandparents, or the train to Inverness, when we stayed with our parents' friends, the Aitkens. That was a more complicated journey, because at Inverness we had to change and get on a small local train that would chuff its way through the Cairngorms to Kingussie and then onto Newtonmore.

Fiona and I belonged, were special, only to our parents. Our guardians had us out of duty, out of kindness, or because they were being paid, not necessarily because they wanted us, or because they loved us as "their girls". But our parents weren't there, so Fiona and I belonged, instead, to each other. We lived as guests in other people's houses, trying to be inconspicuous, but wanting to be noticed and approved of by the two people who weren't there.

Fiona and I have always been close. There is no-one who can make me laugh as she does and we seem, still, to have a kind of shorthand – we just need a look from each other and we understand. We have had some sad and worrying times in our adult lives, who has not, and the long distance phone calls we have made to each other to placate, cajole, reassure, have been legion.

It wasn't nice not to be able to go out at weekends or not being met by anyone on Going Home days. It made me feel a bit lonely, but the really lonely-making thing was to have no one to report to. "Dad, Pamela Murdoch pulled my hair and bit me." "I'll tell my Mum on you." "Mum, I'm scared of swimming. I hate the chlorine and I don't like putting my head under the water." "Mum, Mrs Dunsmuir says I can sing a solo." I was nearly eight when the head mistress Mrs Dunsmuir asked me to sing "Christopher Robin" in a concert the school was giving that was to be held in the Hydro at Dunblane, where we had learnt to swim. My hair looked like Christopher Robin's anyway, with my fringe and bob and I was dressed in boy's striped pyjamas with a white cord that tied up around the waist. I practised the song lots of times and knew it backwards. But I was upset and annoyed that the chorus of little girls behind me, background humming, were out of tune. I kept turning round to scowl at them. If they couldn't sing in tune why did they have to sing at all? I didn't see why they needed to be there anyway. They weren't in Christopher Robin's bedroom humming; he was alone, as I should have been.

But there were other things that seemed to matter when neither of my parents were there. There was no one to complain to on a daily, even a weekly basis. "Do you know what Janet McClure called me?" Nor anyone just to chat with in a friendly, companionable way about school; about my scratchy socks and how I thought Irish stew made of sheep tasted like Afghan coats left out in the rain or the tapal coolie's blanket. There was no one to feel my hurts as keenly as I did, no one to delight in my little triumphs with me – and because there was no one to share them, they felt diminished somehow.

We learned to swim at our parents' insistence. It was a school extra, but they deemed it really important that we should at least be able to keep our heads above water. We went to the Hydro each Monday morning and were put under the supervision of Mr MacDonald, a gruff Glaswegian who took us through the routines and techniques. He had thick bottle glasses and very hairy arms. We clung to little floating blocks as we splashed our legs and tried to become confident enough to attempt a few strokes. I was rather scared of Mr MacDonald. He called us all "puddocks". "Come you, ye great puddocks, let's be having you."

When he deemed the time was right to let us test ourselves with a full length, he took us to the deep end and presented a long bamboo pole. "Right, Blair-Hill puddock, let's see what you can do. You start swimming like I've shown you and if you feel you can't do any more reach out for this pole and I will pull you out. OK?"

I gingerly climbed down the deep end steps and started out. After a few strokes, I found myself sinking and sputtering and choking. I reached out for the pole, but Mr MacDonald pulled it away. This happened again and again, but I swam the full length, somewhat erratically, but I did it. I never trusted Mr Macdonald again, or forgave him for breaking that trust, even though there was some triumph in swimming the length. I still hate swimming, I hate the chlorine in swimming pools, and as for the sea – the thought of swimming through deep water terrifies me. I imagine unseen sea creatures looming up, catching me and pulling me down to the sea bed. Even a sea view doesn't impress me much. The English seaside in winter positively depresses me.

One Monday afternoon, after swallowing too much chlorine and probably at the beginning of a cold, I foolishly complained to matron that I had a sore throat. She looked down it with a torch, found it to be red and decided I had mumps. I didn't. But there was another girl in the school who did, so I was incarcerated in the sick room for five days with the infectious girl and inevitably picked up the bug some ten days later. This time, I was in the sick bay on my own, with a sore stiff neck, a swollen face and a throat so inflamed it was hard to swallow. I felt wretched. I stayed in bed, encouraged to drink lots of water and Lucozade which I liked, but drank with difficulty.

After a few days I began to feel better, but was bored and very, very lonely. It was early spring. I looked out of the window to see the little buds on the trees and watched as a pair of blackbirds flew about picking up twigs and grasses to make their nests. Matron, or one of the kitchen staff, would come up with my meals – otherwise I would be left entirely alone. Even Fiona was not allowed to visit me. There was one book with pictures in it, of Noddy and Big Ears, but no books for drawing, no crayons or pencils. I would breathe on the window panes and draw faces in the condensation.

After a few days, which felt like several months, Miss Scott, the assistant matron, came up to get me dressed and said we could go for a short walk round the grounds, up to the Pineapple (a folly built in the grounds of Dunmore Park, to where the school had moved from Kilbryde Castle). My legs felt surprisingly wobbly as we walked through the watery spring sunshine, but I was delighted by the pussy–willows and the dangly catkins that puffed out pollen if you shook them. I'd never seen them before.

Miss Scott was a kind young woman with red hair and she pointed out where she thought some birds had made a nest in the hollow of a tree and where the wild daffodils were starting to push green sprouts through the grass. We came across a rabbit with bulging eyes that didn't move on our approach but lay panting shallowly, clearly in some distress. "Oh poor little thing, it has this horrible Myxomitosis. I must get Ray (the handyman) to come and put it out of its misery." I didn't like to think what Ray would do – bang it on the head, wring its neck? I backed away in squeamish horror and Miss Scott decided it was time to walk back to school.

The next day I was allowed back in circulation. Fiona came to find me and as we met, I burst into tears of relief and she cried too, that I was once more where she could cheer me, speak to me, keep an eye on me, put her arms around me and hug me.

I tried to make up for the days I had been confined in the schoolwork that was set for me, but none of the teachers seemed to be troubled that I had fallen even further behind in just about everything. I went to find Fiona whenever I could, but she uncharacteristically got impatient, "Isla, I can't now. I am going with Ursula and Margie." It flashed through my mind that I would burden Fiona with my small hurts and troubles, but who would Fiona go to with hers?

"Going out" days, half term and holidays were another problem. Where could we go? There were four "going out" days a term. Parents would collect their children and take them home for the day, out for a picnic in summer to Pitlochry or the Lake of Menteith, or out for lunch at a local hotel if they lived far away. To begin with, Fiona and I stayed at school, which conjured up feelings of shame and envy in us, as the other girls felt pity for us, and we would watch them getting excited as the day approached. There was one occasion when a friend of Fiona's, Janet Gordon, asked us both out for lunch with her parents. It was a treat much looked forward to and Fiona and I were spick and span as we went with shining faces with Janet towards her car after church on Sunday. The problem was that Janet's generosity of heart had failed to reach her parents. They were mortified and utterly sweet to us, but very regretful that we couldn't go with them as they were visiting relatives who were not expecting us. I don't know who was more embarrassed – Janet, her parents or Fiona and me. Back to school we went, tails drooping between legs and a long Sunday stretched ahead of us as the only girls remaining in the silent school.

But not on all going out days did we feel quite so sorry for ourselves. Occasionally, Aunt Doris would come over from Glasgow and not really know what to say to us; it was a trial for us and a torment for her, as she struggled to entertain us and we tried and failed to behave well and not be bored.

My parents hated the notion of our being left behind and arranged for the Hendersons to take us out (for a remuneration of course). The Hendersons, who were the parents of two girls our ages at school, owned a small hotel in East Kilbride So we spent every fourth Sunday in the Golden Lion Hotel in Stirling. The day followed a pattern. Lunch in the dining room, with white damask dining cloths and crisp napkins, candles on the table and melba toast (I loved melba toast – still do) and menus the size of blackboards, or so it seemed to me, bound in green leather. A pianist tinkled on the piano and five minutes into lunch, Mrs Henderson – Betty – requested that "Charmaine" be played. It was always "Charmaine".

The afternoon was spent running round the hotel (what nightmares we must have been) and usually I found my way to the long silent ballroom. On a small stage was a grand piano. I would open it and feel the keys and play, tunelessly, as if I were a concert pianist, longing to make the sound I knew should come from it, but not having the knowledge or the skill to produce it. It wasn't long before a member of staff, alerted by the dreadful racket, came in and scolded me. I was not put off, however, and crept into the ballroom every "going-out" day.

Holidays were more problematic, with our parents in India anxiously making decisions that they felt were the best for us.

Besides, there were the children in upper class houses in England, brought up by a nanny and sent to boarding school, who during the holidays saw little of their parents. Fiona and I knew we were loved and that made the separation from our parents bearable.

SEVEN

Billeted Out

Holidays could be fraught, but often turned out surprisingly well. To begin with, we holidayed with my mother's parents. Staying with my grandparents was not a satisfactory solution. We were ten and six, my grandparents lived on a main road in Prestwick, Ayrshire, and they were unused to small children. We usually went for errands in the morning coming back for lunch at 12 noon. The morning started early with the shipping forecast just before six, played loudly in the bathroom next door to our bedroom, and the smell of a cigarette that Charlie, our grandfather, had on the go as he shaved. So the days stretched somewhat endlessly. In the afternoon, my grandparents rested as they had done in India, and Fiona and I were expected to make ourselves scarce or be very, very quiet.

There was no TV, of course, so afternoons were spent on Prestwick Beach. Winter days are the ones I remember, with the tide far, far out and worm casts on the sand – which rather alarmed me, as I knew the worms would be underneath there somewhere. And it was cold, so cold with the wind chafing our faces and giving us pains in our ears. I tied my long maroon and blue school scarf around my head, but still the wind seemed to penetrate, causing my eyes to water and my head to pound. We would tramp the streets, the golf course too, often in the bitter wind – dreading that it might be toad-in-the-hole for lunch or creamed spinach or bacon and egg pie, with undercooked bacon and those horrid white grizzly bits. Yuk!

I never really liked my grandparents, if I'm honest, although they were kind enough to me. Charlie had a resentment of my mother, because she so resembled the Charles that preceded him, my natural grandfather, Charles Skeoch. Charlie was a dapper man, a teetotaller; he'd had a bad war with memories of lice and mud and drinking so much he got the DTs. Like so many of his contemporaries, he never mentioned the War.

My grandmother had a wonderful singing voice and sang in many amateur productions, but when she expressed the idea of doing so professionally, all hell broke loose – her father threatened to disown her. Her dream never flowered into ambition or reality. It just got locked in a little box of thwarted hopes that became tarnished with bitterness.

She was a plump woman, loud and garrulous, with dyed black hair and too much makeup. I was embarrassed by her. Her powder smelt floury and her cheeks and lips were too bright. She sometimes looked like a Pantomime Dame and smelt old-ladyish – violets or lilac, sweet and sickly. I got the feeling that she didn't like me very much. She was always saying, "Oh, Isla," in a resigned sort of a way as she cast her eyes to Heaven, or "Charlie, tell Isla to behave." Of course, they didn't know us any more than we knew them. My mother thought the world of her though, so I learned to keep my lack of affection for my grandmother to myself; I didn't even tell Fiona. It somehow felt disloyal to my mother that I didn't really like hers.

She did however, give me a piece of advice that I have acted on all my life. "When you get to be a big girl, Isla, when you are old enough to vote – you must use it. Women have not always been able to vote, it has been fought for. A lot of women have suffered to enable us to have the right, the privilege of voting. You should try to find out what you can about the political parties and vote for the one whose policies you most agree with. Never waste your vote." At the time, politics, voting, men in dark suits mumbling together, seemed a dull concept, but I have never failed to follow this advice. How can I protest against anything if I have sat on a fence? Apathy is always an enemy. My voice may not count for very much, but it is my voice – and amongst many others, it can make a chorus.

Once, my grandmother sent me to an old man up the road to have my ankles massaged with talcum powder, as she thought they looked thick and chunky. "You don't want to end up with the Stewart legs!" (Apparently, women on the Stewart side of the family had tree-trunky legs.)

For the first time, I smelt that "old man smell" – sports jacket in need of a good clean, hair oil and that indefinable acrid "old man' scent and I hated having my ankles pummelled by this dour, silent stranger – it felt uncomfortably intimate –and couldn't wait to run away. Although my ankles are reasonably slim, I have quite a thing about them still and tend to wear long skirts or trousers.

To be fair to my grandparents, we must have been a handful. Fiona was sensitive and easily hurt, trying so hard to keep us both 'good', and I was wilful and naughty – not easy to keep in check. Two small girls that they didn't really know, but were responsible for – difficult.

Somehow the person I was, Isla, wasn't up to much – or rather, up to too much, in a getting-into-trouble sort of a way. I was always being scolded, so often I didn't know what for, so it was me, the inside of me, the kernel, the essence that was unsatisfactory. It was hard to change if you didn't know which part of you was unacceptable.

So I decided to be other people. I retreated into the world I shared with Doris Day, Pier Angeli and Jean Simmons; I'd swathe myself in chiffon scarves, make lipstick out of red Smarties and grind Grandad's matchstick embers into powder, spit in it and make interesting eye makeup. I was Audrey Hepburn and Judy Garland ("I am Mrs Norman Maine") with freckles and large sunhat and my hands would make a camera lens. I'd examine my face with scorn that it did not have blue eyes and freckles like Debbie Reynolds. I'd pour water into my eyes and sit in front of the mirror to watch the tears course down my cheeks like the girl in Ben Hur, "Oh Judah, Judah Ben Hur." I'd swish my short hair as if it was Pier Angeli's swaying curtain; I'd be delicate and slow and calm, evoking Jean Simmons in "The Robe" and I'd try to copy her voice with its precise vowels and slight nasality. I'd laugh openly like Doris Day and cup my hand over my mouth the way Debbie Reynolds did in "Singin in the Rain" I'd look at people levelly, like Deborah Kerr, but that would prompt the reaction "What are you staring at Isla?"

I didn't have a favourite doll or soft toy to share my bed and my company – my companions had dimples and eye-liner and preposterous eye-lashes and straight white teeth. I was six years old and I felt that Hollywood might accept the girl that people found so provoking and I wished daily that I might go there. However, it can sometimes be a blessing when wishes do not come true.

I have seen friends and colleagues go to Hollywood and try to measure up to that town's demands. They jog and go to the gym several times a day, have their teeth fixed and their noses straightened, their breasts enhanced and their tummies tucked, bags removed from under their eyes and their faces lifted and tightened until they look as if they are swimming under water. All this and no work, plenty of rejection and loss of self esteem, so that they lose sight of who they are; their reflections in the mirror are strangers. It is as if their talent is of no consequence at all – that it all comes down to looks and being young.

It wasn't long before our grandparents wrote to our parents to say that they could no longer look after us, so next holiday we were dispatched to Newtonmore, near Kingussie, Inverness, to stay with Molly and Jack Aitken, friends of my parents in India who had set up a 'holiday home' for children whose parents lived abroad. Molly was the sweetest, kindest, most gentle of creatures, who stood 6' 1" in her stockinged feet. Jack was rather forbidding, but we didn't have much to do with him.

The beautiful Cairngorm hills were there for us to roam over, there were brown rivers with deep pools that we were forbidden to go near, there was Mr Fusty, the sweet shop owner to whom we paid frequent visits, there was the tiny local cinema, there were rabbits and countless sheep and above all, there was Molly's gentleness overseeing all. We felt secure and safe, although I think poor Fiona was in a constant, nagging state of concern that I would do something unpredictable and unacceptable and we would be asked to leave; this anxiety about having nowhere to go was a constant worry for her.

I remember once we got miffed by Jack's shouted orders about something rather trivial and decided we were being too harshly treated. We saved our tea and a couple of apples, spilled the contents of our not very heavy piggy banks and one sunny afternoon we headed for the hills. We had no idea where we were going. We sat by the deepest of the deep brown pools of the Spey River, leaning against lichen covered birch trees and contemplated our future. A couple of curious sheep stared at us and soon there seemed a flock of them – just looking. with empty eyes and moving mouths – surrounding us. Blank eyes in sheep, or in people come to that, are decidedly unnerving and very soon we realised that we ought really to head home. Besides, we'd eaten our cake and our apples. We arrived expecting the wrath of Jehovah to descend upon us. In truth, no one had noticed our absence.

I wanted my parents at Christmas time and I wanted so much to share my birthday with them, when Mummy had always said "Happy Birthday, Saluki, this is a special day for *me* because it is the day that you were born." And I'd glow and feel glad.

Presents were a source of anticipation that usually ended in disappointment. Not having anyone to explain details of a longed–for gift, it was left to a surrogate parent who didn't care hugely if they got the gift right; it was nearly always a let-down.

I longed for long, tumbling hair, but my fine hair was always cut short. I loved Jean Simmons' looped-up hair in "The Robe" and Rita Hayworth's of course – her hair was always ripply, shiny and gorgeous. Debra Paget and Pier Angeli had shiny, swingy hair and I ached for hair that I could brush and pile on top of my head and stick with pins. The next best thing was a wig. I asked for a wig, a long haired wig. I had no idea that a real hair wig would be very expensive (I know now, being a regular customer at all the theatrical wig makers and indeed, when I lost my hair, briefly, to typhoid, I got myself a very expensive one) and acrylic wigs had not been invented. What I had not expected was a woollen wig from a joke shop, the colour of the sick-bay's beige carpet; it was set in plaits, Heidi style, and it couldn't be brushed or altered. It seemed sort of knitted. When I put it on, it only covered three-quarters of my head; my own hair was very evident and made the woolly wig look even beiger. It was horrid. Hot tears of disappointment stuck in my throat. Mummy would never have bought me such a horrid thing; she would have known, because I am her baby Saluki with hair the colour of conkers. But of course she wasn't there and the wig went immediately to the back of the wardrobe.

Then there was the musical box. I had in mind a musical box that opened up to reveal a woman in a ball gown, dancing with a man in a uniform, like the one Edmund Purdom wore in The Student Prince, or a ballerina spinning round and round in a white tutu with a mirror behind her reflecting her spinning, making two of her. I imagined the box to be in white or in rosewood with delicate marquetry. These were the musical boxes I had seen in other people's houses, or in antique shop windows. I opened my special present on my birthday and found a tiny box made of light pine with a picture of a sleeping hedgehog pasted on the top. When you opened it all you saw was the workings of the little metal strips ping pinging out the tinkling strains of Brahms' "Lullaby". It was a baby's box – not the box for a girl, not one with a ballerina or a dancing couple. I was lucky, I suppose, to get a musical box at all, but somewhere in my heart I knew it was not the box my mother would have chosen.

Most disappointing of all was the bicycle I had asked for, for Christmas. I'd seen them in shops; Fiona had one and so did most of the people at Newtonmore. All the children were older than me and zoomed about leaving me behind, and I wanted to join them. Their bikes were shiny red or blue or green and they had Raleigh or Hercules written across them. The saddles were black leather and polished and the bells and the lights were sparkling chrome. I knew that bikes were expensive, so I'd said it could be my birthday present as well and the Christmas present after that. I hadn't been able to sleep all the night through on Christmas Eve, I was so excited. We opened our stockings of oranges and nuts and sugary things, mice and lollipops and peppermint sticks that looked like those poles in a barber shop and other things, whirring tops and a skipping rope. The time came for the opening of the presents. "Isla, come out into the corridor."

I did, with all the others following. This, then, was it; this was the longed for moment. I'd get my bike. There it was, not shiny, or red or green with Raleigh or Hercules printed on it. It was a little bike, secondhand, painted blue with household gloss that was thick and bobbly, and the bell had small spots of rust on it. It was not new, so it was not *mine*. It had been someone else's, not my very own special for-Isla bike. Spoilt of me, but that's how I felt. Perhaps my parents had said a secondhand one would do, but they would have known how disappointing it was to get this one. Fiona knew of course and said she was proud of me for not making a fuss.

Our guardians lived in Craigerne Hotel, which was a small private hotel in Newtonmore that overlooked the hills and the ravishing swoop down to the Spey River. There was a dining room and the guests' lounge and a little sitting room at the back that was Mollie and Jack's that we were allowed to visit. There was the sun lounge, or wide conservatory, which was where the wireless was and where I would hear "Listen with Mother". The stairs led up to the bedrooms and against the wall on one of the landings was a ladder that reached the loft and the bedroom I shared with Fiona. Frankie, the Aitken's sixteen-year-old daughter, had a little room just off ours, which was separate. Ours was airy and light with two skylights, but it got quite hot in the summer and, as there was no blind, the light woke us at about 5.00 am by shining on our faces. We had twin beds and a chest of drawers that we shared, where we kept our clothes and what treasures we had.

I was usually sent to bed before Fiona, so I lay awake until she came up and we whispered long into the night until Frankie would shout, "Shut up, girls". I was not a good sleeper. I'd wake up and sometimes clamber down the ladder in the night and frighten Mollie by sitting in a chair in the sun lounge looking out at the dark. It troubled Mollie that I didn't sleep and she sent for the doctor who pronounced that I had too much imagination and must have no stimulation before bedtime. So Mollie would sit with me as I bathed and sometimes, when she wasn't too busy with hotel business, she would see me into bed and we'd talk as she stroked my hair. I loved Mollie, but I didn't feel comfortable with her attention, as I felt she was distracted and wanted to be downstairs, sorting out tomorrow's problems, so I would pretend to feel sleepy and turn over, muttering "Good night, Aunt Mollie," I turned back once she had gone down the ladder again, and waited for Fiona to come up. Sometimes I was asleep before she came, but often I would stare into the dark and think things.

Mollie taught me how to iron, listened to the wireless with me, tucked me up in bed and helped me curl my straight hair for what I considered special occasions. It always looked awful. Mollie learnt of my love of singing and she and her mother, Mrs Dickie, would actually pay me to sing to the guests in the hotel. I'm not sure this was very good for me. I was given attention, which I liked, and praise, which I liked even more. Some of the guests would ask me to sit on their laps and sing a song especially for them. I didn't like that quite so much. But I liked it when the little sitting room was crowded and I started my repertoire of "The Girl that I Marry", "Christopher Robin", "Somewhere Over the Rainbow", "The Man that Got Away" and "Gilly, Gilly, Ossenfeffer Katzenellen Bogen By the Sea", "Bless this House" and "In a Monastery Garden". Fiona wasn't too sure it was good for me either, but she and the other children enjoyed the cache of cash that grew and that we all shared out at the sweet shop, but she was constantly anxious that I would forget the words or sing out of tune – or simply be embarrassing.

I don't think she thought I was showing off. I didn't think so either. She was fearful that I would let myself down in some way. I liked the way that people would clap and pat me on the head. Some of them hugged me, even kissed my cheeks. I wanted so much to be hugged and kissed, but not by people I didn't know. Now, as an adult, I love to hug and kiss my own close loved ones, but I'm not a touchy-kissy person with friends or colleagues. I don't constantly touch arms or hands, I don't kiss on every meeting and feel vaguely uncomfortable if people are overly tactile with me or invade my space in conversation.

Summer days were lovely at Newtonmore, with light, long evenings, purple hills, lots of wild rabbits that I tried to tame, midges of course, highland midges, but the rain was soft and the light golden. We went for bike rides to Kingussie (actually, as the youngest, I usually got deposited on the side of the road on a bank, as I couldn't keep up, and was instructed to await the others' return). Those sheep again. By now I was used to them and tried to talk to them, even sing to them, and was quite aggrieved that they paid no attention, not even blank eyed stares.

I loved those days and then, one glorious summer when I was eight years old, our mother was home from India and shared them with us. I learned to sew on buttons and to play tennis, I sang songs for anyone who would give me money. Mummy decided that this was definitely not good for me and put a stop to it. Not only because of the petting I was subjected to, not because she thought I was starting to preen, but because she noticed the joy of performing was starting to wane; I wasn't enjoying it anymore – and besides, Mummy felt I was being turned into a performing seal. She had always been alarmed rather than charmed by Shirley Temple and here was her daughter becoming just like her.

We had picnics by the river, tormented by wasps and midges, but we swatted them and laughed and cared not a jot. We were happy and heady with excitement that the beautiful young Queen Elizabeth had been crowned in a golden coach with a "heart of gold". We would all laugh, chat and hold hands. I'd brush Mummy's hair and she would comb mine and say "Hello, Saluki." It was so lovely having our Mother with us and even in this hotel that wasn't our home it felt as if we belonged, because she was with us and she was ours – and even without Daddy, we felt like a family again.

But the holiday came to an end and this time we were taken to Central Station in Glasgow to meet the "Glasgow Escort" by our mother. That awful cold sick feeling started in my tummy when I knew the moment had come to part from her again. This time I wasn't brave and stoical at all, but clung to her like a baby monkey. I cried, but silently; my grip on her arm was like a vice. Fiona, who was usually the tearful one, was dry eyed as she pulled me away and told me to "Stop it! Can't you see it's just as awful for Mummy?" And it was. I could see it was. Her blue eyes looked nearly black as she held me in arms that shook and she was crying too. She wiped my eyes with her handkerchief and told me to blow my nose. By this time, the deputy headmistress, Mrs Cock, had come forward and had taken our hands and told us to wave goodbye. The last I saw of Mummy was her slight frame in her green suit with her arms folded over her chest hugging herself as if to keep her heart from escaping. I felt ashamed of causing her distress and I shouted out "Sorry, Mummy," but I don't think she heard above the train's whistle and the puff-puffing as it pulled away. That picture of her lived with me; there was no opportunity to ask forgiveness, for her to say it was all alright, the regret and the guilt were part of the pain of loss.

Abandonment is a word that people, through the years, have thrown at me, accusing my parents. Although we were in truth sent to boarding school and left to survive the pleasures or loneliness of various holiday homes, hotels or relatives' houses, I didn't feel abandoned. Lost sometimes, yes, but I always knew that my parents loved me. They didn't want to be rid of me. I have no reason not to believe that lots of people had lives like mine, went to boarding school, and had long separations from their parents. I think Fiona suffered more than I did; she was older and she must have felt very alone sometimes. But it never occurred to me to blame my parents; these separations were just a time to be got through until we saw them again. Besides, my imagination was coming to my rescue and I spent more time day-dreaming with Debbie Reynolds, Jean Simmons and Audrey Hepburn – and I didn't complain about the company I kept.

EIGHT

Monsoon in Munnar

We were going home! Home, home, home. We were going to
the sun, to the lime trees, the eucalyptus and the tea, to Boy
and Matey and maybe we could visit Ayah and we were going
to them, our parents. It was five years since we had been away.
I knew that my father had moved from headquarters office
to a different tea estate, Kalaar, so our home wouldn't be the
house we grew up in, not Ailsa Craig with a view over the
valley that looked blue in the evening light, where the swing
still hung from our lime tree and the lilies bowed their heads
against the monsoon rain. But we were still going back to our
familiar Munnar with the bright sounds and the dazzling light
and the air that tasted of lemonade; besides, our parents were
there and where they were was our home.

I packed, unpacked, and packed my suitcase again, quite
tidily for me – I wanted so much to pack presents, like
strawberry jam or peppermint sweets, but Fi said they'd be too
heavy and probably get smashed on the journey, so in the end I
didn't pack anything. I fluttered with excitement, feeling a bit
sick all the time, planning, imagining, anticipating, expecting –
and soon it was time to begin our journey down to London, in
order to catch the plane (our first ever flight) from Heathrow
to Bombay, as it was then.

We didn't have quite enough money for dinner at the
Grosvenor Hotel where we spent the night before departure.

When we found ourselves in the huge dining room with peach-coloured tablecloths, the waiter gave us an enormous leather bound menu each. We tried not to feel intimidated and babyish. Fiona scanned the menu and then looked into her purse. We only had enough money for the soup (Brown Windsor) but you got the bread and butter free. We had lots and lots of bread and butter. We breakfasted on cornflakes, and toast and then left by taxi for the airport, to Heathrow. There was a constant whirr of excitement, intoxicating, making my heart beat fast, my breathing becoming a little shallow, but everything was in sharp focus, as if I had been wearing sunglasses and had taken them off – smells, sounds, sights dazzled me.

It's difficult now to imagine Heathrow Airport as just a series of Nissen huts with corrugated iron roofs and rather empty linoleum floored halls, but so it was in 1956; glamorous girls with their hair in French pleats, BEA or BOAC uniforms with nipped in waists and cheeky little hats and crisp white gloves greeted us. I thought they were the height of sophistication and if I hadn't set my heart on wowing theatre audiences, I think I would like to have been an air hostess – even if it meant having to get French O Level, an unlikely aspiration. The hostesses' eye makeup – well, all their make-up, come to that – was a sort of wonder to me: thick, black eyeliner that tilted up at the ends, and very red lips or very pale lips, almost white. The girls wore quite thick foundation too, and powder, and had a scent of Mitsouko by Guerlain or L'Heure Bleue – anyway something sophisticated, not like Yardley's Lavender Water or Californian Poppy. They smelt slightly musky, heady, tuberose-y or spicy, glamorous and shining, with white teeth and confident smiles.

As unaccompanied children, we were gathered under the ground hostess's wing and taken to meet our friends from

143

India – last seen five years ago and almost unrecognisable. The boys with their thin, scabby knees and down on their chins, or slightly hippy, budding-breasted girls, round eyed and giggling. The Beaumonts, the Duncans, Desmond McIntyre.

There were stopping-off places where we all had to be rounded up again as the plane was refuelled. Paris, Dusseldorf, Geneva, Rome, Beirut, Bahrain, Cairo.

I remember Fiona giving me the window seat in her generous, older-sister way – she was squashed in the middle next to a man in a dhoti who jiggled his legs for the whole journey as he worked on his worry beads. It must have been infuriating, but Fiona endured it with forbearance and never complained. I loved seeing the little houses disappear as we took off and appear again as we landed. In between times, I remember being bored, feeling a bit sick and sleepy. I was never very hungry which, poor Fiona again, felt was a bit remiss as it was *free*, so she ate my untouched or picked-over food, more out of big sister duty than hunger or greed.

It was the first time we had been on a plane and the journey took over twenty-eight hours, with constant re-fuelling stops. At that time, air fares were hugely expensive and could only be afforded by our parents on rare occasions. It seems unimaginable now with non-stop intercontinental flights and "no frills" cheap airlines. There was nothing cheap about flights to India in 1956 and there were plenty of frills – meals beautifully served by gracious hostesses, with cotton napkins and plenty of silver and glass; there was cologne and hand cream in the toilets and the cabin crew never seemed tired or bored, but welcoming, warm and attentive.

At Bombay (Mumbai) we were met by an unknown woman, one of a group whose duty it was to meet English children off

Isla and Fiona arriving at Mumbai airport 1956

the plane from London and to put them on the dawn flight, Indian Airlines, to Cochin.

That single night in her house brought India back to me – the light, the textures, above all the smells – slightly musty and monsoon-y, wood smoke and snuffed out candles and kerosene oil lamps, Sunlight soap and floor polish. We had billowing mosquito nets around our beds and I tried to fight off the notion that there was a snake in my bed, a scorpion in my shoe and another snake coming up out of the lavatory. Snakes seemed to be the thing to look out for – the enemy – and any rustle would goad my imagination into further extreme scenes of horror. But it didn't put me off sleep. We were both so tired and so excited. Tomorrow we would see them; our parents. We had so much to tell them.

Dawn came and we were brought sweet tea and plantains and we got dressed. The drive to the airport in the dawn light was interesting, to say the least: rows of men defecating on the side of the road in a companionable sort of way, with no shame or embarrassment. Bullock carts with tired, resigned beasts plodding through puddles made by the rain the night before, shanty towns – houses made of tin and corrugated iron tumbling one on top of another, and naked children and pye– dogs with sticking–out ribs, women washing their hair, pots boiling over smoking fires. It was as different from Dunblane and Inverness as it was possible to be, not a sheep or a pine tree in sight. Not a rhododendron bush or a ploughed field with orange turnips.

The plane ride was a bit hairy as it was wobbly and turbulent, bumpy and sick-making and we had to stop off in the middle of a field in Belgaum; there was no explanation as to why. I don't think it actually was a field, just a small stopping off place where the pilot gathered his thoughts and picked up a few more passengers. But soon Cochin was in sight; the harbour, the thousand year old Chinese fishing nets, the clumps of palm trees that made up the backwaters and, yes, there they were on the tarmac, blonde head and dark head, stripy cotton dress and short sleeved shirt and khaki shorts – our loved and missed parents. We seemed to tumble out of the plane into their arms. My father with his pipe and slow grin, my mother, beautiful and blonde and high cheek boned and, yes, there it was, lilies of the valley – the smell of home and safety and love and all the choked up missing seemed to melt away. To be replaced by an unfamiliar, unexpected shyness. I had so much to say to them, but seemed unable to utter a word.

We went to our rooms in the Malabar Hotel and there was that India smell again. We unpacked a little, got into our swimming costumes and headed to the little swimming pool, where we showed off madly – jumping, diving, butterfly stroke, crawl, back stroke – "Look at me." "Daddy, Daddy, watch". "Look at me, Mummy."

We'd had so long without their attention, let alone their approval, that there wasn't enough we could do to prove we had grown, were clever, good, funny. We wanted to be all of those things, all at once – we wanted their pride and approval in great gulps. I couldn't get over the notion, despite all my excitement at seeing them, that maybe they were a bit disappointed in me. I was no longer the slender, shiny haired little girl with wide eyes, I was gawky, yet stocky, and my eyes had gone puffed up and slanty and I had this quite prominent bosom and lumpy legs. I bit my nails. I think, though, that it was me who was disappointed in me. I was no Jean Simmons or Audrey Hepburn, no Debra Paget or Debbie Reynolds – I wanted so much to be the sophisticated film star girl and I was just an eleven year old who had already stepped over the threshold from childhood into a rather pudgy puberty.

We ate sandwiches and nuts and fruit at the poolside and had to fight off the very vocal crows. They swooped and snatched the bread off our plates, which was funny at first, then a bit annoying and finally, rather threatening. But I loved the sound they made, sort of "caw-cawing" – nothing made that sound in Scotland.

Morning arrived and with "Bye, see you later," "See you in the Club tomorrow," as we piled into the little black Ford and made our way up the winding ghat through the plains, up the creeper-clad hills, waving at the monkeys and wondering at the darting green birds, up and up through the mist and into the mountains and through the rubber trees and pepper groves. The scent and the air changed, wood smoke again, now fir and gum trees and then the sweet scent of the tea – laid out like sloping lawns, green, ordered, manicured, immaculate. The tea bushes and the hills beyond meant one thing – we were nearly home.

Our bungalow was a long verandahed house with red polished tile floors and white columns, nestling beneath the cut–back jungle. A small stream waterfalled onto the rocks beneath, and there were the usual Indian sounds of cicadas and birds and buzzing things. We'd taken our English summer holiday in late July 'till mid September so, of course, it was monsoon time in Munnar. My father's estate was called "Kalaar" and it and Letchimi had the highest rainfall of anywhere in the High Range Hills. Each tea estate had its own factory and lines of houses lived in by the tea pluckers, factory workers and their families. The floors of our bungalow were cool; the sitting room was plain and – I thought – elegant, with sofas and chairs covered in thick, cream woven linen and cushions with blue hydrangeas all over them. The curtains, too, were thick cream linen, with soft billowing muslin ones behind them – and all the windows opened out onto the verandah.

Mummy showed us into the bedroom I was to share with Fiona. It was whitewashed and clean with the same red tiled floor and the two single beds had yellow counterpanes on them made of heavy cotton. There were thick towels folded at the end of each bed and a bathroom that was off the bedroom which was ours alone. It was like the impersonal room in a hotel, because there was nothing special of ours in it that we had left behind five years before. This didn't unduly surprise me; it was what I had expected. It wasn't the home I'd left; it was the home where my parents lived now and that I was visiting. There was a strange growl behind us, just one low growl that preceded the entry into the bedroom of a small cream coloured cat with a coffee coloured face and feet.

"Meet Mr Chang," said our mother. We made cooing noises and went to greet this tiny creature who wanted to make his presence felt. Mr Chang became our companion and friend and where he led we followed. He soon became the dominant one in our trio.

It took a few days to become re-acquainted with our parents. They were shy of us, too, and to begin with our conversation was polite and rather stilted. But in time Daddy started to tease us, ruffling our hair and commenting on our Glasgow accents and I was proud to notice all over again how handsome he was, especially now that he was in his own working environment. He wore long khaki shorts and check shirt and long socks and shoes and a khaki sun hat and his metal–strapped watch. I thought he looked like some of the movie stars in my film annuals, especially Jack Hawkins, for he was sun tanned with white crinkled lines around his eyes. He said to me, "You're so grown up, Isla, quite a young lady. You are no longer my little girl." While I was pleased that I was grown up, I wondered if he missed his little girl.

We sat with our mother on the sofa and we would all link arms as we listened to the BBC World Service, not Children's Hour this time, but dance music, Victor Sylvester and Henry Hall. She showed us how to tango and the one-two-three of the waltz and we'd show her how to boogie and jive. We started to follow her everywhere – to the kitchen and the store room with Boy, out to the cowshed to watch the cow being milked and we went, of course, to the bees – who had somehow been persuaded to come to Kalaar from Ailsa Craig. We told them we were back as we had promised. We would sit with Mummy on her bed as she put on her makeup and her pearls ("Never spray perfume near pearls, it makes them lose their lustre.") when we were about pay a visit to one of her friends for tea or a tennis party and we would put on her high heels and strut up and down the long corridor until she said, "Enough girls, you'll turn your ankles over!" She seemed so very pretty, just as pretty as Debbie Reynolds, prettier than Doris Day or Mitzi Gaynor, or Lana Turner for that matter, and her quietness gave her a serenity. But I sensed that she was as shy of Fi and me as we were, to begin with, of her. It seemed impossible that these good looking people could have a lump like me as a daughter with a spindly pony tail and stumpy hands (peasant's hands, Granny had called them).

I was trying on Mummy's diamante earrings in front of her dressing table mirror as she was tidying out her handkerchief bag. I sighed and she asked me what the matter was. "I wish I was prettier. I wish I looked like you."

She came behind me and put her arms round me. "But you are pretty. Look at your straight nose, see that? It's the Skeoch nose, small and neat, and you still have your conker coloured hair. My baby Saluki – but you know what? It's what you feel and think that makes you pretty. You have seen people with sulky faces, whose mouths turn down at the corner? Granny always says 'A woman of twenty has the face she was born with; a woman of forty has the face she deserves.' You are a lovely girl because you are a lovable girl. Daddy and I wouldn't change a single thing about you." I had been fishing for reassurance and I got it. I was relieved.

It could be a bit dull if it rained, which it did nearly every day, so we sat inside by the wood fire, drawing or thumbing through magazines and papers sent out on the crinkly see–through airmail paper from England. The news was always days late. Each evening, when the tapal coolie arrived with the mail and the papers, he ran down the road, covered only by a cumbli (a thick, not very waterproof blanket), and delivered the mail and made his way to the kitchen where his clothes were dried and he was given a meal. We used to look forward to the tapal coolie and would fight over the copies of *Woman's Weekly* and *Tatler* and *Country Life*. There was a record player and we played songs over and over again, "You Belong to Me" and "Salad Days" which was a recent hit in London. Once the tapal coolie had been, we listened to the news on the World Service and Mum and Dad had drinks, whisky heavily diluted with soda, and we had delicious fresh lemonade, but made of limes. We called it "Nimbu Pani" and we felt very grown up. We would then go for our baths which Michael, our chokra, would run.

I couldn't understand why my parents needed so many servants. There was the syce (the man who looked after the horses), the cook, the dhobi for laundry, the matey who washed dishes and cleaned vegetables and who would chop wood and draw water for cooking, the chokra who waited at table and ran our baths and cleaned the silver and the sweeper who cleaned the bathroom and the kitchen and it was he who also polished the tiled and wooden floors with delicious smelling polish, a mixture of beeswax and turpentine. With felt pads attached to his feet, he would scoot up and down the hall and the corridors as if he was skating on the river Thames, like a figure in a mediaeval painting. There was a tailor who only came occasionally, but who sat cross legged in the sewing room and I don't know how many gardeners there were, two or three certainly. The reason, my father explained, why there were so many servants was the caste system – jobs were delegated to certain castes and this could not be altered; the sweeper could not touch the food, the matey washed up, chopped the wood and cut up vegetables but didn't cook. Besides, being a servant in a planter's house was considered a good job when employment was hard to find.

Ayah was to pay us a visit! Mummy announced this with the excitement she knew we would feel. Ayah, our Ayah, our very own Ayah was coming here to Kalaar. Mummy had sent photos of us through the intervening years but of course, we were five years older – would she recognise us?

We were to have tea and scones in the sitting room. We heard the car scratch over the gravel below the waterfall, the bit before you walked down the long colonnaded verandah. Ayah came down the verandah and Fiona ran to meet her. She was smaller than before (it was I, of course, who was taller) and she had more grey in her hair, but she still had her gold cross on and her gold bangles and she still had that comforting smell of coconut hair oil that enfolded her in a little cloud. She was crying as she held Fiona's face and Fiona was crying too. "My Missy Baba Isla," she said as she embraced me. But of course, I wasn't. I wasn't a baba anymore and somehow I wasn't Ayah's. I was a young lady who wore a bra and I belonged to myself.

Ayah wore the white starched sari we were so familiar with and her chupplis and we all went to sit on the sofa and Michael brought us our tea and scones. We were shy of each other as Ayah clasped our hands and patted our cheeks and we all laughed and tried to tell her about our new lives, our new selves. She took out a little bag with gifts in it for us. Wrapped in tissue paper we found a cache of sweets and a small tin of Cuticura powder each; modest gifts, but given with such tenderness, it brought a lump to my throat and I felt ashamed again that I had nothing to give her.

It was soon time for her departure as she was due back at her new employer's house to give her charges their baths. We kissed her goodbye and she cried and waved and in my heart I knew then that, this time, the goodbye was more profound than just that word. For my Ayah had gone, along with my babyhood. She had moved on, just as I had.

We went back to the sitting room, "Wasn't that lovely. She hasn't changed a bit," said Fiona. But to me she had and even then I recognised that the change, rather than being in Ayah, was in me.

What I did not find out until I was an adult was that Ayah had a baby boy who was aged only two years old when she left him to come and work for us. He was left with her parents, who brought him up, and she spent her leave time travelling to Kovalam to see him. What sort of grief can she have endured in such a parting? And she came to look after us, Fiona and me; she loved us, yet all the time she must have been pining for her baby. This separation apparently was quite common (still is) in families in India where the wife's job is more lucrative than the husband's. And I thought I had some separation anxiety? My tears were as nothing compared to what Ayah's must have been. I just wish, as a teenager, I had known.

Sometimes, if it wasn't raining too hard, we would be driven in to Munnar town and we would have the thrill of visiting Maraaka's bazaar and we'd want to buy everything, the trashier the better: dolls with wobbling heads and rather sinister smiles, tinny mouth organs, marradaddi ornaments (marradaddi a Swahili word, meant over the top and rather vulgar; it is such a good word that it is still in constant use in our family), garish glasses and vases in impossible colours and, of course, the much longed for glass bangles – some with cut frilly edges, some plain, some with gold painted lines and squiggles on them – blue and green and ambery yellow and red, even purpley ones. They jangled and tinkled and were utterly irresistible. You could keep the gold ones, the mother of pearl, the wooden ones with a tiny brass clasp, the ones made of elephants hair and indeed ivory (oh dear, there was a lot of ivory about in 1956) – no, the only prized bangles were the glass ones. Our mother bought us eight bangles each; I still have a couple at the bottom of a drawer in my dressing table.

We then set out for the MSA (the Munnar Supply Association). This was then the only shop built for the planters by the planters; things were ordered and sent out from home or sent up from Cochin or Madurai or even from Delhi. It was a red brick, red tiled building with gables, buttresses and a porch and it was built in 1902. Inside it was cool, with white walls and glass and wooden cabinets; you could lean over the glass and see all the household things on display – shampoo and Cuticura powder and Wrights coal tar soap and Lifebuoy and Pepsodent toothpaste "to avoid tooth-drop" and lavender water and Ponds cold cream and tins of mustard footbaths. Under the glass they held the appeal of unavailability and all the more desirable for that. On shelves behind the counter were jars of things and tins and packets with familiar labels: Heinz and Fairy and Yardley and Coty and Tate and Lyle.

There were little packets of Reckitt's Blue in muslin bags, that made white clothes go a bluey white; there were packets of starch and bottles of bleach; there were boxes of Cadburys chocolates, too, which were always a disappointment when you opened them, as they had usually gone white and mottled from the damp – or was it the heat? There were the coveted jars of Bovril, Sye baked beans and Mohan's cornflakes (the latter I thought were pretty disgusting and had an oily cardboard-y taste).

In the middle of the store were long trestle tables, with linen and muslin things on display; napkins and table cloths from the mission, lovingly embroidered by nuns with flowers and fruit and birds with long tails; you could buy linen sheets and the sheerest of sheer lawn nightdresses, with smocking and delicate white embroidery, and those little round net mats that you put over glasses and jugs to stop the ants and bees getting into the lemonade and to keep the dust out of water jugs.

In the corner of the MSA sat a small bald man with legs like spurtles (sticks for stirring porridge). He always wore long khaki shorts and long woollen socks that came up to his very knobbly knees. This was "Daddy" Dupen and he was in charge of the MSA and he seemed to live there; I don't suppose he did, but I never saw him anywhere else. I was rather frightened of him, without reason, as he didn't even notice Fiona or me when we went in to the shop, but would nod to our mother and continue to sit on the stool in the corner. It seemed a strange way to spend a life.

Occasionally there was a gymkhana – rarely in the monsoon months, which were given over to rugby and fishing. They were held on the Munnar race ground and many of the villagers came out to watch the somewhat odd proceedings from behind the railings; all the planters and their families turned up, for this was one of the social events of the year. It would start with a "Handy Horse competition". Here a somewhat cabalistic British ritual would take place – riding through narrow pens and putting on raincoats while mounted and other bewildering shenanigans. There was tent pegging, there were paper chases, there were ladies races and several for the men; all the horses were owner-ridden. There was the enclosure which held the car park, the announcer's stand, the Tote, the place where the riders saddled up, and the bar where the women and children would mingle, sipping shandies, lemon tea, pink lemonade, lime juice and soda, long gin and tonics or short gin and "its". Company news was discussed: who was to be acting manager on which estate, who was going home on furlough; gossip – whose ayah was getting too close to the children? Mrs So and So was seeing a great deal of her husband's SD, "And, my dear, he's an Indian" – was it healthy, was it right? People's reputations were tossed and gored, school reports were discussed, photographs produced and never far from the surface was the yearning for the children –

never discussed, that would be far too dangerous, a flood gate could open, besides it wasn't really playing the game; these emotional things were private and best kept to oneself.

Here was an English way of life that so many of the newly arrived young planters and their wives could only dream about: servants, private horses, cocktails, shooting, fishing, tennis, cricket and golf; a way of life you could not possibly imagine as you left your parents' semi-detached in suburbia, all this and sunshine and log fires in your bedroom and someone bringing you tea in bed every morning. The only price, and there is always a price, was forgetting the sound of your child's voice and not quite being able to remember the colour of his eyes.

We would go to friends houses every other day and there were the weekend visits to the Club, which became our social world rather than whirl. Jane Beaumont was my friend and her sister Beverly was Fiona's. We compared notes about most things. Jane had a crush on Annette Stevens, who was a brilliant horsewoman, and I developed one on Duncan Finlayson, the doctor. I blushed and stammered whenever I saw him at the club, going into the men's bar or at church or on a fishing trip to Devicolom or Kundali.

On one occasion we were invited to Chris and Ann Hickson's for a buffet dinner party after which we all played charades. Chris was mad about Eartha Kitt and would play her records to the distraction of Ann. In fact, Fiona and I had been given the duty of bringing her latest album out with us.

We had drinks and supper (coronation chicken and kedgeree and rice with raisins in it, followed by trifle) and then it was time for the charades. I was rather nervous, as word had got about that I wanted to be an actress and there were good natured comments like, "Well, let's see how good you really are Miss Edith Evans!" I so wanted to impress everyone – Dr Finlayson, my newly re-acquainted friends, the Duncans and the Beaumonts and, of course, my parents – I really wanted them to take my idea of becoming an actress and going to drama school seriously.

I can't quite recall the exact story of our charade, but I know I had to discover a body and scream. No half– hearted mewing for me. I filled my lungs and opened my throat and SCREAMED. The Hicksons' servants came running into the sitting room, where there was much nervous laughter and cries of, "Oh my god! What a noise! Vi, Ian – she has a good pair of lungs on her I'll give her that!" My throat closed over with shame that I'd shown off and over-acted and my eyes pricked, but Daddy came to find me and put his arm around my shoulder. "Well, done Isla. You gave us all a fright but that was the point wasn't it? Well acted." I was known as Sarah Bernhardt after that and I didn't mind at all – even though I hadn't the faintest idea who she was.

* * * * *

It had stopped raining when all the servants came out to see "Missy Isla riding on Sahib's horse."

I had cajoled my father into letting me ride Durban, the only horse that remained in his stables in 1956. He was not keen. "He's a nervous horse, dear, and he has a very hard mouth. I'm not sure he will let anyone onto his back but me."

Durban had been bitten by tsetse flies in his native South Africa before he made the journey by ship out to India and he had little white flecks all over his brown flanks. I was determined and made the request daily until, worn down, my father agreed.

I told him I'd had riding lessons (he knew; he'd paid for them) and felt I would be quite competent at "going for a little trot, just in the garden." So the syce brought Durban out with Boy, Matey and Michael in attendance. Fiona, my mother and Chang watched the proceedings from the drawing room window.

With the syce's help I mounted, wearing my red tartan trousers and no protective hat, and set out at a gentle trot. There was a sudden clattering of pans from the lines where the labourers lived and Durban's ears went back and he was off, at a terrific pace, round the garden. I tried to restrain him by pulling on the reins, to no avail. Durban, I think, was having a game with this cocky little upstart who had presumed to get on his back, and just rode at full pelt around the garden. At least he didn't speed off with me into the tea, or worse, into the dark, impenetrable jungle, he just went for a gallop round and round. The servants fled out of his way and my father, each time I appeared, tried to catch his bridle, but Durban was having none of it. Round and round he went, with me clinging to the reins, his mane and my legs gripped him as hard as I could. With each turn Fiona and my mother said, "Here she comes again," as a patch of red tartan flashed past and Chang put his paws on the glass of the window as if he was trying to catch a buzzing bee. Eventually my father on one side, and the syce on the other, caught Durban's bridle and he was persuaded to stop. I fell into my father's arms, tears of humiliation, rather than terror, falling down my cheeks.

"I told you he had a hard mouth, dear." The understatement of the year,

"But you are not hurt and nor is Durban, so let's go in and settle down."

Of course, I should have got straight back up again, with

my father leading me on a rein, but I was incoherent with excuses and embarrassment and, of course, a little fear. I haven't really ridden since – well, just for work and only side-saddle, which is not as frightening as it sounds. You put your right leg around a sort of pommel thing and make your body face forwards; you actually feel quite secure.

In fact, when I was playing Lady Caroline in a successful 1970s TV series, "When the Boat Comes In", I had to learn to ride like this for the role. I took myself off to the Ladies' Side Saddle Association and when the time came to meet "Fanny", the beautiful grey steeple-chaser, I felt quite prepared. Fanny wasn't though. Normally on films you get given a film horse, one that knows how to behave and will not budge until it hears "action" and won't stop until it hears "cut". But on this occasion they wanted an aristocratic looking horse to go with my aristocratic status as Lady Caroline. Fanny kept looking round to see where my other leg was, as we trotted down to the first filming position. (No rising to the trot, obviously). The scene was a shoot and there were guns and dogs and gamekeepers and beaters and extras dressed as maids preparing luncheon on long tables. I was to ride into this very English scene and disrupt it. The disruption came from Fanny. The first crack of a gun and Fanny was off, heading for the woods; she cleared a small stone wall with me clinging to her back. I wasn't very good at using the brakes on a side-saddle horse (it's all supposed to be done with your bum apparently), but her owner was able to stop her.

"You were lucky, she didn't unseat you. She's not used to a side saddle."

"You mean Fanny hasn't been in a film before?"

"Good God no! She won at Doncaster last week."

I never mentioned riding again and I saw Durban only from a respectable distance.

* * * * *

Once every three weeks a movie came to the tiny Munnar Picture House. Fridays, usually, and they caused flurries of excitement. "The Thief of Baghdad", "King Solmon's Mines", "Rear Window" and "Singing in the Rain". Then, of course, Saturday night was "CLUB NIGHT".

Fiona and I prepared for Club Night all afternoon. We would wash our hair and crimp it into waves with Alligator Teeth clips. Mine naturally hung in straight sheets. It looked even worse when I tried to curl it; it would go into little humps or ridges and pointy Ls. It would have been so much better to leave it straight, but I longed for curls and bows and bunches and Alice bands.

We would go off to the Club in the little black Ford car and straight to the powder room, chintzy, with dressing tables and mirrors and that lurking damp India smell. We would then go into the lounge, a long room with dark wooden floors and sofas and armchairs made of wicker and wood – very Somerset Maugham. We would meet up with my mother's friends (we were too old now to go to the children's playroom) and they would have their gins and whiskies. Wine was not really drunk in Munnar – only on very special occasions, as it was expensive to import. We would have our nimbu panis and bowls of cashew nuts and homemade crisps. We would play skittles and indoor bowls; my father went into the bar from which women were definitely barred.

The men played snooker and laughed too loudly and

ordered more whiskies and the turbaned bar bearers scuttled backward and forward with silver trays. There was a "burra-peg" – large measure, "chota-peg" – small measure and a "pow" – a teeny, measly measure. We would then go into the dining room and have dinner and after dinner we knew there would be cards or games (the men usually went back into the bar). The evening would wind down, with farewells called out to our friends as we made our way to our cars to take us home, yawning as we gossiped over the evening's events. You had to be alert as you drove home, with headlamps on full beam; you never knew what might be round the corner. On one occasion, we saw a large black shape in front of us. My father turned the headlights off and told us to be very quiet. It was a solitary elephant making its slow way across the road and into the jungle. We held our breath. Elephants moved in herds. A chap on his own was a bad sign and could be dangerous. But he moved away without even raising his head in our direction and we, after a while, put the sidelights on and made cautious progress home.

When my mother and her sister Ailsa, as young girls, were coming back from the Peermade Club with their parents, they encountered a very lucky piece of timing. They were in a soft-topped little car when a Sambhur deer leapt from the bushes, impaling itself on the bonnet of the car before struggling, poor creature, off the road and into the tea. Had it been one second later, it would have landed on the passengers, doubtless killing them outright.

NINE

Two Leaves and a Bud

I thought of the endless cups of tea I'd drunk at school, a thick, brackish brew, almost orange in colour, that left your teeth with a film over them and in need of a good brush. Betty Henderson liked tea that was very pale yellow and tasted of jasmine blossoms. The tea at Newtonmore was just tea, not too strong not too weak and on special occasions Molly put a spoonful of Earl Grey in it so that it tasted of bergamot and lemon peel. Jack said it was a sin to adulterate tea in this way, but I liked it and still do. Granny Paterson had tea that she left to stew and she kept heating it up so it was thick and bitter.

Tea was drunk by all sorts of people on all sorts of occasions and was especially enjoyed in Britain, it seemed. It warmed and comforted you when you were cold and it was thirst quenching when you were hot. Tea was a sort of miracle drink and Daddy wanted to teach us all about it – not because it would be useful, but because it was an interesting process and so, indeed, it turned out to be.

It started with the tea pluckers, who were always women. They looked amazing in their colourful saris of vibrant greens and purples and oranges. They wore a light blanket or cumbli over their heads and the rope of their tea basket went on top of this; they plucked their "two leaves and a bud" with dazzling speed.

Their baskets would be weighed at the end of each shift and they would be paid according to weight. I was impressed

Tea pluckers

by how they could stand unperturbed by the leeches in the monsoon months; they just let them bite and then waited for the great, black, blood filled creatures to drop off. Sometimes the bites became infected and had to be treated. Snakes were taken more seriously, but the women only occasionally got bitten and there was usually serum to treat them back at the factory. However, I admired their calm.

In fact, leeches were taken seriously, very seriously. If you went into the jungle, either for sport or to search for a dangerous, wounded animal – perhaps one that had become man-eating, one that had to be put out of its misery or "dealt with" – you never went alone. If you had an accident, broke a leg for example and could not walk, a shotgun might protect you from the panthers, the jackals, or even the snakes – but it could not protect you from the leeches. In a matter of hours, you could be covered in the little bastards and they would not take long to simply drain you; like the worst sort of Hammer

Horror, even Dracula could not compete with leeches. So that was the rule – never go alone. And go with someone you trusted!

Most estates had their own factory. The smell in the factory was utterly distinctive and utterly delicious. It's hard to describe, sweeter, more intense than new mown grass. If you stick your nose in a newly opened packet of tea (posh tea, maybe from a single estate and not blended), you will get just a hint of the scent. If you didn't prune the tea bushes, they would grow to about 60 feet and would flower and fruit. They would produce a single, pure white flower, similar but slightly smaller than a camellia (they are from the same family).

The freshly plucked leaves, two leaves and a bud, so soft, young leaves, are first "withered" in troughs, under strictly controlled conditions of temperature and humidity, for between 12 to 20 hours, depending on the season. The "withered" leaves are fed to rolling machines that twist and break the leaf, thereby releasing the sap. Fermentation is carried out by spreading the rolled leaves in layers in a carefully monitored environment for a specific duration. They are then dried and fluidised in bed dryers, cleaned of stalk and fibre by electric static machines and sorted into various commercial grades by sieving, breaking, cutting and winnowing operations.

That was the orthodox method that was used up until the early 1970s. It all sounds a bit technical, but in truth it was fascinating to watch this in progress.

The tea was then graded into categories. Orange Pekoe was generally thought to be the top category – wiry, whole leaves were used to produce flavourful, fragrant and light–coloured liquor. They would grade downwards until what was called "fannings" or "sweepings". These are small particles, quite rich in colour, and generally used for quick brewing. I remember my father saying he would avoid tea bags as the "fannings" were used in them, making the tea strong, but less delicate in flavour. There were *never* tea bags in our house.

The tea made from Kalaar estate tea alone, unblended with any other, was exquisitely delicate. Tea-time was a time we looked forward to as young teenagers. I relished the tea, which was always served with some ceremony in pretty cups and from a silver teapot. We usually had a newly baked cake with it, or light floury scones and butter from our own cow. (We kept a cow and several chickens). I think teatime was a civilised gift the Edwardians and the Raj left to us. I like everything to do with tea: the china and silver teapots and strainers and sugar tongs and all the accoutrements that go with it. Tea at the Ritz is a serious and posh affair, as it is at the Savoy and Claridges and the Waldorf in the Aldwych.

On visits to London when I was staying with my mother's sister, Ailsa, and her warmly welcoming and accommodating children, my cousins, Pam and Brian, we would visit the Ceylon Tea Centre in Lower Regent Street. It was always packed, as the tea was really delicious, fragrant yet strong, and the taste of it always pulled me back to India and the sitting room at Kalaar with the log fire spitting and the radio crackling with the BBC World Service News.

At the Tea Centre, you had a choice of sandwiches, a bun, a crumpet or scone followed by a choice of cake. The women serving looked so beautiful in their saris and were gracious and elegant. I wanted so much to be like them, reed slim with small wrists and calm eyes.

One of the nicest places to go for tea now is to the Wolseley in Piccadilly. The cake stands and teapots and starched linen table cloths give due seriousness to this brew that began its life thousands of miles away, under the Anamudi Mountain in the blue, blue hills of the High Range, and ripened into two leaves and a bud under the Indian sky.

Tea has many therapeutic uses apart from just drinking it.

If you have a late night and you wake up with suitcases under your eyes, the whites of which look like uncooked egg whites, only bloodshot, lie down for ten minutes with a couple of cold teabags on your eyes. You will get up with your eyes looking and feeling better – really – I've tried it. It works!

Uses in the kitchen:

Rub a pan that still has the smell of onion or fish (the latter never in my house of course, because I hate fish!) with damp tea leaves and the smell disappears.

You can use it as a cleaning agent. Dip a cloth in cold tea and wipe over mirrors or chrome and it will gleam.

And of course feed houseplants on tea; they love it. Not every day, just as often as you would normally feed your plants.

In theatre companies, the wardrobe mistress often uses a dilution of tea to "dip" shirts or lace, giving it the colour of a soft sepia photograph.

On the other hand if you want to remove those stubborn brown circles of tea from a white table cloth, drop a few drops of lemon juice on the stain, leave it a few minutes and then wash out.

For a very old tea stain – water mixed with glycerine. This does work.

Tips on serving tea:

Always heat the pot, but never add "teaspoons – one for the pot"; it makes the tea too strong. Use filtered, cold water to boil up and pour it on the tea as soon as it's boiled. Leave it for three minutes if it is Indian tea, a little longer if China tea.

If you are not serving it immediately and you think it's brewed, strain it, to prevent it becoming stewed and bitter, and stir it. If a cup of tea is too strong, poor some water into the cup first and then add the tea – don't add it to the pot.

Which brings me to the vexed question of milk first or tea first? My father used to get quite animated about this. In posh circles, the etiquette was tea first, followed by milk. Apparently if your porcelain was not of good quality, the boiling tea could crack the cup, hence milk in first. If your porcelain was of excellent quality, it would withstand the hot tea being poured in first. I'm told that is how it started. Who had the best china – the richest, poshest people. So it became a sort of class snobby thing. Very cucumber sandwiches and Lady Bracknell. My father (and I must say, all his tea planter colleagues) insisted on milk in first and to hell with the snobbiness. It was the same thing as putting hot water into the cup then the tea if you wanted to dilute it. The tea mixed better, swirled around more if it followed the milk into the cup. To this day I am fussy enough to have my tea in porcelain cups instead of chunky pottery or thick china mugs. I just like it in cups; it feels more refreshing and gracious, it is more calming – to me anyway.

Tea with lots of sugar was considered good for shock of course. Remember all those war films. "Here you are dear, a nice cup of tea." And who will forget those scenes in *Brief Encounter*, agonising over cups of tea on station platforms, supposed to soothe troubled breasts.

Tea reached Scotland somewhat later than it reached England. In 1785 the Duchess of Monmouth sent a pound of tea leaves to a relative who chopped them up and boiled them and ate them as one would eat spinach. What can it have tasted like?

TEN

Gin and Nimbu–Pani

I've so often been asked by people in response to the story of my upbringing, "Why, Isla? Why did you have to be sent home? Why couldn't you stay with your parents?" I've become quite tired with searching for answers that are beyond "because that was the way of it, what was expected, what happened." Did I mind? Of course I minded, but I daresay I would have minded a good deal more if, when living all the time with my parents, they didn't love me, neglected me, mocked me or put me down. I accommodated the temporary loss of my parents, making each reunion sweet, each parting a little grief, but with the promise of the next reunion full of anticipated and real joy.

Besides, the pain, the real pain belonged to the parents who lived without their children. I am a recent grandmother to two beloved little girls and the pain of parting from them even for a short while is like the pain that only those in love really understand. I miss their smiles, their chatter; I miss it so much it's a physical pain. I think of them both when I wake up and I think about them just before I go to sleep. Love for them makes me sentimental. The anticipation of seeing them when I go round with pounding heart to ring on their door bell and hear their voices cry out, "It's Raderah Isla ... coming Raderah Isla." The door opens and there stand my girls – arms outstretched to me and I fold them up into the hug I've so needed even if I only saw them yesterday. I love being called Raderah, not Grandma.

This is what those parents missed – all of them, not just mine. Perhaps the pain lessened in time; perhaps they simply learned to live with it, even becoming dependent on the pain, because it connected them to their babies. But I don't know and can only speculate by imagining my feelings, not theirs. If they felt the anguish I imagine they did, I can only feel for them and admire their restraint and their stoicism. Stiff upper lips are out of fashion, but I like them. There is so much spilling of emotion and feelings nowadays that would be far better being kept private – in newspapers, on TV, in reality programmes and dramas. In drama – or in life, for that matter – I am far more moved by people trying not to show their feelings than people who exhibit them. I don't think there is anything so very bad about control and reserve and nursing a private sorrow close to one's chest. Counsellors and psychiatrists may tell me I am wrong, but occasionally giving voice to a pain doesn't make it go away, rather it turns it into something solid, that demands attention for something to be done about it, at whatever cost.

Women left behind in India as their children were sent home had had their choice in some ways made for them. Be with your husband and lose your children into the arms of strangers, or go home with your children and lose your husband into the arms of a mistress. The older women in the High Range warned young brides that their duty lay with their husbands, or they could lose them. Besides, "Children are resilient, they get used to anything." But they were left with the loneliness and grief, for it was a kind of bereavement, loss temporary or permanent felt by my parents and their friends on giving us up, knowing, hoping it was the right thing to do for us, for our future. Maybe long, lonely empty days were spent without the laughter of their babies in the struggle to remember the sound of their voices, trying to visualise their growing, changing bodies. So many milestones missed – first day of the holidays, being picked for the hockey team, suddenly being able to swim, getting the solo in the school choir, finding your first pubic hair, getting your first period – all those things they weren't able to see or be told about. So they were excluded by time and distance and lack of – well, being there. Could the tennis parties, nights at the club, gymkhanas, polo matches, walks through the hills make up for this sacrifice? Anxiety and longing filled their mornings, and maternal arms must have embraced many sunny afternoons and found them empty. Maybe my parents learned to shut out pain because nothing could be changed; tradition could not be altered. You would somehow be depriving your children of their Britishness if you tried.

At the turn of the twentieth century and into the 1920s there was a shortage of women in this macho world of the tea planters. So the Fishing Fleet arrived. It became notorious in fact – for hopeful, unmarried, young women were shipped out to India in batches, none of them realising what could possibly be in store for them, desperate to find husbands and a new life for themselves. Most of them were doomed to disappointment. The Fishing Fleet disembarked at Columbo and those who failed to find husbands made the ignominious, long journey home as "Returned Empties."

It surprises me that more people in the tea community weren't alcoholic, nymphomaniac or both. Some, of course, were. Those who found the physical isolation less burdensome than the emotional kind, often left their husbands to return home to civilisation, where intellectual and emotional food could be relished, savoured and discussed at length with like–minded companions. They were "failures", "misfits" … "She drinks, you know, on her own." Reasons were rarely sought for this deviant behaviour and the ones who left woeful abandoned husbands were considered no better than they should be. "Well, she comes from Glasgow, couldn't get used to the silence, the jungle, the rain, the leeches, the isolation." The man, after all, has his job, she doesn't even have the housework, cooking, sewing – servants do all that. Emptiness must have become routine.

I often questioned my mother about her days. How did she fill them? I tried to picture her doing elegant things or ordinary things – especially ordinary things. I never saw her cook or iron a shirt, or clean the bath, or sweep the floor, because someone else did those things – servants.

There was no labour-saving help for the servants. The sweeper brushed and swept the carpets, then took them outside to beat them – there was no vacuum cleaner. There was no dishwasher either; Matey washed the dishes without washing up liquid and there was no washing machine so the dhobi washed the bed clothes and the table linen, sometimes boiling them in a huge pot, then they'd be starched and bleached out on the lawn. They'd sometimes be put through the wooden mangle, but usually they just got dry enough on the washing line at the back of the bungalow for the dhobi to iron. There was no freezer, so the Boy had to shop in the bazaar every day. There was no tin-foil or cling-film, so food was covered in the larder with a cloth or a large net mat with little shells or stones dangling from it. Did we have a fridge? I don't remember one. Bath water was heated with wood by the goosle man, knives were cleaned by Matey with sand and cork and sharpened on a slate. The servants lived in houses behind my parents' white pillared bungalow and they loved my mother and father fiercely, loyally and with complete devotion. My parents in turn respected, felt affection for and cared for them. Of course, it was a form of feudalism, but they were not serfs, but free men and women who chose to stay with my parents out of affection, respect and tradition.

In 1960 when my parents finally left India for good, their young chokra, Michael, asked for a lift down to Cochin with them; he said he was going to a wedding. When he turned up at the airport with a suitcase tied up with string, asking to come to England with them, to look after them, my parents' resolve to keep their upper lips stiff all but vanished and it was with tear-blurred eyes that they saw his small figure still waving at the plane as it soared higher and disappeared into the clouds.

I was nonplussed by the fact that someone (the same Michael aged fourteen who was the cook's eleventh child, who had taught himself to read and write) should run my bath and clean it when I had finished; that the bathroom sweeper was not allowed into the kitchen and had his meals apart from the other servants. I was appalled. Why did my parents allow this?

My father tried to explain: it was the caste system. There was no sneering that the British knew better, no "hurrah for the Raj," but it *was* a different era and Imperialism ran deep. He was not ashamed of the British in India, as we were later expected to be, and he respected Indian culture and customs, so he tried, with what knowledge he had as a foreigner, to explain India's Hinduism and the Hindu's Indianism. I still remember some of what he said.

"We are guests here, Isla. We came as conquerors and we did much harm, but also some good to India. But this is their country, not ours – and while we are here, we will respect and hold dear what they respect and hold dear, even if sometimes we don't understand it. The servants need to know their place because their caste dictates it and they expect me, us, to be their friends without ever stepping over the never discussed border of friendship. I respect and trust them. I hope they respect and trust me. But I sit at the table and they serve me. There is no shame or humiliation, nothing demeaning to them in their service, there is pride. They are proud people. Do not have the ignorance and pomposity to be ashamed for them."

Questions to my mother about her daily routine remained unanswered. But I watched her. She was her own housekeeper. She had to oversee everything to do with the servants and the house, she had to check everything, keep the books, she had to draw up rotas for silver-cleaning, floor polishing, linen changing, ordering provisions, writing out menus, relaying recipes to Boy. She was in charge of paying the servants their wages, enquiring as to their needs, both personal and in their duties in the house.

And she set herself a high standard in her appearance each day. She washed, put on clean clothes, applied her make-up and brushed her hair all before breakfast. She was scrupulous in this. She was taught by her mother that she must set an example to us, when we were with her, and to the servants. That to look slatternly would make her slovenly. She should cleanse her skin scrupulously each night at whatever time she went to bed. My mother persisted with this routine until the day she died. She would apply her make-up every morning even if no-one called on her for days on end.

My mother wasn't really a drinker, but for some women, the gin and tonics persisted throughout the day, and it was considered a very bad failing to be seen in public "pie-eyed" or "squiffy-billy". Your social equals no longer considered you equal, but someone to be tut–tutted over, someone to turn their backs on, or pretend they hadn't seen or heard, someone whose visiting card was returned and to whom no visiting card was delivered.

So the days would stretch out towards a limitless horizon.

I can only imagine with hindsight the despair and gnawing pain of such women, the pain of emptiness that they tried to assuage with gin or whisky and more gin – but instead of the hoped for balm, the little scorch of emptiness just burned deeper.

And gradually, the dinner invitations, even the lunch invitations, would cease. Tea was safer. Cucumber and prized Marmite (sent out from home) sandwiches were served and cakes and Scottish pancakes and potato scones. Tea, after all, was tea and gin was not offered.

The community, being small and closed, was rife with gossip – everyone knew everyone else's business, or thought they did, and judgements were made, sometimes unfairly. Some women were childless, so knew nothing of the misery of sending children home. But their childlessness was its own private despair.

One such woman was Maggie Spence, who put on children's concerts. Indeed, I made my theatrical debut in one, aged two and a half, as a pixie. I had a tall green hat with long ears growing out of it and I was mortified when the audience laughed as I made my first appearance. I was convinced they were laughing at me and I had my first show of theatrical temperament when I pulled off my hat and walked off the stage (a theatrical gesture I was to repeat some 40 years later in Pirandello's Henry IV with Richard Harris, but for

Isla and friends in Munnar concert.

rather different reasons). In reality, the audience was probably laughing at my two-year-old's earnestness, more laughing with me than at me. But I hadn't learnt to distinguish between the two. Maggie was wonderful with the children, coping with tears and tantrums with calmness and a grace that soon soothed hurt hearts and angry breasts. She knew how to cajole and encourage; she had a quiet smile which gave you confidence and you somehow came to believe you were her very favourite child. We all felt that.

People were harsh in their judgement on her and her husband's childlessness. "Too selfish, my dear. Too set in their ways, both of them. No time. No room for children." I imagine that one or other of them couldn't have children and that was Maggie's secret grief, her own private ache and ongoing longing. My mother remembers her looking through the window of the children's nursery at the club from which her childlessness excluded her, watching the little ones running round being chaperoned by their own individual ayahs and she said Maggie had a stricken look on her face. She saw a world she could observe, but could not enter; no little girl's arms would encircle her neck, no sticky lips would kiss her goodnight, no little boy's knees would need to be washed or dabbed with Mecurochrome. She would never look for toys in Maaraka's Bazaar. It was a loss for her and I suspect it was a huge one. This was not the era when divorce was taken lightly and not the community that would take kindly to the scandal that divorce carried. It was a sure way to be shunned. One woman got divorced – in fact, her husband left her – and some years later she remarried, but two women in the district never addressed her again. They saw her every week at the Club for thirty years and spoke not one word.

Some women had affairs. Harriet Denton was beautiful. She was long-limbed, fine featured, with high cheekbones and a luscious mouth. Her hair was a tumbling auburn curtain, like a copper beech swaying in a soft summer breeze. She had green eyes and an Irish accent that wasn't quite a brogue, which sounds bucolic – she had a Dublin lilt that had a flirtatious quality to it, filled with promise and possible secrets.

But Harriet was an innocent, as unaware of her sexuality as Bambi was of hunters in the forest. Harriet was fearful of everything. She screamed with horror at the cockroaches on the train from Delhi to Mussourie, she was afraid of the thought of the rat snakes on her roof protecting her from the rats. She was dismayed by the monsoon and the leeches that came with it. She didn't know how to address or "order" the servants. She was a city girl and was ridiculed for asking where the nearest Woolworths was. She needed some new makeup. Woolworths? This was the jungle; makeup, clothes, perfume, English food had to be ordered months in advance from the homeland. Harriet was, at first, unnerved by the attention of the men in the Club and the hostility of the women in the ladies' powder room. But who could blame her from turning from the coldness of the women's stares and sniggers to the warmth of the men's admiration. My parents were certain she had affairs – several, one supposes. It was thought she had had an affair with Maraaka the shop owner in Munnar town. I hope she did. She remained childless but loyal to her husband Stanley Denton, who was bald with bad teeth and who I thought looked like a cod.

And some women couldn't cope with the life at any price, even if they held their husbands in affection. Phyllis Saunders awoke to the silence of the jungle, became terrified of the whispers, wheezes, cries, moans of the night and headed for the traffic and din of her native Glasgow. She had been a working girl, used to taking responsibility for her own professional actions – and indeed her own pay cheque. She tried to make a go of the imagined romantic life and marriage, but it wasn't like the books or her dreams. It wasn't like anything she could endure. Of course she was blamed. She didn't have the stamina. She didn't have the bottle.

But she got out.

So many didn't. They got paler, thinner and became shadows of themselves – their personalities consumed by the jungle that engulfed them. Some were defiant for a bit, but could foresee no escape. Some grew bitter and brittle and bitchy; some were resigned and wore patient resignation as a shell to protect them from the little sulphurous pool of disappointment within. Some flourished of course. Usually those who had a passionate love for the man they had married. They took up painting, tennis, jobs in the library in the club, flowers for the church and club. Not many of them, or so it seems to me, even with hindsight, thought of trying to improve the lot of the children or the women in whose country they had come to live. They had very little to do with them. They were part of their lives, but a life apart.

Luckily, Violet's love for Ian and his for her was passionate and constant. They loved each other's company and were only lonely when they were deprived of it. Ian would come back for lunch each day (his horse would later be replaced by a motorbike), come in and wash his face, have lunch and half an hour's "rest" and head out again.

Whoever knows what goes on in any one's marriage? There were women who got huge pleasure from painting, in the extraordinary light, the vibrant colours of their Indian landscape. Scrap McKay was one of them, as was Gwen Brook. Gwen was a smoker with a smoker's voice and a slow unhurried way about her – she was a languid Australian, not a fast-talking one, and she was immensely proud of her Australian-ness. She was married to Tommy Brook, a dapper man, gentrified and stylish and probably rather snobbish. He was an expert rider. He would enter all the gymkhanas and usually win. He played polo with speed and confidence – he was a dashing figure who wore tweed jackets and yellow cravats and shining black riding boots. He always looked immaculate. He and Gwen enjoyed the Indian life, shooting, riding, she painting – and she was always re-decorating her

Ian and Violet

bungalow. They returned to a small village in Sussex, where the riding was too expensive, and there was no shooting, polo or gymkhanas. Tommy was to die a slow death from throat cancer and Gwen was to outlive him by only a few years amongst her blue china jars and paint brushes, looking out on the alien view of daffodils and primroses and yearning for the brightness of the morning glories and the canna lilies. Life seemed pretty dismal without Tommy, so with little fuss, Gwen left the polite English countryside behind and joined him.

* * * * *

When the sun shone, which it did only sometimes in the monsoon months, we would venture onto the tennis court and walk round the garden. But you had to be careful. Because there was so much rain, leeches were only a heartbeat away. They would smell blood as soon as you set your foot outside and would seem to stand on end, waving their horrid leechy-ness, waiting to latch onto your legs or, God forbid, get too close to a bush and they would find their way onto your neck. I found them repulsive and although the bites didn't hurt exactly, you couldn't pull them off once they had taken hold. You had to wait until they were full of *your* blood and then they'd fall off. Cows and horses seemed immune to them, as did the tea pluckers; but I became mesmerised by the sometimes moving carpet on the lawn; they would always find their way over your boots, under your trousers into your socks.

One day I was in my mother's bedroom, trying on her earrings and necklaces, when there was a great shout from Michael: "Madam, Missy come quickly – elephants." And indeed there was a herd of wild elephants in the lower part of the jungle, a large herd, about twelve of them, and there was a newborn baby, a calf, with them. We piled into the car and headed to the sighting with our binoculars around our necks. There they were – red? covered in the red, rusty mud – not grey and elephanty, but like proud warriors in their paint. We whispered with delight and awe as these proud magisterial creatures made short shrift of the bamboo. There was one large one that seemed to be the boss. Daddy said it was the oldest female, the matriarch – she was bossing the others. It surprised me; I thought it would be one of the great tuskers, but it was grandmother Baba who pulled the others' strings. They started to move further into the jungle, pushing the baby into the middle to protect it, and reluctantly we had to let them go, as we could no longer see them clearly.

We made our way back to the car but Oh! Oh! My God! The ground, it moved and all the way up our legs were leeches – thick and dark brown, some of them with yellow stripes on their backs. Screaming ensued. The more we stopped to try to pull them off, the more climbed onto us and soon we were just leech-legs. We ran and ran and got to the car. Michael had given us bags of salt to pour onto the leeches, should it be necessary, but that didn't work, so my father got out his lighter. We were hysterical, but the lighter worked!

Leeches are used now in hospitals, as they were long ago, but I'd have to be given a general anaesthetic just to let them near me with their arching, looping bodies, soon to become swollen with ME. All sorts of things were tried by my father and the servants to keep them off: mustard oil on the skin, bags of salt to drop on them. The itchy bites would sometimes suppurate and when you tried to pull the leech off, they would stretch like an elastic band and there would be a round reddy/

blue circle left on your skin, from their teeth presumably, and the blood would go on oozing for ages, despite loo paper and cotton wool swabbed on them.

Arriving back home, we settled down and pulled our boots, socks and trousers off – any sign of leeches? We had tea and buttery toast and started to feel calm. I went to the loo and there, embedded in the topmost part of the inside of my thigh was the largest, blackest, swollen-est leech ever seen. I was mesmerised with horror, unable to make any sound, but I could see the leech's head underneath my skin – bluish, bruised looking, under my paleness. I had to wait, paralysed, till it dropped off.

ELEVEN

Learning to Fly

St Maray's, our school in Scotland, was to be closed down. It was being such a happy day when we received this news; we were picnicking at Top Station, a lovely place high in the High Range hills, isolated and cut off from all the other estates. My father had been born there. Pine trees and eucalyptus gums grew in profusion and there was a beautiful river that fed into a lake where we would fish for trout and cook them over a bonfire – not eaten by me obviously.

Daddy read out the letter and we all went into shock. Mrs Dunsmuir had written that the school was to be closed from the moment of her writing; there was to be no reprieve, no-one would buy her out and, as we had left no personal belongings at the school, there was nothing she needed to forward to us. That was it. Our life at St Maray's was over.

Fiona went into hysterical shock. Tears flowed, rage glowed – understandably, she was fifteen and coming up for her O levels, a terrible time to change schools, leaving her friends who had become her security, her little corner of belonging, and all without warning. It transpired that the Ministry of Education had been made aware, and therefore concerned, that there were so many unqualified teachers at the school. Indeed, Mrs Cock – the English teacher and deputy head – was the only member of staff who had any training at all. This apparently was not uncommon just after the war. But what was to become of us? Phone calls (very unusual) and telegrams were sent backwards and forwards to my mother's sister Ailsa in England. Might it be possible to get us in to her daughter Pam's school in West Sussex?

I wasn't unduly upset at the school's closure. I had not been especially happy at St Maray's; my friends had not been particularly close. Only one thing troubled me. I held a secret to myself which no-one knew of except Fiona and she never spoke of it. It was a silent secret, lied over, acted around, bluffed out by me. And a change in school meant that it might now be discovered. I mustn't think about that. It was enough dealing with the certain knowledge that our time in Munnar with our parents was coming to an end.

But where would we go in the holidays? Would we stay with Aunt Ailsa – and where?

Would I be lonely? Would I make friends? Or would people find out about me and not want to be my friend? These were the imponderables, but I couldn't ponder them now. I had to make the most of every minute with my parents and the newly re-discovered joy of being home. I tried to imprint every pineapple, every banana frond, each patch of dappled grass under the lime trees, on my memory. I wanted to remember how my parents talked, the soft, slow way my father had, the lilting, fast talking way Mummy had when she was excited. I wanted to remember the feel of the soft fur of our cat Chang, the rough weave of the linen sofa. I wanted to hold in my head the scent of home and the lavender water Daddy put on his handkerchief, cut up limes, the beguiling smell of starched cotton sheets, Daddy's pipe tobacco, Mummy's perfume and the scent of the tea in the moist monsoon air.

Before we knew it, we were driving down the ghat once

more, through the misty hills and the rubber, the coffee and the pepper groves and we would be in the warm sun of Cochin, waiting for that little aeroplane to take us from these parents we'd only just started to get to know again. All day there was a heavy sick feeling in my stomach. I tried to do the remembering thing; the bougainvillea creeper by the side of the swimming pool, the way hair curled in different directions on my Dad's neck, the mole by my mother's mouth. We clung to our parents and laughed for the camera, even though our sickness inside was growing and rising into our throats. It was impossible to eat. All one's effort went into not crying or looking stricken, but all too soon that treacherous little plane swooped us up and away leaving them tiny dots on the ground – Daddy in his checked shirt and khaki shorts, and Mummy in the grey dress with white spots on it that I loved. That morning she had let me comb her hair and put on her earrings for her, clasp the little string of pearls around her neck. Little offices, intimate and terrible because they would be the last I could perform for her, until when? Another two years? I would feel the warmth of her neck under my fingers, try to imprint on my brain the little blonde hairs on her nape, another little mole under her right ear. I was so full of love and a violent tenderness, I wanted to crush them both to me and beg and plead to stay. But British reserve always came to the rescue. British reserve was needed.

I know why they call it the British Stiff Upper Lip. So tight and painful is the effort of not betraying your feelings, let alone crying, that your lips become paralysed and painful – like a block of wood – rendering speech impossible. And you don't betray your feelings, because the consequences would be disastrous – floodgates would open and all sorts of pain would be spread about like a tumultuous river, like a plague. So you bore it. Whatever the grief, whatever the pain, you bore it with stoicism and fortitude. It's easy to laugh now at British reserve and apparent lack of emotion, but actually I think there is something rather admirable about it. Besides it wasn't lack of emotion, it was having too much, an excess of vulnerability; to let it loose, unbridled, uncontained, would have brought the Empire "on which the sun never sets" to its knees.

* * * * *

A new life awaited me at West Preston Manor School for Girls in Rustington, Sussex. I was to come out of the dark and cold of our repressed Scottish school into the gentle English sunshine.

I was eleven years old when I met Miss Boykett.

Dorothy Boykett was short and stout, with white hair pulled into a tight bun. She had piercing blue eyes that really looked at you. I'd never been looked at like that before; it was as if she was really seeing me. It was intimidating, but fascinating too. I felt I wanted to please her. She was round, like a little grey wren or a fierce little merlin with a beaky nose, which was patrician. She smiled rarely, but when she did, it transformed her from the ferocious little hawk into the comfortable little wren.

She got a First Class Honours Degree at Cambridge and she believed that teaching was not just a vocation, but a gift she had been given, something precious to share. She had a very firm belief that children should learn self-esteem by honouring themselves and others. She believed that education was a birthright all children deserved, and she would deliver it. She believed that you achieved if you endeavoured. That even if you failed, work could be its own reward, that confidence was encouraged by genuine praise, that kindness/gentleness was a strength, that a thirst for knowledge should be encouraged, that hope kept you buoyant, that every child had something special to give the world, that we were, all of us, unique.

She was a Christian Scientist and a Spiritualist. Our meats were carefully worked out; our diet was organic and a lot of it was raw. We had homemade wholemeal bread, raw salad of cabbage and carrots and currants and seeds and nuts and chopped up apple. I loved it. Pilchards were served once a week, but they were easy to palm off onto someone else. On the whole the food was good, not the sticky grey gloopiness of porridge and herrings and tripe.

I knew I'd like this school, where the girls termed my Scottish accent quaint, and liked my straight auburn hair and called me "film star". I loved the nickname, even though I knew it wasn't true. I'd always wanted to be a film star, I loved film stars, but I was starting to get plump and plain and a bit of a lump. My breasts were getting larger and were encased in "parachutes" and, at eleven, I had already had my periods for nearly a year. I was physically ahead of my age, but inside I was still such a little girl, still willful, still defiant.

My secret was discovered on my second day at West Preston.

I couldn't read. I'd been able to copy the shapes of letters, but I had no idea what they meant. No one in Scotland had taught me and my parents were not around to check. There were such long gaps between seeing them, two years would pass – a holiday filled with activities, swimming and running and cycling, then another two years of separation then another. And here I was, an adolescent girl, and I wouldn't have been able to tell you that Peter Rabbit loved radishes in Mr

McGregor's garden if there weren't pictures. I loved Jemima Puddleduck, but mostly for the drawings of foxgloves and the silly darling expression on her face. It had nothing to do with words. In "writing letters home" to India, Fiona colluded in my secret by writing out sentences which I copied. It would have been much easier to just read. But I didn't know how, so I just pretended I did. I can't think how the bluff persisted, or how I got away with it. I wish, of course, that I had been sussed earlier. I have tried to fathom what stopped me. Fear? Stubbornness? I think it was that I was always in trouble, standing in a corner with a rebelling heart, busy with behaving or not behaving, working out ways of answering back. We had never been praised at St Maray's. Praise was perceived as leading to arrogance, to vanity. (The reason why we were not allowed mirrors.) And most of us need praise, or at least encouragement, like we need water or food – look at plants, a bit of plant food and a watering can and a good talking to and see how they grow.

Anyway there I was in Form 3b on my second day at West Preston with Miss Evans taking the class. The girls were copying out from a book, neatly and slowly, and girls were taking it in turns to read from the book. It was "Lorna Doone". My heart pounded. What was I to do? For my turn would surely and inevitably come. Perhaps I could pretend to faint? My mouth went dry; I sweated as the adrenalin pumped through my veins. Juliet Palmer sat down – I tried to listen to the story. Lorna Doone, Carver Doone, Lorna, Carver, Carver Doone. It was my turn. I stood up. I told the story as I imagined it would turn out; I kept going, even though I felt the silence in the room become a force like a dam about to break. Inevitably, it did break. First giggles, then laughter, then sh-sh-shushing. Of course I stopped speaking because of the lump that had risen up in my throat, hard and shutting out air and tears did fall now. From my eyes and from my nose – fear, humiliation, relief I'd been discovered, but shame at the discovery, too. I was grown up, I was "Film Star" with swishy hair and I couldn't read anything. I was on the edge of a huge and black hole – I was about to fall into it … Miss Evans' voice pulled me out.

"Isla, sit down. You are a brave girl and you must be a frightened girl, because you can't read, can you? We will help you to read, won't we girls. We will read with you in break and at playtime and you will enter a world where you will be transported."

The class applauded. I cried again. Miss Evans said my life would change and of course it did. It didn't take me long before "The cat sat on the mat" became Jane Austen, George Elliot, Dickens, and Shakespeare. Girls in their breaks vied to hear me read. I became someone to know, someone they'd "improved", been kind to. In fact, they were kind and patient and utterly supportive.

It was not long before I was quite accomplished at Janet and John books, feeling a little humiliated that girls in my class who were reading Black Beauty and Jane Eyre were taking it in turns to help me pronounce things. S-C-H-OO-L, "You don't pronounce the H and it's not CH as in church; and you pronounce through and thought differently and there's bough as in BOW, but the bow you wear in your hair is pronounced B-OH." I would sometimes throw the book away in frustration that I couldn't do it. As I stumbled and got things wrong sometimes the girls would laugh involuntarily and then say "Sorry." They would get frustrated too. "Why can't you SEE that that says BEAN and not BE-ANN," and I would reply, "Well, last time it was I have BEEN to church – with two 'E's." I can't do this."

Miss Evans would intervene, or Miss Williams or Miss Stromwall, and we'd have a "quiet time" in the small staff room when there was no-one else there. It didn't hurt so much if I got things wrong in front of them. And they didn't expect me to always get it right. What was easy for Wendy, Juliet or Sally was hard for me and my teachers recognised that. It was more than once that they said, "Has no-one taught you this, Isla? What about your times tables – do you know them?"

I learned to read and then – miraculously and quite suddenly – it all fell into place. I read all I could – Ethel M Dell as well as Dickens, Georgette Heyer and Anya Seaton, in rotation with the Brontes and Evelyn Waugh. I read Agatha Christie and Lettice Leaf in *The Girl* newspaper. During prep (our homework, usually presided over by Miss Williams), I would have my exercise and text books open on my desk and Ryder Haggard on my lap (not literally of course). The frustration when I was discovered was not the 100 lines I had to write, "I must not read novels during prep," but the fact of the book being confiscated for three weeks, by which time Amber in *Forever Amber* was forgotten in favour of Cathy in *Wuthering Heights* – not a bad substitute.

Soon I was reading out loud with the other girls and to my astonishment I became quite good at it. I didn't drone as some of them did, I relished the words and I tried to make the passages live. Sometimes the girls would stop writing and just listen, and occasionally Miss Evans would let me read on, her head up from correcting our exercise books, and she'd listen too. It was my second experience of drawing in listeners, an audience, and it made me feel a tiny stirring of power; it took me back to that day on board ship when people clapped me for singing.

It wasn't long before I was appearing in small parts in plays – "A Christmas Carol" and then a large one – Brutus in "Julius Caesar" (disappointed I wasn't cast as Mark Anthony). Brutus is a good man, no doubt of it, he comes forward and eloquently addresses the crowd – in prose. Then up steps Mark Anthony, muttering that he's not very good at public speaking and wins the crowd's hearts by speaking in verse. Poetry beats pragmatism in rhetoric, certainly in drama and often in life.

At the end of my second term, each class was asked to choose a one act play and produce it themselves, covering all departments – director, actors, stage management, costume, lighting – and present it to the whole school at the end of term. Local people and patrons and governors of the school, parents and friends were invited, too. Our play's title was "The Bathroom Door". I was given the main part, as my reading aloud had impressed our chosen director, Wendy Madley. The character was, unsurprisingly, called The Prima Donna. I did no work on it. I had the impression that it would all fall into place, come easily, as the reading had done once I had found the key. We rehearsed and I thought I would just pick up the lines. My colleagues got a bit anxious as the day of the performance grew nearer. But I was confident.

Of course, it was awful; I was awful. Being on stage where the words don't come, sensing the stiff, embarrassed silence of the audience starting to cough and shuffle their feet, that feeling – being alone under the lights, marooned, utterly at sea, opening my mouth and no sound coming out – has become a recurring nightmare in my adult life. I was so conscious of letting down all my friends, betraying myself with my arrogance and utterly misplaced confidence. I was so ashamed – apologies could never be enough. I went to bed, but mortification kept me awake for most of the night.

After Assembly in the morning (where I tried not to see the gloating looks of "serves you right", or worse, pity), Miss Boykett called me to her study. I prepared for the worst. But I was asked to sit down in the armchair and she sat on the other one, facing me.

"Well, Isla, what a big lesson you've learnt. That you had to learn it so publicly will be more painful, but it will guarantee that it will not be forgotten. You let us down last night, your colleagues of course, and you also disappointed and embarrassed the audience. Most of all, you let yourself down. You are not without talent, but talent needs hard work to help it blossom. Hard work will nourish it, polish it; nothing just happens by chance. Now go back to class and put this behind you. I won't say forget it, for I know you won't. But you will never, ever, not prepare for a part again." Nor have I.

But I did go in for poetry competitions and bible reading at the Worthing Festival and to everyone's astonishment, especially mine, I would very often win. We were competing against all the schools in the district, Convent of the Sacred Heart, Farlington School for Girls, Roedean and schools in Littlehampton, Rustington, East Preston and Ferring. I liked words. I liked the taste of them on my tongue, as well as the sound of them; words like relish and beleaguered, sonorous, gratifying, muffin and melancholy....If I was reading out loud as opposed to reciting by heart, I learnt that it was a good idea to keep my face out of the book as much as possible. I took my time and noticed that if I spoke in a clear voice, not too loudly, but distinctly, as if I was imparting a secret, people would lean forward to listen to me. Being told I was good at something made me want to try harder at everything else; confidence didn't make me conceited, it made me believe that achievement was possible – I had a certificate to prove it: Isla Blair-Hill, 1st Prize in Bible Reading.

Most teenage girls go through a pretty horrible phase and I was no exception. I was rebellious, of course; I was defiant, I was passionate and proud and willful. I was untidy, competitive and expected people to fall in with my ideas. I was bossy and found it hard to forgive hurt or betrayal. My reports home repeatedly said, "She lacks grounding." And one of my reports read "Isla is a very good leader, but in the wrong direction." I expected people to follow me and usually they did and I got them and me into trouble (not serious trouble, not boys or booze or even smoking – just being a bit silly).

But then Miss Boykett (nicknamed Bucket) played a master–stroke. Common, I'm told, in a lot of schools with an imaginative Head, she made me a Council Member. Council Members were like prefects. We were in charge of the other girls, to help them, persuade and counsel them; we did not punish, but occasionally we scolded – very occasionally. I was on the verge of turning into a bully and Miss Boykett showed me another way. I started to take an interest in the other girls, rather than just being preoccupied with myself. I helped some of the younger ones with homework, comforted them if they were homesick, hurt or rejected, or someone had been cutting or cruel to them; I would secretly help them to wash their hair. (We were only allowed to wash our hair every three weeks, unless we had a doctor's certificate to wash it once a week. I prevailed upon my doctor to give me a certificate in the first term I was there. Now I wash my hair every day.) I would compose poems for Valentine's Day on behalf of yearning girls for unavailable boys.

I began to really notice other people's feelings and mind about them. My anger would flare if I saw injustice or cruelty and I would storm in to stop it. To this day, I find it difficult to watch plays or films where there is overt cruelty. I was sick, literally, as I watched "Midnight Express" in a cinema in Australia and never saw the end of the film. On the whole I became calmer, kinder, I hope a nicer person. I was probably a little prig. I found it oddly touching the way some of the little girls got crushes on me and the other councillors and asked if they could borrow a hanky or a letter to put under their pillows. Council members "ran the houses". I was in the Red House, Arundel, and I was able to issue red stars for good behaviour and black stars for bad behaviour. I learned quite quickly that the red stars seemed more effective than the black variety. As one knows, a little bit of Baby-Bio makes plants grow, stamping on them crushes them. Obvious, really. And so it is with people. Most actors respond to directors who give them confidence, not those who taunt, humiliate and bully them. I am always surprised that some theatre directors don't know this. Nothing is worse than being inhibited and made to feel foolish by the very person who should be helping you to spread your wings and fly. You need this help with every play, especially when the role is not an obvious piece of casting.

I would sometimes lead the prayers in Assembly, take reading and writing classes; yes, me, who only a few years earlier was struggling over the hieroglyphics myself. I would choreograph some of the younger girls in songs from the shows – "I'm Gonna Wash That Man Right Outta My Hair" and

"America" from "West Side Story". No one was very good, but we had fun and laughed a lot and at some poignant moments we'd cry a little too, in a companionable way, and we'd dance together to the strains of "There's a Summer Place", and long to be dancing in the arms of boys with down on their top lips and who emanated the distant whiff of Eskamel (the ointment for acne), let alone in the muscular arms of Tab Hunter and Robert Wagner By this time in our lives we were desperate for any male company, even the butcher's boy on his black bicycle and stripey apron had us all hanging out of the dormitory windows saying, "Oh! He's gorgeous!" He wasn't gorgeous at all. He was just a boy, but that was enough for us.

Fiona was at West Preston for only eighteen months. With so little grounding in her school work at St Maray's it is remarkable how well she adapted to life in Sussex. She worked hard to make up for all the studies she had missed. It only became apparent how very poor the schooling at St Maray's had been, when it was noticed by all the staff at West Preston. I was illiterate and we were neither of us very numerate; we both had a great deal of catching up to do, but with Fiona it was more pressing, as she had a deadline if she was to get any O levels at all. My breakthrough with reading was not referred to in my chats with Fiona; she was pleased, but there was no acknowledgement of my long-term inability; we just never mentioned it. Being so much happier at school, we made our own friends and were less dependent on each other for companionship.

In the summer term, Fiona got glandular fever and was shut away from us in wretched isolation. I would talk to her through a long glass window and watch her legs getting thinner, her face drawn and grey – woeful and dejected in her incarceration. She was sent home to recuperate with Aunt Ailsa, but of course becoming ill meant she was unable to take her O level exams and would have to come back for one more term in September to take them just before Christmas. Luckily she got the required passes enabling her to become the nurse she so longed to be and she entered the Middlesex Hospital as a student nurse aged nineteen. Miss Boykett and West Preston had changed both our lives and we became strong in the belief that we were capable of achieving whatever goals we set ourselves.

TWELVE

One Collar and Two Socks

The relief I felt that I no longer had to pretend to read when I couldn't was so huge, I wondered why I had held this secret to myself for so long. With fifty years of hindsight, I still wonder why no-one at St. Maray's picked up what Miss Evans at West Preston could hardly help but notice on my second day. And, in truth, my memory of actual lessons at St. Maray's is so sketchy that it seems like a form of amnesia, for I can hardly remember anything about them. I remember NOT going to lessons, I remember "prep", but what on earth did I do there? Now that I could read, it was as if everything had sharpened into focus. I imagined I even heard things with more clarity. It was as if I had been stumbling about wearing someone else's glasses that were as thick as bottle tops, or that my eyes had been blurry and now, with spectacles or contact lenses, I could focus properly and blink away any shadows.

I liked the shape of words as well as the sound and I began to take pleasure in writing the letters out, carefully – between ruled lines at first and I made decisions about the shape of the letters that would inform my handwriting all my life; for example I write "r"s in a sort of Roman way, not in the up and down English way, I wanted the letters and the words to belong to me and not for them to be prescribed. I liked loops, which sometimes developed into rather self-conscious twirls; I enjoyed writing and learned to write in italic script with thick black ink and a selection of pens in varying sizes. It didn't matter that it was often a mess; it was the fact I was doing it at all that made me excited and want to practice until I became reasonably proficient.

Much of my pleasure in writing has persisted with me into adulthood. I have spent time and, I'm afraid, more money than I should in stationery shops. A wonderful shop called Papyrus has recently closed down and I miss it. I liked their hand-made paper, envelopes lined with tissue paper, thick, thick cards, A4 writing paper that a fountain pen glides over as if over glass and sealing wax that sizzles, sending up black wisps of smoke when you plunge your signet ring into it. I love sealing wax, its smell and the smooth feeling of it when it's set – of course, it's a bit affected to use it now, which is a shame. At a huge branch of a supermarket I was in recently, that sold everything from saucepans, sunglasses, cuticle clippers and ready-made meals for one, there was no writing paper of any description in their stationery section. A sign of the times.

I don't know if it was this early deficiency, this late coming to words, paper, pen and ink, that resulted in my being one of the last remaining letter-writers I know. I write long. detailed letters rather than emails; I like the formality in a letter, I like too that, contrarily, one can be more personal, poetic and go deeper into one's feelings in a letter.

I write all the time; I write a thought on the back of an envelope, or even on a bus ticket; little scraps of paper litter the house. Has all this come about because of the late discovered joy that reading and writing have conjured up? I often wonder if that is a contributing reason for being an actress. Words are the tools of my craft; feelings too, of course, but I'm not a mime – I use words every day as a performer and my delight in them has never gone away.

During our years at West Preston Manor, Fiona and I spent school holidays with our mother's beloved sister, Ailsa. Despite their very different personalities, Ailsa and my mother looked very similar, with their pale blonde hair and their periwinkle blue eyes, and they sounded alike, the soft burr of their Scottish accents noticeable and comforting. Where my mother was introverted and shy, Ailsa was extrovert and vibrant; my mother had an air of calm about her that so often covered a fluttering heart and her eyes, so like Ailsa's in colour and shape, wide and round, would look at you with a composure she had schooled herself to feel. Ailsa's nose was like her mother Jessie's, gently aquiline; Violet's nose was straight like her father, Charles Skeoch's. Ailsa became beloved to us too; she was warm and generous spirited and enthusiastic and she opened her home, her arms and her heart to us. She lived in Bury near Arundel with her husband, the 6' 5" tall Patrick and her children, our cousins, Brian and Pam. The house was small, but room was found for us and we shared in all the family activities. Looking back, our cousins were remarkably hospitable and kind. I think we took Brian's room, but if he minded, he didn't show it. He was funny, he played rugby and the ukulele, he was constantly joking – which disguised a kind and sensitive heart. Pam was mature for her age, she had beautiful legs and an almost old fashioned grown-upness; she didn't suffer fools. They were our cousins, but soon we would do everything together as friends.

We now belonged to a family, not ours directly, but as relatives, they were the next best thing to our parents. We did normal family things, like take it in turns to wash up or clear out the dreaded Rayburn, feed the cats, Binty and Bwana. We rowed down the river Arun in summer, taking sandwiches wrapped in checked napkins; we went to Point–to–Point races in the winter and spring with headscarves tied in a knot under our chins and in the summer we rode our bicycles into Fittleworth, where we had riding lessons and came back sweaty and smelling of horses.

I was starting to get puppy-fat plump, with stocky legs and a round face. My hair was still straight, despite the newly discovered "rollers", so I decided to have a perm, giving me the curls I longed for. What a mistake! My fine hair became not curly, but frizzy – and my head resembled a burst sofa. I had to live with my mistake and disappointment until it grew and I was able to cut the perm out.

I went on enjoying the feeling of relief that I could read, that I was no longer looking over my shoulder fearing discovery. I could read, I could write. I was free. My parents' weekly letters gave me added pleasure now that I no longer had to rely on Fiona, patient though she was, reading their contents to me. My letters home belonged to me now, not written out by Fiona for me to copy. They got longer, more descriptive; I even enclosed bad poems (discovered in my mother's attic after her death, wrapped in cellophane bags, done up with rubber bands). Embarrassing, rather bum-clenching poems about bluebell woods and daisies freckled in dew.

I enjoyed writing essays about almost anything from buttons and ribbons to the role of dogs and horses in our lives, Harold's march to Stamford Bridge and Katherine Swynford, John of Gaunt's second wife. I enjoyed commenting on characters in books, Jo in "Little Women" and the extremely nauseating Nell in "The Old Curiosity Shop". English grammar was interesting too – where to put apostrophes and semi-colons, "I before E except after C." "Necessary – one collar and two socks." Little rules like that. I looked forward to history lessons. History was just stories about people with long hair and beards, but who, doubtless, had the same joys and sorrows that I felt in my life and yet their lives affected ours; stories with the dates thrown in – I loved history lessons.

I liked the bible stories too, not just the parables and the miracles, but all the letters to the Corinthians and the Romans and all those other people, the Sermon on the Mount – that was pretty good stuff and sensible: be kind, be humble, thoughtful and loving – that was what it amounted to. Jesus sounded a good man. but was he the Son of God? I'd never thought about it. But if he said he was, then it might be true, unless he was mad or bad or both.

I started to believe in Jesus, in God. I am not sure if it was religious fervour, or just delight in the church services and the bells and smells. Church going in Scotland had been a dour, bleak affair – no stained glass windows, no bells, not much colour and the hymn singing was pretty minimal and dismal; a choir of elderly ladies, plump girls and a smattering of embarrassed-looking youths sang "All in the April Evening" and "In a Monastery Garden", but it was hardly transporting. I used to stifle the urge to giggle, not usually successfully. At East Preston church, the services were High Church, much swinging of incense and bowing and I would swell out my ample chest singing the lovely hymns and soon learned all the prayers, including the Creed, by heart. I used to look forward to church; I loved the smell of the burning candles and the incense and the old prayer books and the general damp, herby, mossy smell in the little church. The stained glass windows became familiar, as did the names of the fallen in both World Wars listed on the wall beneath the clutch of flags. I would wonder, vaguely, about Thomas Strawn and Benjamin Pilver, Robert Knox and Peter Barker; what had become of their families, their wives, their mothers? The wall of names made me feel sad, so many names for such a small village.

I went to religious instruction classes with Father Fincham, as I had decided to be confirmed and I gave myself to the instruction with absorption and enthusiasm. The preparation for my confirmation was thorough. I grew excited as the day approached. We were told that as the Bishop's hands touched our heads to bless us, we would be filled with the Holy Spirit (I hoped I might even speak in tongues as the Apostles did in the Bible, when the Holy Spirit entered them). I was about to be Jesus' child, not quite a bride of Christ, but certainly his friend.

We wore white dresses and white veils that were to cover our hair "Not an occasion for vanity," said Miss Boykett. This was a time when we were to think deeply about what we were doing. The trouble was, we looked so silly with the veils nearly meeting our eyebrows, we were self-conscious and thought of little else, so vanity was at the forefront after all. There was a lot of incense swinging, the candles were lit and the choir sang something lovely but incomprehensible in Latin. We all lined up. I was behind Juliet Palmer and was somewhat disconcerted to see that she looked rather fetching in her veil. I was once again a "puddock" and on this occasion the name suited me perfectly. It was my turn; I knelt in front of the Bishop, kissed his ring as I had been instructed to do, and then I felt his hands on my head. This was the moment I would be flooded with light by the Holy Spirit; I would be changed forever as I was embraced into God's chosen circle. Nothing. I felt nothing. Not spiritual, enlightened or close to Jesus. Nothing. But I didn't let on. As the other girls went on about how amazing the experience had been, I agreed.

"Did you feel anything, Isla?"

"Oh! Yes, full of light. I felt it was as if a light was switched on, shining from inside me."

I didn't become full of light, but I did go to communion at 8 o'clock every Sunday. I liked the Madeira-tasting communion wine and saying the prayers in a whisper all alone with God. There was a tiny red glass hanging lamp that always had a candle lit in it. We were told this was where God was when we came into the church and we should make that our focus. In truth, it did look like a small, red, beating heart, suspended apparently from nowhere, just above the altar.

My belief in God stayed with me throughout school, but always with a little question mark above it. I wish in some ways that I had faith still – I see so many people sustained by theirs, but my question mark remains.

I would like to believe in a power greater than myself that has a pre-ordained path for me, with the odd foray and diversion through freewill. I'd like to believe that what goes around comes around, but, as my mother would often say, "The wicked flourish like the green bay tree," and so often it would turn out to be true. I think of all those nuns and monks and the Cathars in France who denied themselves any sort of earthly pleasure hoping for a huge reward in heaven and I want to shout down the long arc of years, "Do it now, for this is it. You will be a long time silent in your cold dark grave." But they believed it so perhaps that is all that counts.

But I love churches: the tranquillity, the smell and the cloak of calm that descends – it does make one imagine that God is about. I burn a candle and think of all the people who lived before me on their knees with their prayers and supplications;

I think about my parents and my good fortune in meeting both my husband and my beloved son so early in my adult life and I whisper gratitude for the unexpected joy both my little grandgirls have brought into my life and a fervent prayer to keep them safe. And I pray for Fiona and her family and I catch myself and think "What AM I doing?" But it comforts me and whether or not there is anyone there to receive my prayer I am glad I have prayed it. I go to church occasionally, at Christmas and sometimes just to feel quiet and it soothes me so who knows…? That question mark again.

One Mothering Sunday in March when I was fourteen, our mother was in England without our father for a short visit. We went to church with her and at one point in the service all the children went up to gather posies of primroses and violets for our mothers from a big basket near the altar. I rather grumpily took the tiny posy of flowers to my mother (surely I was too old for this?), but I saw her eyes prick with tears as she smiled and thanked me and I felt I wanted to fold her up in my ungrateful arms. These were the small rituals and offices she had missed.

I wanted so much to love her with all my heart, but I knew subconsciously that if I gave her my unfettered love, it would feel as if my heart was being ripped out of me again when she had to leave. I had got used to being without her, now that she was back with me, all the choked up longing for her would surface and it couldn't be pushed down again without feeling as if I were suffocating. So I tried to push *her* away instead.

I was so pleased and relieved to have her with me, my own mother, to kiss me goodnight and for her to notice my improved prowess as a dancer/tennis player/cyclist, that perversely I was cruel to her and found deeply wounding things to say, usually about her not being there, not in the routine of the household.

"You don't do it like that, that's not the way it's done," and I'd watch her hurt expression, but that didn't stop me. "How on earth would you know?" I'd cry. "You weren't here." and my mother would go quiet and retire to do the washing up or go upstairs for a cardigan and when she came down, I'd notice her eyes were red and I'd feel horrible and hug her a bit too hard. I loved her so much and wanted her to love me so much, but I had a teenage girl's capacity for cruelty and I would get in little barbs all the time or lash out at her with my unbridled tongue. I've never fathomed why. Was I like a cat who, faced with the owner's return after a holiday or a time of absence, punishes with a turned back and a disdainful shrug of indifference disguising hurt and fury? It's only with hindsight that I can see my behaviour and feelings were a mass of contradictions.

For just at the time children of my age were flexing their muscles, spreading their wings to fly the nest, my parents were returned to me.

In the Spring of 1959, Aunt Ailsa informed Fiona and me that our Mum and Dad were returning to the UK unexpectedly and for good. I was overjoyed that we would be a family again, sharing a house that was ours and not one rented for a six week stay on the rare occasions they were here, but ours, our very own. Joyful, too, that I would just be with them as their daughter and they would watch me grow and I could tell them of my burning desire to be an actress.

In the summer of that year, when I was fifteen, they came home. It was twelve years after India's independence and unrest was spreading throughout Kerala (The only democratically elected communist state in the world) and when it reached the High Range and Munnar, there were rumblings which grew into riots. It was considered that it really was time the British went and that all the tea estates should be run by Indian companies, not a Scottish one, which was hardly a surprising view, and one with which my father had some sympathy, but the manner of edging the British out became quite fierce. There was rioting in the factories, and strikes, some of the managers' offices were set on fire with the managers still inside them and their servants were threatened. There were all sorts of disquieting and upsetting scenes.

However justified the reason for the riots, it must have been wounding to see the people you considered your friends being the ones to shout the loudest and throw the largest stones. I was not there, and I didn't witness any of this, so I have no first-hand knowledge. But my parents made the decision to leave India one year before my father's official retirement, twenty-nine instead of the thirty years. This was hastened by the fact that my mother had amoebic dysentery that would not clear up and the doctor advised her that only by returning to the UK could she get the correct treatment to make her well again.

They hardly spoke of their departure and the events leading up to it, and I was too busy in my now English world and too glad to have them home to ask any probing questions. They brought little with them, not that there was much to bring, for most of the furniture belonged to the Company.

On a visit back to the High Range with Fiona in the 1990s, it was disquieting to find our bungalow and Kalaar unchanged. There was the same sideboard, the same lamps, even the same wind-up telephone. I hadn't realised that all these items were not ours. The past echoed around me and everywhere – down the red tiled corridors, in our bedroom; along the verandah, I collided with a five year old sandaled ghost with hair the colour of conkers. As the driver took us back to Munnar, I sat with my left arm out of the Ambassador car window and remembered the sunburnt pain of it that distracted from the pain of saying goodbye to Ayah as I left the bungalow four decades earlier.

If my parents were leaving India for good – would Fiona and I ever go back, or would our childhood be buried in the monsoon-soaked Indian earth at Kalaar?

At fifteen I gave it a moment's thought and passed on, not realising then how deep my Indian roots had wound their way round my heart, but where did I belong? Where was home? Would my parents be different living in England instead of India? Would they find me very different?

I was soon to learn about my parents, and my respect for them was to grow as I watched them come to terms with losing their Indian identity and trying to embrace their English one. They were both intensely shy and reserved characters, which could have been mistaken for diffidence, even timidity. They never announced their arrival into a room with a fanfare, rather they would slip into it, observing other people and, finding small talk with strangers rather a strain, they would often end up talking to each other. They were made of strong stuff. Their gentleness belied their strength; they were strong and they were brave.

THIRTEEN

How to Boil an Egg

A precarious, rather frightening and unemployed future lay ahead for them. They hadn't lived in the UK since my mother was thirteen and my father twenty-one; she was now forty-two, he was forty-nine.

As soon as they reached Tilbury Docks, indeed the very day they disembarked, they raced by taxi to catch me as St. Joan in Shaw's play at the annual prize–giving event at West Preston Manor – "Light your fires, do you think I dread it as much as the life of a rat in a hole?" I must have been pretty awful in the part, but, again, I felt empowered as the audience went quiet. I won the Acting Cup and saw my parents beam with pride, the first time they had witnessed me collect any prize. I glowed inside.

Fiona had already done a year at the Eastbourne College of Domestic Science, a sort of finishing school, where she learned to cook, sew, darn, iron, arrange flowers and fold guest towels and pillow cases; how to answer invitations and how to address Archbishops, how to organise a household and how to get in and out of cars without showing her knickers. She had just started her training as a nurse at the Middlesex Hospital.

We shared that summer with our parents and although we were all relieved to be together, and this time for always, we were sometimes diffident in each other's company. It was odd that I should feel shy of these longed-for people. In truth, they were almost strangers. They had lived so long in my imagination that I couldn't completely recognise them in reality. My father was concerned about money, getting a job and finding a house. I wanted to be the centre of their world, but their world was an uncertain one, money disappearing like sand through a sieve, there were my school fees to pay and a house to find; my father wrote off for countless jobs and never got an interview, rarely even a reply. There was an undercurrent of anxiety, even in the laughter we shared, and I'd hear my parents' muffled discussions going on into the night, hushed and whispered, and I'd hear the worry in it. But in the morning I'd pretend I hadn't heard their mutterings and that we were a normal, happy, English family living in our rented house in England – which we were really. We'd make plans about what we were going to do, not just for that day, but for the months ahead. Now it was the four of us together forever and ever.

I said we were to have the best, most elaborate Christmas when the time came, with a huge tree hung with glass icicles, silver balls and tinsel and we would buy the most beautiful fairy for the top, or it could be a star, shiny and silver, but it had to be the most beautiful, for it was to be ours, our very own tree, not shared with other people, but our tree with our very own decorations on it. Daddy laughed and scratched his head in the way he did when he was nervous or anxious – I was just learning these little mannerisms and they were becoming dear to me. "We have to be a bit careful, dear, as we don't have much money."

I had missed my parents from that hollow bit inside me that only now was filling up with emotional vitamins. I had memories of my father's smile and his pipe. I'd held my mother's fragrance in my head for so long that she had become an image, a mind-photograph – with her blonde head resting against my father's shoulder. The real person, whilst just as lovable, was a constant surprise. There were so many things about her of which I was unaware; that she couldn't whistle, that she hated milk and – worse – junket or yoghurt. That she didn't shave her legs, but used a little pad like a soft emery board that she would rub round and round; she wouldn't pierce her ears and her clip on earrings would hurt her and leave little red marks on her lobes. I learned that she loved marshmallows and chocolates (I share her affection for the latter). When she didn't like something – coffee, champagne, oysters, red wine – she would say it disagreed with her "I love it darling, but it doesn't love me." I'd stand beside her in church on Sundays and hear that her voice was lilting and sweet, I don't remember going to church in India. I'd not often heard her sing before, just things like "Baa baa Black Sheep" and "Twinkle. Twinkle Little Star" and "The Girl That I Marry", which we sang together, along with "The Road to Mandalay". But in church she sang out clearly and I was touched and rather thrilled by the quality of her voice. "You should have been a singer, Mummy, like Granny." And she would smile and stroke my hair and say "Oh! Darling." And I have no idea if she felt wistful about it or not.

"What would you have liked to have been if you had had a job, Mummy?"

"Oh, I don't know, I would like to have been an archaeologist I think, and go on digs and find exciting things, even ordinary things, sometimes the ordinary things are the exciting things. I was good at geography, and started to learn about geology when I was taken out of school, but I never learned any science, so of course I could never really have been an archaeologist." Although she never voiced it, I sensed that she minded about her loss of education.

"What about you, Dad? Did you dream of becoming something when you were my age, or did you always want to go back to India?"

He'd puff on his pipe, smile and scratch his head and say:

"I'd have liked to have been a banker or a stock broker. But if I had been, I'd never have met your mother."

These conversations always came back to that, that his life properly began when he met our mother and his daughters had made things complete for him. I asked him why he had given Mum a blue zircon ring when Fiona was born and that my birth had not merited a gift.

"Did you want me to be a boy? Were you very disappointed that it was me? I know you had a boy's name all ready. Alan Stewart. Well, I have to say, I am jolly glad I wasn't a boy if you were going to land me with a name like that."

"No," said my father scratching his head again.

"I never wanted you to be a boy, I wanted two girls. I wanted you to be you and here you are."

"Yes, but I must have been a disappointment after Fiona," I said – fishing for a further confirmation of his love – "because when she was born, you kept a book about her for a year, well Mummy did, about how much she weighed each month and when she first walked and got her first tooth and the first word she said and stuff like that, and there was no book about me. Mummy can't even remember what time of day I was born."

"There was no book about you, dear, because it was the war and we weren't at home in the High Range. I was stationed in Bangalore when you were born in a hospital, not like Fiona, who had a midwife, Truttie, to help her into the world. You were in the Lady Curzon Hospital and a very grand doctor called Colonel Aspinall delivered you at about 10.00 in the morning. I wasn't there, but Mummy told me all about it. I went to see you with Fiona as soon as I could and there you were with Mummy and you were sucking your thumb. I was so proud of Mummy for giving birth to someone, my daughter, who was already clever enough to suck her thumb."

"That's nothing," Mummy said "She's been sucking her thumb since she was half an hour old and when Colonel Aspinall came in, he asked what we were going to call you. Isla Jean. We named you after a river in Scotland and there's a Glen Isla too and Jean just seemed to go with it. Colonel Aspinall said, 'Good gracious, with a name like Isla Jean Blair-Hill, she will have to be a film star.'"

"Did he? Did he really say that?" I was delighted. "You see, that's what I'm going to be, an actress."

I wanted so much to sit on Daddy's lap, but I was too grown up for that and it would have embarrassed him, I think. Physical affection did embarrass him; I suspect if I'd been a boy he would have shaken my hand at greetings and farewells; as I was a girl he kissed my cheek and patted me on the back.

He asked me what I liked about acting, having told me for the umpteenth time what an unstable profession it was, full of rejection and disappointment and scathing criticism. I replied that it was hard to explain, but I'd try.

"It's as if a little door inside me clicks open and I can release all my feelings through somebody else, that the character I am playing, while different from me, still has my voice, because I am saying her words. I try to imagine how she will be feeling, even if I've never had an experience like hers and I bring something from my own life and emotions into hers to make it real, so that people are seeing me, but I will be a sort of cipher for her. Oh, it's too difficult to explain."

"No, go on," said Daddy.

"Well, when the audience goes quiet and I feel they are feeling what she might be feeling, when I make them laugh, or feel sad, it is as if they are sharing our emotions – mine, mixed up with hers; sometimes I feel as if she is acting, being, feeling outside my control and I become more her than me. And at the end of the performance, I feel sort of cleansed. I'm not explaining it very well. I'm not sure I can explain it at all."

"I can't pretend to understand it, dear, but I see it means a lot to you."

"It does, it does. It's strange, but when I'm being somebody else, is when I feel most myself. I've got to be an actress Daddy, I've got to be."

"Well, we'll see dear. Your mother and I will look into it, but meanwhile study hard at school; you've got to cover your options. Perhaps you can do a typing course, just so that you have got that behind you."

It was best not to argue. But I think he understood more than he admitted.

I was learning tiny details about my father, too, that other children would have grown up knowing about theirs. He didn't like cheese and he ate too many Polo mints and gave himself mouth ulcers; he was not fearful of snakes, tigers, leeches or spiders, but he was nervous of bats and moths and wasps (he swallowed one as a boy and it stung him in his throat which became swollen making it difficult to breathe). He loved watching and listening to birds and he thought keeping them in cages was a cruelty which he couldn't abide. He invested small amounts of what tiny savings he had in stocks and shares and he bought the *Financial Times* every Saturday. He wore a tie every day of his life, Brylcreemed his unruly hair each morning, refused to wear after-shave, but sprinkled lavender water on his breast pocket handkerchief. He was strongly superstitious – would allow no peacock feathers in the house and would never buy or hire a green car deeming it unlucky and accident prone. On a home leave, on one occasion, he had to have a dark green little Austin, as it was the only car available. When he was involved in a minor accident he, of course, blamed the car.

People often ask me why I didn't have things out with him, about his decision to leave us behind in Scotland when he and my mother went back to India – but what was the point of asking the question, when I knew the answer? It was something that all of us Raj children knew. That was what was done. I just felt it was a time to get through as well as I could without them. And I did. Perhaps I wasn't always as sanguine about it then as I am now looking back, but I don't think I was unduly disappointed if they missed a concert, a sports day or a little milestone; I accepted it, although sometimes I wished I was just a girl with a Mum and Dad who turned up for things like everyone else. But I got over it and, who knows, maybe gained strength because of it.

Before we became settled there was much to sort out, come to terms with; life in England took some adjusting to before we felt even vaguely secure. My parents had to find somewhere to live, but my father also had to find a job, any job, but which should come first? The house or the job? As a tea planter, even as the manager in headquarters office (which he had been for several years), he did not qualify for many jobs in England, not even as a postie in Auchtermuchty. Eventually he was employed as a clerk in a small firm that made ladders in Slinfold near Horsham. My mother washed his shirts and made him tea in the room at the Station Hotel as she looked out at the rain and the endless greyness of November days. It was very different from the High Range.

Thereafter my parents progressed to a room in someone else's house as paying guests, near to where my father worked, right out in the country. It must have been acutely depressing for my mother. She didn't drive then and there wasn't any transport to speak of to take her away from the dripping leafless trees, the chatter of her landlady and the unheated bedroom that was all she could call home.

England was not the welcoming place my mother had looked forward to and she felt lonely and isolated. England was, after all, an alien country to her. not yet her home. Like all of us, she had faults, and on several occasions she drove me wild with irritation. She could be vain and she could be indolent (as indeed can I), but self-pity was not one of her faults. She never complained as she read cook books by Marguerite Patten and tried to follow the recipes. She had never cooked before, as she had been in India since she was thirteen years old, where people had cooked for her. She learned to dust and polish and scrub and wash clothes, darn socks, and to do all the things most of us learn before we are ten. My mother was forty-two years old.

At last they found a small bungalow in Horsham with a large garden full of trees, that they called The Estate. Their house cost £2,500 in 1959, the first proper home they had owned, loved and lived in until my mother's death in 2005.

The ladder firm in Slinfold closed down and my father had to find other work. He wrote countless letters and had just as many rejections (your age ... so long abroad ... lack of qualifications ...). It was a bruising time, rejection always is, and he started to get dejected. But my mother wouldn't allow him to plunge into anxious self-pity.

"We can live on soup and bread, we have the girls, we have this house and something will turn up."

It did.

At the age of 52 my father got a job as a junior clerk in the firm that made Wright's Coal Tar soap and he commuted daily to London Bridge, rising at 6.00 a.m. and getting back at 7.00 p.m. It must have been trying in so many ways – the loss of status, getting used to the crowds and the unreliable trains and just the length of hours. But he had my mother to come home to and that made it all worthwhile. On one occasion during my school holidays he came home, tired of course, but with his face wreathed in smiles. He had won the office sweepstake of £15 – quite a considerable sum then. He handed £5 to my mother, £5 to Fiona and £5 to me. That gesture in that snapshot of time has stayed with me, as it was so typical of him.

The days started to get shorter and the leaves on the trees got crinkly and brown round the edges and some were already turning yellow and I knew it was time to go back for my last year at West Preston Manor. I was quite looking forward to it now that our family was together. Even if we weren't physically together, if we were all in different places, we were still together somehow. No stiff chins and pebbles in the throat feeling as we waved goodbye. My parents were here as part of our lives now. They lived in England not India; they were home. India was left behind a closed door.

Going out days at school were quite different too. After church on Sundays we would come out in our grey and blue uniforms with our panama hats on, still smelling of incense and virtue and there they would be on the other side of the road from the lychgate of the church, standing by their new car, a little Ford Prefect, Dad pulling on his pipe, wearing the now familiar tweed sports jacket and Oxford Bag trousers and there would be Mum in a dark grey coat, her blonde, shining head hatless. She would smile and wave and I would pretend to be cool, when in fact my heart was racing.

"There they are, there are my Mum and Dad," I'd say, trying to be casual to Sally Kingsmill or Sheila Gaffney, and I'd feel like any other girl whose parents had come to take her out for the day.

In my last term, the summer term, on going out Sundays I was allowed to get on the train home for the day from Littlehampton and I passed through all the tiny stations until I came to Horsham and there would be Dad wearing a jacket and tie, puffing on his pipe of course. I'd hug him before I ran down the steps of the station in front of him and out to the waiting car.

Mum had usually been to the WI market on Friday and came home with armfuls of fresh spinach and squidgy meringues. I'd only just started to like spinach, fresh spinach being so different from the creamed sort that came out of tins and tasted of bad breath. She'd make a special raspberry blancmange and we would have it with fresh raspberries, meringues and cream all squished up together. After lunch we would saunter up to the top of the big garden and look out for the fox hole under the big fir tree. Dad would say "Damn foxes," but Mum would tell him how much she loved them, especially when the cubs came out at night to play, and that was usually enough for him. Mum's regard for them was the foxes' reprieve.

At St. Maray's I learned that being Isla was a very unsatisfactory person to be. I had too many faults that needed correcting – even at West Preston I was told there was a great deal of room for improvement. But I began to learn from my parents that they felt differently. It was enough for them that I was Isla they never wanted me to be anyone else and even at my most toxic teenage grumpiest they accepted me for myself. Knowing that your parents believe in you, trust you and admire you gives you a sense of confidence and wellbeing, a proper sense of yourself. I felt more blessed in this than many of my school friends who saw their parents every day.

On clearing my mother's loft and her desk after she died, I came across a cardboard box that had once contained an electric blanket, and in it were cuttings from newspapers, reviews, photographs, postcards from me, poems I had written – yellowing now and curled at the edges. But they told me of my parents' pride in me, and their love that had no conditions at all.

FOURTEEN

Number Four Hundred and Eighty–Four

West Preston Manor days passed quickly. I played many more roles in school plays – Saint Joan of course, Oscar Wilde's Salome, Coward, Shakespeare.I even played a few men, including Edmund in King Lear, with a moustache, and solid Brutus, not charismatic Mark Antony, in Julius Caesar; they both walked like a flat-footed, rolling hipped, enormous-bosomed girl.

Miss Boykett and my parents wanted me to go to university but I ardently put the case for drama school. Although my father knew of my passion and he felt we had already made a deal, RADA was the only college my parents had heard of, so it was decided I'd audition there and if I got in (I was the only one with confidence that I might), they would not go back on their word and they would support me. Not financially, though. They were unable to do that, so it was imperative that I should get a grant from West Sussex County Council.

Before I went for the big audition at RADA, I had to audition for three men, local officials in navy blue suits, in a dark room in Chichester. They sat behind a long table and asked me why I wanted to be an actress. I found it much more difficult to explain this to them than I had to my father; I said something idiotic, like I felt it was God's plan for me. To their credit, they didn't blink and asked me to do a couple of speeches. I felt self-conscious and nervous and a bit humiliated that these elderly men should decide my future. What if I got a place at RADA but failed to get a grant? I remembered to smile and say thank you before I closed the door on their deliberations. I went over my speeches every day when I was alone, but I didn't really know how to prepare them. I relied on the emotion, the feeling coming to me, and some days it didn't. I felt dry and detached. Other days I overacted and had to stop myself and start again. I knew the lines backwards and could have said them in my sleep.

I had my drama "elocution" lesson every week with Miss Pocock and she gave me notes. In those days a list was sent out from RADA for you to choose from three Shakespeare pieces, three modern pieces, and you could have one piece of your own choosing. What on earth made me choose that poem? Why not St. Joan, Salome, Nina?

Now I sit on the auditioning panel at RADA and I know how frightening the audition experience can be. What I hope it will never be is a humiliating one. The applicants come with a spring in their step and hope in their beating hearts as they embrace the day they pray will change their lives. It is surprising how few people who come to audition have got that special something that makes you sit up, the thing that you know could move, uplift, or make an audience laugh. Sometimes they are too moved or amused by themselves to include us, the audience; sometimes they are too afraid, or too schooled and coached. Only rarely do you think, "Yes" – and a green pencil marks their application paper. At this stage it is usually unanimous amongst the panel.

Recently on an "auditions day", applicants trudged through the snow to make the appointment that would last just a few minutes. Your heart breaks for them. The ladies' loo had an aroma of nervous tummies, perfume for confidence, mouthwash and hairspray. Some of them were lined up in the corridor, pretending nonchalance and cool when in fact you knew their pulses were racing, their palms sweating and their insides were in a churn. One girl came in barefoot thinking, I daresay, that she was being bohemian – just as I had when I was at RADA, with my black fishnet tights and a ridiculous rubber elephant tucked under my arm. I wanted to hug her and smooth her hair and tell her everything would be well, but of course it wasn't. She wasn't very good.

All of them are full of dreams, as I had been, and ambition and the desire to act. How those same hearts would sink when the letter with the RADA logo came through the letter box with the R for rejection. What they should know is that most of them WANT to act which is different from NEEDING to act. Of course, we, on the auditioning panel, are sometimes mistaken in our judgement; sometimes we are very, very wrong.

When I auditioned for RADA there were about 800 people auditioning for 40 places – now it is just under 4,000 for 28 places, so one has to be quite strict even to allow them in to the next round. There are four auditions to get through at RADA, each one leading to a more expansive one until a whole day is spent work–shopping with other hopeful candidates and several members of staff. But at least you want the applicants to have a pleasant experience auditioning, so we try very hard to be friendly, we chat, they do their pieces, and we chat some more. My heart aches for them, as I know how I felt that hot June day waiting for my future to be decided by anonymous strangers sitting in the dark of the little theatre

My mother and Fiona came with me. I sat by the side of the stage where "Sergeant" said he would announce me as my turn came. I felt a bit light headed. Just before me a tousled man of about 26 with a rich sonorous voice was doing something that sounded Welsh. It was by Dylan Thomas. His voice cast a spell; it was poetic but muscular – the speaker was Anthony Hopkins.

I was suddenly aware of my silly print dress, my too short hair, my knee socks in sensible shoes and being only sixteen. Sergeant announced me: "Number 486."

I think the people in the dark were having tea, because tea cups clattered and there was much whispering. Mr Hopkins had caused a stir. I did my Shakespeare piece and came to "The Assyrian came down like awolf on the fold …" I spoke with passion, but was aware of what a dreadful choice Miss Pocock and I had made. It seemed so babyish and dum-de-dum, not like Dylan Thomas at all.

I was still blushing with humiliation, frustration and disappointment as I sat on the steps of RADA in Gower Street, waiting for my Mother and Fiona to collect me. I'd blown it, my one chance and I'd blown it. I was inconsolable, because it had been up to me and I had muffed the moment. It was hot as we trudged back to the train and I was disagreeable and monosyllabic and refused to be cheered by the notion that I couldn't be sure, maybe it was better than I thought. It wasn't. My chances and my dreams were shattered.

I had no other idea for my future. I was going to be an actress, but how could I without training? I was sixteen and I had dreamed only one dream since I was six, since I'd sat in the dark at Drury Lane theatre and listened to "I Hate Men".

In my last term at West Preston, I had been boarded out to stay with the vicar, Father Fincham, and his wife in the vicarage about a hundred yards from the school. I loved it. I had a room of my own, the first time I had not shared a room with Fiona or several other girls. The curtains were flowery and chintzy, as was the bedspread and in the early summer mornings, the light gently touched the pink and blue flowers on the curtains, as the soft breeze wafted them in and out. It was soothing. At night, I would walk back from school through the fading July light avoiding little puffs of midges and seeing the evening star appear and wishing on it. I would come into the vicarage at bedtime and Mrs Fincham had said I was allowed to make myself cocoa and have a biscuit and maybe I would listen to Radio Luxembourg on my transistor radio. I felt independent and grown up, as if I was holding my breath waiting for my life to begin.

But what was my life to be without being able to train to be an actress? Could one become an actress without training? Had Jean Simmons or Debbie Reynolds trained? I could write to all the repertory theatre companies, all the theatre agents. I couldn't possibly give up so easily. What was I made of? Sterner stuff than this, surely. How could I let myself be so easily defeated, let my dream drift away? I contemplated the notion of trying to write, learn journalism, but that meant going on a typing course and a typing course would lead me, not into journalism, but to being a secretary and...STOP. Could I train to be a florist? My parents and I had chatted about Constance Spry's Flower School, but it seemed very expensive and although I loved flowers, I didn't want to be a florist. I wanted to be an actress.

One Saturday morning we were about to get into the little mini-van to journey over to Farlington School in Horsham, for yet another tennis match our school would probably lose – we usually lost. I was couple three with my partner, Juliet Palmer. We piled into the van with our tennis racquets, little white dresses and shoes, when someone came running out of the front door, down the steps, "Isla! Isla! A phone call for you." My heart lurched; I perceived that phone calls usually heralded bad news. I took the receiver into my trembling hand. It was my mother; she was gabbling.

"Isla, we've had a letter from RADA; you've been accepted. You start there on September 20th. There is a list of things you have to get, tights, practice skirt, character shoes ..."

Her voice became distant. I had got into RADA, I had been accepted. I was good enough to get into RADA. I was a DRAMA student! The day was already bright with sunshine, now it was dazzling. I was radiant, I was walking on air. Now everything was in place, I had a future; I was going to RADA to train to be an actress. My name was already in lights ... I even got the West Sussex County Council grant, which would pay for my fees and give me £5 a week living allowance.

One of the best things was hearing the most important news of my life thus far from my mother. She told me, "We'll celebrate when you come out for the day next weekend, darling. We'll have your favourite lunch and we will open that bottle of Mateus Rose Aunt Bet gave us for Christmas. You clever, clever girl – Daddy and I are so proud of you!" It was a novel feeling to hear her pride, because she was here to voice it.

FIFTEEN

Look, Move, Speak

I started at RADA nine days before my seventeenth birthday. Of course, I felt adult – a drama student – but it was not long before I realised how young I was for my age. I had been protected in an all-girl environment, never met any boys, I didn't know much about drama, nothing at all about life and here I was with everyone older than me, prettier, more confident; many had been to university, some were married. I was suddenly conscious of my clumpy legs, my baby voice, my middle class-ness and my Sussex boarding school accent. I bit my nails, wore no makeup and my first day in tights for movement class was like being stripped naked and being thrown into a bear pit. Of course, all the other students were just as self-conscious as I was and no one looked at me. They were too busy willing people not to look at them. I began to regret that I hadn't heeded my parents' advice and gone to some sort of college before I came here. Every year at school I had won the Drama Cup, I'd had the leading role in nearly all the school plays. I had been the big fish in a tiny pond. Now here I was a minnow in a huge ocean without, it seemed, the ability to swim.

All my reports said "Despite being so very young ..." "Isla is such a young student..." "When Isla is more mature ..." I tried hard, but didn't know what Yat Malmgren was talking about with the Laban Theory. I never seemed to have enough breath in Catherine Fleming's voice class and Shakespeare suddenly became technical, so I stopped understanding it. Mary Phillips, who taught mime, made me stiff with inhibition and fear. But it was more than fear that I felt for Anthony Hopkins and another classmate, Victor Henry (known then in class as Alex). I was terrified of them. They drank heavily when classes were over and would smell of alcohol in the mornings. They had an air of anger, not always suppressed, and they were really talented – they seemed to be able to do anything, they had such passion, an instinctive raw ability to make whatever they did utterly truthful. Anthony was a very good mimic, which was funny, but scary, too, as you never knew when you'd be the object of his observation. I was so easy to mimic and mock with my posh girl's vowels and my primness. But he didn't "do" me – I doubt if he even noticed I was in the same class. Well, of course, I wasn't … in the same class; he was towering and powerful, unpredictable and unafraid. So was Alex. I seemed like a well bred mouse in comparison, with no talent at all, not even a voice.

On one occasion, in the mime class given by the stiff and terrifying Mary Phillips, she of the cold eyes and, I thought, cold heart, we were told that we all had to mime an animal of our choice that we had observed and the rest of the class had to guess what we were supposed to be. I chose something pathetic and sugary like a fawn or a lamb or something and got the scathing comments from Miss Phillips that I'm sure I deserved; I had been rigid with inhibition throughout, anyway. It was Tony's turn.

He sat in front of Miss Phillips staring at her. He never broke his gaze and he didn't move a muscle. We began to shift uneasily. So did Miss Phillips. Eventually when several minutes had passed, she said. "This is a mime class, Anthony, you are supposed to be improvising a mime."

"I am, Miss Phillips. I am a rabbit being hypnotised by a snake." The class ended. Tony became our hero.

The end of the first term drew to a close with a promise of a RADA Ball at the Savoy Hotel – the cabaret was to be the "Beyond the Fringe" guys, which caused a great flurry. I was relieved the term was over and excited by the prospect of the Ball.

About five of us girls were to stay in Lynne Ashcroft's house in Kentish Town. I was commuting to Horsham each day and didn't know London at all. My mother and I had hunted the shops in Horsham, Crawley, even Brighton for a dress.

"If it's a Ball, you will need a ball gown, a party frock won't do," my mother said, and we settled on a long white organza dress with a full skirt with deep pink hydrangeas all over it. It was rather crinoline-y and "Gone with the Wind". It sort of whooshed and rustled when I moved, with masses of underskirts, and I thought I looked like Grace Kelly in High Society. I wore my mother's long white kid gloves, my right hand self-consciously covering the tiny gravy stain on the left as I made my entrance at the Savoy. Almost at once I realised my dress was all wrong. It looked as if I had borrowed it from my mother, along with her gloves, was far too old for me, and seemed from another century; my friends were in short black numbers and wore bright red lipstick or slinky red sheaths with high black heels and glossy stockings.

We greeted each other and some of the girls seemed embarrassed to be with me, as if I somehow spoilt their image, just by being in their company. No one asked me to dance, no one – which was sad, because I was quite a good dancer and I longed to dance. I had a little bit of the buffet, but had no appetite at all. I didn't drink either – I was encased in a bubble of humiliated misery. I went to the loo for long stretches, but had to keep going back to see if it got any better, if anyone would notice me, or want to be with me. They didn't. I sat all the time on my own, smiling, pretending enjoyment.

I watched the cabaret of excerpts from "Beyond the Fringe" and as soon as I could, I rushed away and got in a taxi to Kentish Town (my first taxi on my own – my Dad had given me money "in case you get separated and need it").

I arrived in the darkened house and found my way to my mattress on the floor in Lynne's room. The tightness around my chin and the lump in my throat gave way to great gulping sobs of disappointment, humiliation and grief at being so plain and undesirable, so young and babyish, at being a wallflower – well actually, a great pink hydrangea – at being such a failure at my first big social event.

I heard the others return in the early hours as they whispered, a bit drunkenly, and did lots of sh-shushing and "Isla's asleep." But I wasn't. I just couldn't face the post mortem of their triumph, my lack of it, their fun and my failure.

It was very dark as I left Lynne's house with my overnight case and offending hydrangea dress in its bag and walked down the hill to the tube station. It can't have been later than 6.30 a.m. I left a note and Christmas cards for Lynne and Cath and the others, expressing how "jolly" it had been, but "I felt rather poorly and I had to be home early ..." It was a bit lame and I'm sure no one believed me, but they soon forgot. Here were the holidays and in a few weeks we'd begin another term. Oh God! Another term...

I never wore the hydrangea dress again and I never told my parents what a disaster it had been, I had been, although they guessed from my "trying too hard to be jolly'" expression and my lack of details about the Ball. What had seemed an appropriate dress had come from my mother's era of elegance, a time warp of early '50s and this was the liberated '60s; her choice had pulled me into her world and I didn't yet know how to cross the bridge into mine. Many years later, I found the dress in my mother's attic – still in its muslin cover and wrapped in tissue. I realised the hydrangeas weren't pink, but a delicate dusky lilac with soft green leaves. It was, in fact, very lovely – but its soft filminess held the scent of anguish and defeat, and wrapped in its layers of petticoats were tears of humiliation and just holding it brought the hurt back. It went to a charity shop.

My first term at RADA had been a trial for me. I was wretchedly miserable about everything. There was nothing I was any good at. I was the baby, naive, a virgin, I didn't drink or smoke, I was too young to be allowed into a pub anyway. I was wet, and I had the wrong accent for 1960. I sat alone in the canteen at lunchtime, longing to wear black eye liner and white lipstick like some of the other girls. I tried it, but the black eye liner was wrong for the shape of my eyes and closed them right up and the white lipstick looked as if I'd burnt my lips and had applied Germolene and Jackie and Lynne laughed. Not unkindly, but they laughed. My clothes were un-cool and looked as if they belonged to my mother. Some of them actually did: a grey flannel pencil skirt that I wore with a wide elastic belt and a grey and white striped blouse that looked, I thought, rather New York business woman. In fact, it looked like my mother's borrowed blouse. I was fearful all the time, of not keeping up, being humiliated by not understanding, or just not being any good, of looking wrong and sounding wrong and thinking wrong. I couldn't do the breathing in voice classes and I didn't understand what I was supposed to be doing in movement classes, which were taken by Mr Fettes – a frightening man who wore black leather trousers, the first I'd ever seen, and who shouted things like "Punch, punch, dab, dab. Now slash, slash," as my tights-clad legs flailed in the air out of time with everyone else. One day, I overheard him speaking to another teacher, the elderly Shakespeare teacher, Nell Carter, about me.

"What on earth were they thinking of allowing her to come here? She's far too young; she should have waited at least a couple of years. It's unfair to her, she can't keep up – and I'm not even sure she has any talent."

Miss Carter said something like "Give her a chance, it's only her first term ..."

I didn't really hear any more, because I was too mortified by Mr Fettes' comments, for he was only voicing what I was starting to believe myself. I was out of place here, I was lonely, I was self conscious, I should never have come – maybe they had made a mistake in accepting me and I felt certain they were going to ask me to leave. And all the misery of it had culminated in that hateful ball. I would always be out of place here, so I would leave before they chucked me out.

My decision leaked out to my parents two days into the Christmas holidays. Mum and I had been shopping in Horsham and she asked me if I needed anything new for the next RADA term.

"I won't be needing anything, because I'm not going back."

Mum stopped walking, looked at me, hugged me without speaking and propelled me to Wakefields in the High Street for a coffee, where it all came out in great gulps of shame and defeat. She gave me her handkerchief and told me to blow my nose and forget about the coffee, we'd go home and talk about it there.

I told her about my loneliness and self-consciousness and how I was rubbish at everything and I thought they were probably going to ask me to leave. I couldn't go back, because everyone knew I was the worst in the class, I would never make an actress and nobody ever wanted to partner up with me, I felt that everyone was laughing at me anyway. Mum hugged me again and said if I didn't want to go back, then I didn't have to, there were plenty of things I could do with my life. I think she was secretly relieved that this whole actress/theatre business was coming to an end, that although it had lasted a long time, perhaps it was just a phase after all. We awaited my father's return.

At 7.00 he came in, saw our faces and poured my mother and himself a whisky, and some lime juice for me, and asked to be filled in. I told him what I'd told my mother, only in the repeated version I made it darker and exaggerated so that the only conclusion he could possibly come to was that I should never go back. Dad listened in silence and his eyes never left my face. He drew long and hard on his pipe, sipped his whisky, drew on his pipe again. "Is this what you want Isla, to give up?"

I nodded that it was. There was another silence.

"Well, I'm disappointed in you and surprised at you. You were never a quitter. You have always been strong and determined, willful even, and adamant about this ambition of yours. And I've gone along with you, because I believe you could one day be a talented actress. I know nothing about the theatre world, but it seems to me that people who do have given you a chance, and that it is you who is not allowing yourself to take it. You deserve more from yourself than this. Do you imagine all the other students feel as confident and clever as they let you believe? They are all probably just as nervous and frightened as you are. But they are able to hide it better. I don't know if you will have success as an actress; I don't even know how good you are, but I do know one thing: if you give up now you will never forgive yourself for the rest of your life because you will never know. You won't have given it your best shot. You won't have given it any sort of shot, and when you are a disappointed old lady you will look back at this moment and wish you hadn't thrown everything away by being afraid. It will take courage to go back, but I think you have got that. I think you should go back and do two more terms, finish the year. If you then feel the same, maybe the life isn't for you, but you will know for certain. I think next term it will be different."

And so it was. I was moved from class A to class B. The year's intake was split into streams of A and B. In stream A I had been with Tony Hopkins, Victor Henry and an older group of students, who scared me, not just with their drinking and their ferocity, but because of their talent. The students in stream B were probably just as talented, but I felt more like one of them. I started to laugh and become less inhibited, I wore fishnet tights and a grey pinafore dress with a black polo neck sweater, it didn't matter that I didn't wear eye liner. I was not copying anyone; I was starting to be me.

There was one teacher at RADA who knew I was young, but didn't call me a baby. He said my voice sounded velvety, not high and girly. He said I had a quality that was engaging and if I trusted myself to be still, I was watchable. He taught a class called "Technique" and although he made me nervous,

Isla, Simon Ward and Charlotte Howard
in "The Two Bouquets" RADA

he gave me confidence too. His name was Peter Barkworth. It was ironic that a teacher who taught "Technique" was the person to liberate me from my self-consciousness, my inhibitions. Peter (or Mr Barkworth as we called him) was a very distinguished actor, who spoke in a quiet voice, nearly always with a smile. He was a dapper man; he always wore a suit and polished shoes and a clean shirt every day. He had an air of quiet authority and gave structure to what we were trying to do. I knew nothing about technique, none of us did; indeed, some students started by scorning it. The "Method" was what they spoke about. Stanislavsky, Lee Strasburg. "Acting should not be technical; it should be natural, immediate, from the heart." Of course, that's what we all aspired to; how come, then, we were so wooden, awkward? It wasn't long before we all started to look forward to his classes.

Peter suggested ways of bringing an immediate past on stage with you. What had you been doing before the scene began? Peeling potatoes? Reading a letter? Crying? Then maybe you could be wiping your hands, putting the letter in a pocket, wiping your nose as you entered. You didn't just arrive in a room – you brought what you were just doing in with you. He would suggest a displaced activity while talking, arranging flowers, putting photos in a book, sharpening a pencil, folding clothes. People don't just speak at each other – sometimes they look away, don't meet your eyes at all – it's up to you to discover the secret life of the character. You could counterpoint a scene by saying something while doing something else. He taught us about sub-text too, and having an internal life, while acting out the life the playwright had given you. LOOK, MOVE, SPEAK became a mantra. LOOK at a character on stage – MOVE to the piano, pick up a sheet of music and SPEAK the question. LOOK at the door, MOVE to it, SPEAK "Goodnight" and leave.

He taught us the technique of kissing (oh! the embarrassment). How to cry if you are saying "Goodbye" – no, not by staring at a light for a long time, but how to be moved by something tiny about the person you are saying goodbye to, focusing on it – a speck of food on their tie, a little mole above their mouth, something that makes them vulnerable and the moment of parting poignant and unbearable. He taught us how to react and how to listen. He made us improvise and discover our own spontaneous explorations into character by creating an atmosphere where we all started trusting each other.

I began to be able to work on a role, not just learning lines, but thinking about the character's background, parentage, accent, clothes, shoes she'd wear. By giving things a structure, rules if you like, suddenly I became less awkward, less wooden, less theatrical and more natural. I began to be truthful. Slowly my shoulders opened, and I stopped being fearful of making a fool of myself. Much later, not at RADA, someone taught me the rules of Shakespearian verse speaking (Julian, my husband, actually). There are rules and they should be followed and ditched later, once you have learnt to speak in Iambic pentameter (five beats to the line), not breaking it up but observing the line endings; it sounds more natural than a lot of prose. It flows and sounds as if you are making it up on the spot, just invented the lines, it sounds immediate and easy on the ear.

The RADA course was two years in those days (it's now three) and for the first two terms, I commuted daily from Horsham to Victoria where I would catch a bus to Tottenham Court Road. The days were long and unpunctuality was noticed, frowned on, and continued lateness merited a discussion with the Principal as to whether or not you were serious about the course. Sergeant policed the entrance hall and clocked you running in breathless with seconds to spare. There was no excuse accepted for being late unless it was very serious. Buses and trains' haphazard timetables, leaves or people on the line, accidents, even illness, would not do. It became exhausting. I'd catch the 7.28 train which meant rising at 6.00 to allow for the 20 minute walk to the station and I'd often get back at 9.30 in the evening when my father would pick me up from the station and I'd have soup and toast and fall into bed to start all over again the next day. My parents could see me growing grey and thin and started to fret about my health. So when I mentioned that a girl in my class was looking for a room-mate, they chatted it through with me and reluctantly but sensibly agreed it was the only option, as in my second year the hours would become longer still, with shows to rehearse and productions to be in.

I shared with a girl called Heather who was in stream B and we found a bleak little basement room in Torrington Place, a three minute stumble from RADA. We had to share a kitchen and a bathroom, the floor was covered in linoleum that curled up as it got to the walls and there was a smell of damp and decaying food. The floor of the communal kitchen was always greasy and you couldn't see the bottom of the loo, as it was stained a dark brown and in need of a good soak in bleach. Of course I didn't eat properly. I ate white bread and butter and Mars bars and so it was not surprising that I got constant colds and a boil on my bum (agonisingly painful) and once I got flu. This was during a public performance of "Prison Without Bars" – it was an all-women play and not very good, but my mother came to see a matinee with Aunt Hazel and

237

was shocked that I should be performing with a temperature and the sweats. I told her I had to, I was sharing the role with Lynne Ashcroft and it would be just my luck if agents and prospective employers came when Lynne was on because I was off. No, I could not be off.

She was even more shocked when she came to my room and witnessed the squalor her little girl was living in. I think it was the lack of a pillowcase and the soiled pillow from heads other than mine, with just the striped ticking covering the soggy contents, that made her suggest that I move. And so I did with Heather again, to a flat in Earls Court.

It can't have been easy for my parents to watch their daughter enter a world of which they had no comprehension, a world that to them seemed threatening, immoral and possibly dangerous. And their daughter was young and vulnerable, for all her lofty protestations that she could look after herself.

I tried to be bohemian. I walked to and from home barefoot on many occasions, or with just my fishnet tights which were starting to become very hole-y. I'd visit Fiona in her nurses' home and she would be embarrassed by my appearance, although she never scolded me. Once I appeared with a pink rubber elephant under my arm. I even started to smoke a pipe. It made me feel sick, but I liked the image. I thought I looked eccentric, but cool – I must, in fact, have looked quite idiotic.

Fiona and I met up at the weekends when she was not working. We were starting to inhabit such different worlds, but we were always glad to see each other. We were following our dreamed of careers. Perhaps it was no surprise that she became a nurse. She had spent so many years caring for me, it must have become a habit and she was good at it. School had been her security when our parents were abroad, which was why it was such a blow when St. Maray's was closed. And now, her security became another institution – the nurses' home, the structure of the ward with the Sister in charge, timetables and rules.

Our parents had been back from India for two years, Fiona was safely at the Middlesex Hospital and here was their youngest girl, little more than a child, in an alien and frightening landscape that they had no control over. But they let me find my own way and supported me through it. I am reminded of C. Day-Lewis' poem where he states, "Selfhood begins with a walking away, and love is proved in the letting go." And they loved me enough to let me go. Not long after we had been re-acquainted they let me go.

Because they let me go, of course I went back. Every weekend, when we weren't working, I'd go home to my bed in my room and I'd tell my parents of the week's antics; lessons, humiliations and little triumphs. I'd eat properly and sleep twelve or thirteen hours and on Sunday night we'd watch Roger Moore in "The Saint" on TV as we sipped chicken noodle soup and munched on toast. A little flutter would start in my tummy as I knew it would soon be time to go to bed to be ready for the 6.00 start next morning and the train to Victoria to begin another week.

For all the nervous tension I expressed, the undoubtedly long hours and hard work, there was something exciting, even glamorous about the life I was starting to lead, in my parents' eyes anyway. My horizon was expanding and theirs was somehow reduced – no polo matches, no cocktail or tennis parties, no gymkhanas or soirees at the Club. Instead there was the daily commute, the washing and cooking, with the occasional weekend away staying with friends from India and reminiscing about days that were already being bleached out in their memory, friends with whom they had less and less to talk about.

One Friday evening I was going home to my parents for the weekend when I passed Mr Lazlow on the stairs. He had a tiny room in Earls Court next to ours that he shared with a canary.

"Bye, Mr Lazlow, have a nice weekend," I called as I went down the stairs.

"I'll spend it in bed, as I always do. It makes the time pass quicker."

I was stopped in my tracks. Here was a middle-aged man (in truth he was probably about forty) and he was so lonely he was wishing, sleeping his life away.

Mr Lazlow's ghost has hovered over me throughout my adult life – perhaps because loneliness is the one thing I fear and the one thing I will doubtless have to endure like countless others, like most of us, in fact. It is hardly profound to say that we are all really alone – if we are lucky, we've enjoyed closeness, love, companionship, but our own company is usually the company we end up keeping.

To my surprise and delight I got several letters from agents (it was "Prison without Bars" and a musical, "The Two Bouquets", they had seen) – I hadn't heard of any of them, but John Fernald, the Principal, picked out the good, reputable ones and I made appointments to see them.

I found myself in the offices of Plunkett Green, Eagle House, Jermyn Street. Terry Plunkett Green came in wearing a green velvet jacket and asked me to join him in the office of his colleague, Julian Belfrage.

Julian was pencil slim with thinning hair, a cigarette in his hand and the bluest eyes I've ever seen, fringed by the longest lashes on anyone since Bambi.

SIXTEEN

A Long Way to Fall

Julian was the hot-shot agent of the time and remained so until his untimely death aged 60 on 28th December 1994.

The other RADA students were amazed and envious, "Julian Belfrage wants you? Good heavens! He's the best." He was and I grew incredibly fond of him (but that's another story.).

He put me up for various jobs and the last few weeks of my RADA term were spent auditioning. He made it a rule that as soon as you had finished your audition you had to call him to report how it went. "Always have four pennies ready and look out for phone boxes."

I went to the Theatre Royal, Drury Lane, to audition for "The Boys from Syracuse" and afterwards I made the call to Julian from Covent Garden (which was still a vegetable and fruit garden like the scenes from Pygmalion/My Fair Lady) to report in.

"Isla, don't get on the tube home. Don't go anywhere. Walk down to the Strand Theatre. Go to the stage door; they are waiting for you."

"What? Now?"

"Yes, now, do whatever you did at the audition you have just been to." It transpired that "The Boys from Syracuse" producers had called their opposite numbers at the Strand Theatre and my agent to say I was far too young for their show, but seemed perfect for the understudy in "A Funny Thing Happened on the Way to the Forum."

I trotted down the road (I was wearing Fiona's black stilettos) – it was no more than fifty yards – and checked in at the stage door.

"Go down to the stage Miss," said the stage doorkeeper. I sang "I Have a Love" from West Side Story. They asked me how old I was, "Eighteen, but I'll be nineteen in September," feeling as I had always felt that my youth was somehow a handicap. And that was it.

I made the second phone call to Julian. "Put the four pennies in and press A when someone answers," and Julian said, "They want to see you again tomorrow, but I want you to wear a pretty dress and get your hair done. The audition is at 4.00 pm, so you will have time for that in the morning. Have you any money?"

"No, Julian, I have no money at all."

"You can borrow some from me and we will set it against your first paycheque if you get the part. Get on a tube to Piccadilly Circus. My offices are closed now, but there's a bar further up Jermyn Street, called Jules Bar. I'll meet you there in 20 minutes."

I met Julian, declined a drink, and stuffing the ten pound notes into my bag, completely unaware of how shady it could have looked, I made my way back to my flat in Holland Park that I was now sharing with three girls. I bought the dress (far too old for me, a sheath graded blue, light blue at the top which darkened into midnight as it reached the hem) and I had my hair cut and set at a hairdresser Julian had recommended in Bond Street.

At the audition there were rows of us sitting on chairs in the wings, and waiting on the stairs by the stage door. My turn came.

"I have a love and it is all that I have, what else can I do…"

I finished and they asked me to read a bit of the script with the stage manager, enquired what my age was again, and thanked me for coming.

It was two days before Julian called me to say the role of the understudy was mine if I wanted it.

Rehearsals began at the Strand Theatre. The director was the great and legendary George Abbott. Mr Abbott, as we all had to address him, was born in 1887 and died aged 107 in 1995, but he seemed pretty ancient to me when he was only 75 in 1963 – he seemed very formidable.

I was thrown in at the deep end, because the actress I was understudying, Sally Smith, was delayed on a film she was making, so I had to stand in for her for the first five days. I don't think I was very good, but I enjoyed singing the song "Lovely" with John Rye, and the cast of comedians were rather remarkable, starting with Frankie Howerd, Jon Pertwee, Kenneth Connor, "Monsewer" Eddy Gray and Robertson Hare. The girls playing the courtesans were beautiful, leggy and busty, wonderful dancers and they were kind and patient with me.

Half way through the second week, I was told I needn't come in to rehearsal. I assumed they were not doing the Virgin's scenes that day. Julian rang me. "Isla, apparently Sally Smith's film has to reshoot some stuff with her, and she will not be available to play the part of the Virgin. Mr Abbott and the producers want you to play it. Do you think you are up to it?"

I was silent.

"Isla, are you still there? The producers want you to go to the Savoy Hotel tonight at 7.00 to talk to them about it."

I found my voice. "Really? Me play the part? You mean, open in the show? To do the whole run?"

"The whole run. Your salary will go up from the £10 a week you are getting as understudy, to £40 a week to play Philia. They want you to sign for the run of the play. Go to the Savoy tonight. I will ring your parents and speak to them about it."

I borrowed a pink and white gingham dress from my friend and flatmate Suzi and found my way to the Savoy Hotel. Mr Abbott was there to greet me, Vicky Brinton, Hal Prince, Mr Sondheim and the two writers. They asked me how I felt. "Are you alright about this, Isla?" I said that I thought I was and that I would try to do my very best. With that Mr Abbott ordered champagne and I had the first glass of it I had ever tasted.

The evening passed without me saying one word on my own initiative. I was so awe-struck by the occasion, it must have been like drawing teeth to get me to speak at all. At the end of a very short evening, Vicky Brinton put me into a taxi and told the driver to take me home and that it was "on account".

There was a great deal of publicity about me taking over the role, sort of 42nd Street "understudy takes over star role". It was hardly a star role! "From understudy to leading lady" – it was on the front of every newspaper, for it was late July, the silly season, with not a lot of news. I saw my face staring back at me from people's papers on the tube, but no-one recognised me. BBC News sent a journalist down to interview me. I was suddenly a celebrity and was photographed with all the comics and on my own outside the theatre, in Covent Garden market buying fruit, swinging from lamp posts, in Hyde Park rowing on the Serpentine, standing outside the Chelsea Potter in the King's Road (London was just about to swing with the King's Road and Carnaby Street the addresses you just had to visit). I was photographed for Tatler and Harpers magazines by Terence

Donovan and Tom Hustler. What I remember feeling was foolish and embarrassed. I didn't really enjoy the photographs, the interviews, the celebrity bit; I felt shy and as if I was being set up for the most almighty fall, as if I wasn't really ready for any of this. But I kept these feelings to myself, for people insisted that I must be so thrilled, and I was, but I felt that there was too much "fuss" being made (an expression my father could have used). But my parents and Fiona were incredibly excited and proud, encouraging and completely supportive

The show opened in September 1963, when it toured for four weeks to Oxford and to Manchester. I was very lonely on tour (I still am if I tour today) as I was too young to spend time with any of the girls and the comics were all stars in their own fields, why should they bother with me? People were kind, but I felt very alone and a little bored during the day. I went to the big stores and wandered around the perfume counters. I walked around all the colleges in Oxford, I read Georgette Heyer, and in Manchester I spent longer and longer in bed during the day, not because I was tired, but it made the day pass more quickly. I thought of Mr Lazlow and wondered if he still had his canary, poor Mr Lazlow.

We came back to London and had a few previews before our opening night and "notes" each day with Mr Abbott, who had not seen the show for four weeks while we were on tour. "Isla, what on earth has happened to you?" My heart stopped. Mr Abbott's voice told me he was not about to be complimentary.

"I cast you as Philia because you were young and innocent and sweet and natural, she is a virgin. What has happened to you? You are now arch and coy and playing the vamp."

I knew it was too good to last. My first job and I was about to be sacked. But Mr Abbott was made of fairer stuff than this.

"I will work with you all afternoon. We will do all your numbers, all your scenes and we will find together those things that made me want to cast you in the part. You could be a good little actress, you will be a good actress, when I have finished with you, but you will have to work hard, you will have to work very hard indeed if you are to be ready for our opening night."

On the day of our last preview, the Royal Preview, which Princess Margaret was to attend, Mr Abbott asked me to come down to the stage just before the half; my heart was beating so fast I felt sure he could hear it.

"Isla, you have worked hard and I am proud of you. I am glad I picked you and you have repaid me by being mature and professional. Good luck tonight".

I floated up the stairs to my tiny dressing room, sat in front of the mirror and looked at my reflection and said, "Phew!"

* * * * *

Press night arrived. Everyone was nervous and expected me to be the most nervous of all. People put their heads round my door, "All right, Isla? Don't be nervous." "All right, Isla? You'll be fine."

Actually I was all right. I was nervous of course, a little, but I was mostly excited. I felt as if this moment had come and it was my moment.

The orchestra was tuning up (I remembered Drury Lane and *Kiss Me Kate* and asking my mother why the music was "jangly" and she said "They're tuning up.") Then the call came through the tannoy.

We assembled in the wings, Frankie and the Proteans were

singing "Comedy Tonight", there was some vigorous shaking of hands and feet to relax, stretches, deep breathing, people humming, others telling each other to "break a leg." All of us wished each other luck and despite their own nerves on this occasion, the grown up actors showed me concern, "OK Isla? Enjoy it; it will be over so quickly."

Linda Gray playing Domina in a bright red wig and very dark red lipstick and a lot of black eye makeup took my hand, "You are good, Isla. Believe in yourself. I am certain this will be the first of many first nights."

The music was rising up and Frankie was talking to the audience over the drum roll. I knew my parents and Fiona were in the stalls waiting for me, willing me ...

"And now, ladies and gentleman, the entire company ..."

SEVENTEEN

The Wrong Way Round

Through all these new experiences, a different world was opening up to me. It seemed I was getting to know my parents the wrong way round somehow. Most children learn about their parents during their childhood; I had had just short snatches with mine. It wasn't until I was on the verge of flying the nest that my relationship with them became intimate, common place, taken for granted. In my brief bursts of family life I wanted to treasure the time with them, so our relationship had been somewhat tentative, polite, as if we were afraid of offending each other. Caught off guard, I had said horrible things to my mother, to both my parents, and lived the long lonely months without them full of regret and shame that they weren't there to bestow forgiveness.

Now, in our time together, we had quarrels as well as confidential chats, arguments that were allowed to be fiery because we knew our regard for each other was deep; we were beginning to respect as well as love each other. I was touched and irritated by them in equal measure. There were more little things I was discovering about them. Dad liked whisky, but only drank two measures a night, never more. He liked kippers, but was rarely allowed to eat them because of the smell they left in the house. He had only ever eaten English fruit from tins in India; these had been treats he savoured, tinned peaches, pears and mandarin oranges, and indeed he preferred them now to the fresh variety. A creature of habit.

He had beautiful handwriting and kept his papers ordered and his documents neatly filed. He was a gentle, courteous man, quiet and deep. His sense of humour was dry and his laugh infectious. He had a wisdom about him that I trusted; if there are such things as old souls, I think he was one.

But he was impossible to have a row with, which in itself could be infuriating. I'd be getting heated and argumentative, for example, about his irrational contempt for the Roman Catholic Church and he'd terminate the argument by changing tack and agreeing with me. "But Dad ... you just said ..." It was no good; so far as he was concerned, the row was over. It would happen sometimes if we weren't rowing, but just passing the time of day: "I think those new houses are really rather nice."

"Oh, Dad! How can you? They're hideous. Characterless, charmless, all the same little boxes."

"That's right dear, they're hideous." He hated confrontation.

We spoke every day on the phone and he would sometimes act as the peacemaker in rows with my mother; we didn't row often, but when we did, we both said things that would be calculated to wound.

My mother was something of a hypochondriac; her way of getting her mother and stepfather's attention as a girl was to be ill and it had become a habit. She would cry wolf and it was hard to believe her when she really was ill. I was impatient and brushed away her ailments unkindly, even harshly. Dad would scold me. Mum's honest criticisms of me could sometimes bewilder and wound me and she knew she was not doing it always just for my own good. She wanted to say it. Dad would try to stop her. If I had appeared on TV in something she didn't like, she would sometimes ring me up immediately afterwards and tell me that the programme was no good and that I was no good in it. Dad could be heard in the background saying "Vi, dear, don't say that. What on earth can she do about it now? It's over." She'd tell me she didn't like my hair or the costumes, that I looked as though I hadn't slept for weeks with the bags under my eyes. She was usually supportive and encouraging and I should have been able to take her criticism; she was proud and she would say so, which made her little barbs all the more bruising. We were both volatile and quite voluble with each other, which I suppose was better than being just polite, which we were in the early days of relationship when they first came back from India. But one row was to last for several days.

Some years into my career I was married, and my son Jamie must have been about ten, when I appeared in Malcolm Bradbury's "The History Man" adapted for TV by Christopher Hampton and starring Anthony Sher. I had the really good role of Flora Beniform and for two scenes I was to be in bed stark naked with Tony getting up to all sorts of shenanigans. The series was good and I was proud to be in it. I didn't enjoy stripping off, it's very vulnerable-making, but it was required in the scenes and I had to do it. I told my parents about it; they didn't like the idea, but agreed that if that was what I had to do, then I had to do it. They decided not to watch the four part series and I was much relieved.

There were no phone calls after the episodes, but the series did cause a furore (there were even questions asked in the House), but I kept my head down and didn't read the papers. Some weeks later I had a phone call from Mum:

"There's a letter here, Isla, from Miss Evans. She has enclosed a letter to you in a letter to us. It's about 'The History Man'."

"Oh that's nice," I said.

"No, it's not nice at all. It says ..."

And she read the contents to me. It was an unthought-out, unkind, biased, scolding letter from Miss Evans. My Miss Evans, who had stopped me from falling into a black hole of despair and shame because of my illiteracy; who had given me the gift of literature and drama; who had opened my eyes and had given me confidence; who had taught me to read and so much more. Miss Evans, who was my saviour and my friend, who had encouraged me to become an actress. This Miss Evans was writing of her surprise that I could do such a disgusting and ignoble thing; that I was a talented girl with promise. It was such a shame. I should be ashamed, but how could my parents not be ashamed? I had let them, her, the school and myself down. The letter covered six angry sides and my mother ended it breathing heavily.

"The letter is to me, Mum."

"But she sent it to us to give to you. And she's right, she's right. We are embarrassed, Isla, and you have let yourself down."

"Are you taking her side Mum, against me? Why did she send such a horrid letter for you to read? That was not an act of kindness. Her criticism is for me – it was ugly of her to want you to share it, and petty of you to agree with her." I ended by putting the phone down. I was angry and hurt.

For the next few days when the phone rang and I heard my mother's voice, I churlishly replaced the receiver. I was still smarting and I was having a tricky time with the tabloid press, which made me vulnerable, thin skinned and easily wounded. After several days of this, Dad rang: "Isla, your mother is very distressed. This rift between you is hurting her deeply. I am asking you to make it up. How often have we told each other not to let the sun go down on our anger?"

Mum had sent me a card and written inside were those New

Testament verses about love being patient and not proud. Of course I forgave her as she forgave me and we hugged and kissed and shed a few tears. Miss Evans was not to get off so lightly.

I was coldly reasoned in my reply to her and expressed my surprise that she did not seem to understand the nature of the work that she had encouraged me to do. She mentioned Jennie Linden (who had been to the same school): "She has had a great success in her career, she's a very good actress and she hasn't found it necessary to take her clothes off." I wrote back saying that Jennie had made her name in Ken Russell's "Women in Love", which had launched her career, and we all knew how explicit those love scenes had been.

We had a rapprochement and corresponded till her death.

* * * * *

My parents were wise about my boyfriends by not making a fuss, not being judgemental, not expressing dislike or concern, and goodness knows, they must have felt it sometimes. They doubtless knew me well enough to believe that their doubts and criticism would drive me to defend the said boyfriend and deepen a possibly shallow flirtation. My first boyfriend was someone I met as I was leaving RADA. He was nice, older than me, and a good actor. When I got "Forum", he said that I must not accept the part of Philia if I wanted to go on seeing him. The publicity that surrounded my landing the role didn't overjoy him either. He presented me with an ultimatum: Forum or him. My CV shows the decision I made, much to my parents' relief.

I had a few more boyfriends after that, but none of them were serious – and although the sixties were starting to swing,

I still had a fifties head above my mini-skirted body and looked on promiscuity with alarm. I felt oddly embarrassed about not indulging in this sexual liberation that was almost forced on us. It was unsettling to feel that I was out of step with everyone else of my age and circle, that there was something wrong with me. What I sought was intimacy, which doesn't come with anonymous sex. I had a one night stand with an army officer friend of my flatmate that made me shudder with shame for days. Dad had once said, "Don't do anything that makes you afraid or ashamed to look at your reflection in the mirror."

There weren't that many blokes I really fancied, I suppose, and I behaved in a "Come on but come no further" way to several of them that makes me hot with embarrassment when I look back on my twenty-year-old self, what a little prick-tease I must have been. One man in particular, who was the nephew of one of my parents' Indian friends and who worked for a company that owned a string of theatres, would take me to first nights and smart restaurants, L'Ecu de France in Jermyn Street, the Savoy Grill, the Caprice, the Mirabel. He started to educate me about wine and I learned about regions and vintages. However, I enjoyed the food and wine more than I enjoyed his company and usually couldn't wait to leave. And on one occasion I surpassed myself for rudeness. After an evening with him. climbing into his low E Type Jag, I asked to be taken, "No, not home please. I am meeting someone else at The Saddle Room. Could you take me there?" He was nonplussed as I leapt from the car, managing to get out of even the brush on the cheek he was expecting. Shame on me. He was amazingly forgiving – my 21st birthday present from him was 21 driving lessons from BSM and a diamond brooch. A few years later he married and named his first born daughter Isla.

EIGHTEEN

Sausage, Mash and Picking Sweetpeas

During the London run of Forum, I got my first film part – a day on a film with Peter Cushing called "Doctor Terror's House of Horrors". I was to spend all day in the company of a precocious chimpanzee who was supposed to have painted a picture hung in the Royal Academy. It was to be filmed in a studio in Shepperton and, as a young unknown with a very small part, I was expected to get myself to the studio; this posed a problem as I was required to be there before the trains started running in the morning. My father collected me from the theatre the evening before and took me, with my mother, to a small hotel in Shepperton, where we stayed the night, and he drove me to the studios in the morning when it was still dark and very cold. They wished me luck and kissed me, our whispered breath little wisps of steam in the chill November morning, before waving goodbye and making the tedious journey back to Horsham; I can only think my father had taken the day off from work. It may seem over-protective of his 19 year old daughter who, for so long had undertaken all sorts of journeys, sometimes with Fiona, sometimes alone, but nearly always without my parents; but he was here now and could help me and I was glad of it and let him.

My £40 a week in Forum was being frittered away. I had

my rent to pay, of course. I didn't drink, but I did spend most nights at the trendy Saddle Room club run by the then famous Helene Corday and I danced there 'till dawn. I would walk home from Hyde Park to Pont Street where I shared a flat, breakfast on a bacon roll from a man in a van called Dan, believe it or not – well Danny actually. We became chums and he had the roll ready for me most mornings

"Bacon done to a crisp, love. No tea?"

There were starlings in London in those days and a few of them and some pigeons escorted me home, hopeful of crumbs. I slept till midday (except matinee days – no Saddle Room on Wednesday or Friday nights). I bought makeup, I bought fripperies, I was profligate and foolish. I was young.

My father, concerned that I should leave the show after twenty months with only a pair of "kinky boots" to show for the good wages I was on, arranged with Julian Belfrage and his accountant, Peggy Thompson, that a percentage of my salary should be put aside in the form of savings each week and this was done – until the event of my marriage, aged 22, when my father handed over a substantial cheque from my saved money. This went towards the down payment on the purchase of our first house in Barnes, which cost an unimaginable £11,000. It is hard to believe, but in those days it would have been impossible to get a mortgage as a single woman without my father or some other man guaranteeing it.

My father was always prudent and sage about savings. He was so fearful of not having any money, as funds had always been tight during his boyhood and he did not have many of the things he needed – a kilt jacket, for example, the right socks for his kilt, long trousers at a time when all his school friends wore them and he was still in his short trousers and cruelly mocked. He made sure that Fiona and I should have the required "everything": travelling rugs, coats, berets, jumpers, kilts, eiderdowns, even the sort of sponge bag, with pockets inside, that we had set our hearts on; whatever was needed, my father ensured that we had it. He was determined we should not do without. We might be deprived of his and my mother's company, but we should not be deprived of school needs, even luxuries – everything the other girls had, we should have. If they needed to come from Forsyth's or Jenners in Edinburgh, so be it. Neither of his beloved girls should be scorned or mocked at school for having the wrong item or piece of clothing.

Shortly after my grandmother (my mother's mother, Jessie) died, my mother went to her funeral in Prestwick and was to spend a couple of days there. I came down to Horsham from Victoria to be with my father. I was in my last production at RADA and on the point of leaving. He met me at Horsham station and suddenly it was just my Dad and me. There was no mother or sister to be a conduit for our relationship.

It was only a few years since Fiona and I had both parents available to us all the time, but Fiona was well into her training at the Middlesex. Dad had prepared pork sausages, which he grilled with a tentative hand, saying he was making "heavy weather" of it and laughing in a self-deprecating way when they got burnt and split. He had peeled potatoes, which I boiled and then mashed with butter. We sat in the kitchen and ate this feast with tomato ketchup and felt pleased with ourselves and told each other it was very nice. My father had never cooked anything before – really never, not ever. This was his first experience of gas and grills and spluttering sausages; that I was his guinea pig, made me feel like a conspirator in his culinary first. We applauded each other on how delicious it was as we ate tinned peaches and vanilla ice cream for pudding. We talked about his job and how he found the routine rather dull and the commuting tiring. I asked him what he had for lunch. It amazed me that it was always the same; roast beef, Yorkshire pudding, potatoes, beans and cabbage and a slice of apple pie and ice cream to follow.

"How can you always eat the same thing, Dad?"

"Well, dear, it is nutritious and not expensive and we never had beef in India. And we never had apples either."

No one had beef in India. Cows were sacred creatures. We had their milk, but no one thought to eat them. We had chicken and mutton and on rare and dreaded occasions, there was goat. Fiona and I were both teased for not knowing what apples were when we first went to St. Maray's.

The day had started shyly, but by the end of it we were laughing and confiding in each other – not deep confidences, but sharing our opinions and thoughts and feelings. He asked me what it felt like to be on stage. He had just been to see me in Eleanor and Herbert Farjeon's musical "The Two Bouquets" and he said he had loved it and he was proud of me. He thought going on stage would be rather like facing a firing squad. I told him I didn't understand the need to act, and although it was sometimes frightening, difficult and could be bruising (certainly to receive horrible reviews and to take the rejection), it was also unlike anything else in the world. I told him about the time on board ship and playing "St. Joan" when the audience went quiet and I told him how it felt to play Helena in "Look Back in Anger" with Tony Hopkins at RADA. How I seemed to feel as if things were coming to me from outside – it was like flying, uncertain of where I would land, but just responding to what transpired on the flight. We had rehearsed of course, and knew what we were doing – the moves, the lines, but this was nothing to do with the newly learned technique. Something happened to change the temperature and we found ourselves in a different emotional place, always aware of the audience, but responding to each other, really listening, taking the audience with us, aware that we were sharing a secret with them in a little bubble of time. This by no means happened every time one acted, but occasionally it did and made all the trials and anxieties that went with the process worth the struggle. I was just starting, with so much to learn, so much to wrestle with – and anyway, the feeling seemed to defy description; it was elusive, like trying to catch a shaft of light; I was inexperienced and inarticulate and found it impossible to explain, as I didn't understand it myself.

I'm not sure my father got it at all, although he tried. It was bewildering to him that I could remember so many lines. Something that actors always have to explain is "How do you learn your lines?" People don't want to know that that is the easy part. Learning lines comes with practice. I do not find it a nightmare, as some actors do, although I am not blessed with a photographic memory like Derek Jacobi or Stephen Fry. That is an enviable gift.

And so we chatted throughout our day together and had tea and crumpets with marmite and butter and we washed up and he smoked his pipe. He spoke proudly of Fiona and her nurse's training and called her "a remarkable girl" and he talked with such love for my mother, clearly missing her even though she would only be away for forty-eight hours.

He helped me cut some roses from our garden and we got some sweet peas from Mr Budgen down the road. We picked them together and cut down some runner beans and paid Mr Budgen his money, wrapped the flowers in some tin foil and rested them across the top of my bag and the runner beans we wrapped in newspaper and put into the bottom of my little weekend case.

Soon it was time to say goodbye. Daddy drove me to the station and stood waving until the train went round the corner and we became invisible to each other. I sat back in my seat and smiled at his dearness and how nice the day had been. I could not know then that that was the only day in my life that my father's company would be exclusively mine.

I enjoyed many days alone with my mother. She would come up from Horsham on the train and we would meet at Victoria Station by the Grosvenor Hotel: the same Grosvenor Hotel where Fiona and I had had brown Windsor soup and rolls and butter before our first flight to India. I would see my mother from afar, because she always arrived early. She was elegant and sometimes wore a beret, but she had an air of vulnerability about her too as she looked out for me, standing alone with her handbag over her arm, twisting her gloves in her hand. We would go to Harvey Nicholls or Fenwicks and we would pad up and down New Bond street and Knightsbridge admiring or tutting over the clothes in the windows. We sometimes went to Harrods where we would get ourselves a light lunch from one of the interior cafes or the health juice bar (just introduced). Only occasionally did we grace the restaurant. In the restaurant at Harrods, oak panelled and rather stock-broker Tudor, models wandered around the tables wearing suits and dresses that were for sale, with little labels with a price-tag on them round their wrists, while music played. We would eat open sandwiches and sip tea and then go round each floor chatting and being companionable. Here was my mother just being my friend. Yet somehow the roles were starting to reverse. I knew London and "the shops" better than she did and led the way to places her imagination had only dreamt of in India: to a beauty salon for a facial in Beauchamp Place, Fortnum & Mason for tea, where a late middle aged, rather effete man in 18th century costume – complete with white wig, a black patch and eye makeup – teetered around the tea tables chatting to the elderly ladies and "making their day." The afternoon tea at Fortnums at that time was not very nice, leaden scones and tea that tasted of hay; usually we would go to the Ceylon Tea Centre and there we were never disappointed.

On one occasion, I decided to pick my mother up in my new car. It was a bright orange mini and had a black drop head roof and a number plate that read 8PUR. It was an adorable, funny, cheeky little car and I whizzed about London in it believing I was one of the swinging, cool, mini-skirted trendsetters who was about to change the world. The mini – the car, not the skirt – stayed with me for many years until one day, on a drive back from Horsham, the battery fell out onto the road at the Robin Hood roundabout.

The plan was to meet my mother in a road that ran beside the Grosvenor, open the door to her and whisk her away to San Lorenzo in Beauchamp Place for lunch, then to Harrods. I felt grown up and responsible for her, for her pleasure in the day, for showing her this new London that I was starting to discover and I was in the driving seat after all!

I was early. Her train wasn't due to arrive until 11.15 and it was only 10.00 as I found myself driving through Belgravia en route to Victoria. I slowed down and parked. What lovely little shops, a bakery that wafted delicious smells, bread and – new to me – chocolate croissants; a vegetable shop with aubergines, courgettes and red and yellow peppers in boxes, laid out on pretend green grass on little trolleys on the street; there were fat garlic bulbs and brown onions – it looked familiar, like the bazaar in Munnar or Cochin, but I hadn't seen such exotic vegetables in England before.

There was a charming shop, later to be called a boutique I daresay, with one dress in the window, a dark deep blue, the colour of the night sky in the tropics, beautifully cut, elegant in its simplicity. Although I could never afford such a dress, what harm could there be in going in and having a little look around.

The carpet was white and deep, the counter was white with a bowl of full blown cream roses resting on it. The air was delicately fragranced with Jean Patou or Guerlain and only a few dresses and jackets hung from the rails protected from hands like mine by thin sheer veils of cellophane. I started to look through them and noticed labels I'd heard my mother speak of: Dior, Balmain, Chanel – here was the poshest of posh shops. I was still leafing through the clothes when a woman with a chic black bob straight from the '20s (early Vidal Sassoon probably) in a very short black dress appeared and looked at me enquiringly. I think I appeared guilty, as if I had no right to be there – she thought so too as she asked, "Yes, Madam, may I help you?"

"Oh, I'm just having a look about, if I may." There was a silence you could drive a doubledecker bus through.

"Madam, this is a dry cleaners!"

I made for the door, feeling sick with humiliation, and out to the safety of my little orange car. How could I have been so clutzy and unsophisticated? It was only when later I'd collected my mother and we were speeding to Beauchamp Place, and I told her of my gaff, that we both started to laugh. I had to stop the car as we laughed and laughed and because she, my mother, was with me, it became funny and not embarrassing.

Sometimes we would go to a matinee and at the interval, if

ordered beforehand, small trays of tea and biscuits were handed down the rows of the audience and we would sip and nibble and discuss the merits of the play. We were companionable, we were friends, we were mother and daughter doing things mothers and daughters do together.

We would go Christmas shopping too. We'd look at the decorations in the shop windows, the lights in Regent Street and we'd buy secret things for each other's stockings – sugar mice (my mother had a collection of mice, as that was her nickname, Mouse) and chocolate Santas, bars of soap and glass tree decorations. We'd have mince pies for tea and toast each other with our tea cups. We would people watch and play the "he looks just like..." game. She was always enthusiastic, always appreciative of small gestures of kindness or thoughtfulness, always ready to laugh.

There was an element missing though. Fiona. She had done her three years' training at the Middlesex, her midwifery course, when an opportunity came to work at the King Edward VIII hospital in Bermuda with some of her newly-qualified SRN-ed friends. It was a long way away, the other side of the world from England or India, where her days would start just as our days were ending. There was much debate about whether or not she should go and finally it was decided it was too good an opportunity to miss, and besides it wouldn't be for long.

And so my companion, my confidante, my sister who had always been at my side through thick and thin, good and bad, was to step out of my life for a bit. I felt unreasonably aggrieved and a little fearful – how would I manage without her? I knew in my soul I was being illogical and selfish, my career was up and running, why should Fiona not take this chance? And she did. We waved her off at Heathrow where she went through the departure gates alone and her tears fell straight onto my heart like battery acid and I kept hoping she would change her mind, turn round and come back. But she didn't and she looked tiny and vulnerable as she walked into her new life thousands of miles away.

Christmas was spent without her, just the three of us in Horsham, and we toasted her and realised at that moment she was probably fast asleep. I could feel my throat close up a little as that familiar little lump of loss and missing lodged itself there. I had never felt it for Fiona before – well, not since those early days in India when she went off to school without me.

Most weekends I'd go home to Horsham. I was still getting used to the concept of home; my home with my own room which was painted the softest primrose yellow, with venetian blinds and green and yellow curtains and a little creamy-coloured bedside lamp on a small table by the bed. There was a wardrobe where I could hang my clothes, just my clothes and not share the space with anyone else, and a chest of drawers where I could keep my jumpers and knickers and stockings and I could put tiny lavender bags in between them and in another drawer I could keep my diary and letters, photographs and my film star albums and the glass bangles and the bracelet with the four leafed clover and all the treasures that weren't treasures at all, really, but just things that were mine, which in the past I'd had to trundle about; I could keep them here in my home forever if I wanted to, even though I had a flat in London. There was a bookcase where I could keep all my books and the plays I would probably never be in – Tennessee Williams and Noel Coward and Eugene O'Neill – much read. It was good being able to keep them there in case I needed them. Good being able to keep them there even if I didn't.

NINETEEN

Lemons, Laundry and French Tobacco

I've fallen in love twice in my life. Both times it has been at first sight, in an instant. When I fell in love for the first time, I was 21 years old and my career was going well. I'd just finished a six–month TV series for Granada and I was repeatedly being asked to do musical theatre. But I had in mind a different path. I wanted to learn about Shakespeare, Chekov and Ibsen – in fact, all classical theatre – and so I signed a contract with The Prospect Theatre Company to do a new play about Dr. Johnson, James Boswell and Mrs Thrale called "Boswell's Life of Johnson' (I was to play Fanny Burney and double the role of Louisa, a mistress of James Boswell.) There was another play called "Thieves Carnival" by Jean Anhouilh (in which I was to play the ingénue). The cast included Timothy West, Julian Glover, Martin Potter, Sylvia Sims and James Aubrey. I confess I hadn't heard of any of them, except Sylvia Sims, a bit of a heroine with her blonde hair, good bones and blue eyes – I remembered "Ice-Cold in Alex" and how simply lovely she was.

We assembled in a rehearsal room in Victoria on the 22nd May 1966. May had been hot, everyone was tanned and in shirt-sleeves and cotton blouses. I was nervous meeting "proper" actors, not that the actors I had worked with before weren't "proper", but these ones felt high poweredly classical.

A tall, rather gangling man came through the door. He was blond with a determined chin and a roguish smile. He stood in the doorway waving greetings to Tim and to Toby Robertson, our director. The sun shone on his blond hair and made it seem to glow. He was wearing a French workman's blue denim shirt with the sleeves rolled up and jeans and a navy blue cashmere jumper slung round his waist. We shook hands and when he looked at me, something happened to my legs. I gradually became aware of the scent of him, lemons and freshly laundered shirts and a whiff of French tobacco. This was Julian and I will never forget that moment.

Julian came with baggage though. Being ten years older than me and newly divorced from his wife of nine years, Eileen Atkins, some of the baggage was heavy and would cause me a bit of anguish in the months to come. Not only had he been married to Eileen, but he had left her to have a relationship with Sarah Miles, a beautiful, wild and unpredictable 60s icon. Although the bruises from these break-ups didn't show, they were there under his skin, close to his heart and he felt them. How could I possibly enter the frame with a brilliant actress (Eileen had just won the Evening Standard Award for "The Killing of Sister George") and a beautiful movie star – for I knew in that instant that my heart no longer belonged to just me. It was being stealthily and invisibly lassoed by this man in the denim shirt and however hard my head tried to convince my heart to slow down, it floated away – all caution thrown into the shafts of sunlight in the doorway on that hot May morning.

I'd always said that I had to marry a man whose voice was strong, mellow, rich and low – although I'm not sure I specified the qualities when I was ten years old. I just knew my husband had to have a good voice; good voices mattered. So often

Julian

handsome men have been spoilt by high pitched or sibilant sounding voices; their masculinity reduced to Minnie Mouse squeakiness, rendering them, to my ears, a bit ridiculous.

I remember doing a film in Glasgow and standing in the lunch queue behind a huge 6'.6" red-haired highlander with bursting biceps and a red beard of spectacular effulgence. A Viking, a formidable fighter at Culloden, was the character he presented. He had hands the size of tractor tyres and arms that had clearly tossed many cabers. It was his turn to step up to the serving hatch of the catering van to be asked by the caterers what he wanted for his lunch. His voice, falsetto, as if he had just inhaled helium, came back with, "Have ye any cheese toasties?" It was a struggle not to laugh. I've always been disconcerted by high pitched voices in both men and women and won over by deep, rich melodious tones. Julian's voice had all the qualities I liked. I just knew I wanted to listen to him all the time.

It was a scary thing falling in love with Julian. For as well as delight, he would bring me quite a lot of unsettling anxiety. We started living together in secret. I stayed every night in his studio flat at the top of a Victorian house in Fulham and beetled back to my flat in Kensington to change, shower and be there in case the phone rang and it was my parents. The uncertainty Julian brought me was my own insecurity. He was experienced and bright and he was married, for God's sake, when I was still at primary school. I did unforgivable things – I steamed open Eileen's letters to him that she had written from New York and I remember once jumping off a bus to follow her into Mary Quant's shop – Bazaar – in Knightsbridge. Just to see her – her skin and hair, watch her blink and breathe – here was Eileen, Julian's still-married-to-wife and I had turned into her stalker for five minutes. She was unaware of me, but I was in anguish, my insecurity not allowing me in any way to measure up to her. How could he want to be with me? I was quite pretty (a word I was beginning to despise, it felt so insipid somehow), but I was young and I was afraid of her. It didn't occur to me that she could be alarmed by me. She has since become a friend; I admire her work hugely. She is very funny and she has shown generosity to my son and therefore to me.

After two years of tears and fears, sun-wrapped days in France and in Deya, Majorca and drizzle-damp days in London, Julian asked me to marry him. He didn't need to ask twice.

Julian is impulsive, enthusiastic and passionate, he is funny and warm with a sense of honour that some could consider quaint. He is also without envy, he is genuinely pleased when friends, even rivals, do well – if someone gets a part he has been up for and he thinks they are better for the role, he will admit, and mean it, that they deserve it. He even lacks *schadenfreude*, which can be quite annoying when I'm having a good old bitch about someone. He is loyal and kind, but he can be fantastically tactless. This springs from a curious innocence – he sometimes doesn't think before he blurts out a remark he occasionally lives to regret. But because his heart is warm, people forgive him and laugh with him. Julian is well known for playing villains, but he is soft really, open and honest. Tough, he might appear, but his vulnerability is child-like and it tugs at my heart.

I remember in the first years we were together, I used to feel suffocated when we had to be apart; I felt as if I couldn't breathe, and that hasn't gone away. It was different from the choking feeling of the gundamulley bead in my throat that I experienced as a little girl. This was as if I couldn't get enough air in; no amount of air was enough to fill the empty space in my chest. Yes, love makes you vulnerable and open to pain. Separations have become trying and frightening for both of us and we both dread, with silent, unspoken foreboding, the longest separation of all.

Julian and I married on September 1968 and we were to honeymoon in Bermuda. Well, that was the plan but it didn't turn out quite like that. The Friday before our wedding, on 27th September, the Registrar from Chelsea Register Office rang us and said, "So, you have changed your mind about marrying on Saturday."

"What do you mean we've changed our minds? No, we are flying to Bermuda on Sunday."

"I'm afraid not. There must be, by law, one clear day between your divorce and your remarriage. To marry on Saturday, your divorce should have been registered on Thursday." On registering his divorce from Eileen, Julian thought one clear day meant 24 hours. However, the Registrar was persuaded by my father's soft Scottish voice and, I think, a small handful of notes, to marry us on the Sunday. So we had a wedding lunch on the Saturday at San Lorenzo in Beauchamp Place with close family and friends and then we went to our friends Miranda and Edward de Souza's house in Barnes for a wedding reception. I wore my wedding ring, we cut the cake, toasts were made in champagne, Julian made a speech that made everyone cry – and we weren't married at all. We had a secret private moment when we put the rings on each other's fingers and vowed to love each other always. And we have. The reception was happy and sunny, the rain came out at the end of the day and caused rainbows – a tiger's wedding on *our* wedding day. It seemed auspicious.

Julian and Isla's wedding

We were officially married at Chelsea Register at 10.00 the following morning, Sunday, September 29th – my birthday. Very hung over. There was a very large sign with a pointing arrow to the "VD Clinic". Not quite so auspicious. Our little wedding group is photographed looking remarkably cheerful, if a tad rough, bags under eyes and hats askew. My beloved Mum and Dad are standing right behind me.

Only Fiona was missing, but we were soon to join her in the sunshine as we honeymooned in Bermuda, where she and her husband Chris were living. Riding our mopeds, sailing, swimming, fighting our way through the red land crabs as we made our way to the beach each morning for our swim. At night we would listen to the tree frogs and felt distressed when we saw a lot of them squashed on the roads in the morning. I liked the tree frogs and their night music. One evening there was a plop in Julian's wine glass and a tiny frog appeared, really tiny, the size of my thumb nail, but with huge eyes and suckers on his feet. We fished him out and deposited him at the foot of a tree. I don't know if he was too pissed to clamber up it. The other frogs kept on singing.

We saw a lot of Fiona and Chris and we had barbecues and beach parties and drank a lot of champagne and did quite a lot of the things you are expected to do on honeymoon. I found myself swimming through the turquoise ocean looking at my wedding ring through the water and marvelling that I was now Mrs Glover. I was married to Julian; I was no longer Isla Blair-Hill but Isla Glover. Suddenly I was part of a unit, I belonged, I was now more important to one other person than anyone else in his life. I was safe. I was home and I would never be lonely again.

We returned to London, Julian to do a television play; I was to start rehearsals for Nora in "A Doll's House". I was feeling a bit odd. Not ill, just odd. I knew I couldn't be pregnant. Julian had told me when we met that he was unable to have children. When he and Eileen had failed to have any, they were both tested for fertility to find out that Julian was unlikely to father a child. It must have been a blow to him. But when we married I felt I'd rather be with Julian and not have children than have a child with anyone else. I was young and had no yearning as yet for children. We had never used any contraception. I decided secretly that I should have a pregnancy test. I met Julian at the front door when he arrived back from rehearsal with, "Hello, Daddy." I shall never forget the look on his face.

I spent nine happy, utterly contented months before falling in love for the second time.

TWENTY

Oh, It's You

It was in the hot summer of 1969 at 12.50 pm on July 10th that I met him. This time I knew at once that my life would never be the same again, *I* would never be the same again, for in that moment, that hour, that day, I was reduced to a state of awe and panic, joy, fear and elation. Hot protectiveness flooded through me and love so intense, its fierceness frightened me. I knew that in its power I was capable of anything, of opening bolted doors, running through fire, I knew that it was even capable of killing me. I looked at the sleeping baby with skin like a white fleshed peach, smooth, with tiny white dots the size of pin pricks on his nose, a faint fuzz of blond hair on his round head – not misshapen by the drama and traumas of birth.

He opened his eyes and I swear he peered steadily into my heart. I felt a stab of recognition and said, "Oh, it's you." For this was precisely the person I had been expecting. I had somehow known he was going to be a boy (no scans in those days) and I had called him Jamie for at least six months. And now, here he was, my Jamie. My source of anxiety that would last my life, this boy, my boy was here. I had the not uncommon primal urge that most mothers feel – that I would give up my life for his. I knew in that moment that I would passionately try to protect him from all harm if I could. I think I knew too that I would have to watch as he made his own mistakes, suffered hurts and slights and rejection. I knew that

Isla and Jamie

Photograph by Frazer Wood

part of my love for him was to give him the confidence and strength to be his own man, carve his own path, walk away. I thought of C.Day Lewis again: "Love is proved in the letting go." Of course, I didn't really think that at all. Well, not then. Those thoughts only came with convenient hindsight. In that very moment I was too overwhelmed with love to even face the possibility of being parted from him for an instant.

I think I did know then, though, somewhere deep and far away, that just as I held him close he wasn't really "mine" at all. He was his own person and part of my journey as his mother was to watch the struggles and challenges *his* journey had mapped out for him. As I gazed at him, it seemed impossible that one day he would go to school, that I would hand my precious boy into the hands of strangers. Of course, he could always come home and tell me of his triumphs and failures, his fears and forebodings and he knew I would take his part when the school bully lay in wait for him, when he wasn't picked for the school cricket team... I would be utterly partial and partisan. And that thought took me right back to my parents and a surge of compassion for them, for I knew then how very much they had to give up, give away – when they let me go.

My parents had been concerned when I first told them about Julian, ten years older, married but separated and unable to have children. When I declared, aged twenty-one, that I would rather be with Julian and without children, they must have wondered if I would regret my decision when I was forty-one. I daresay they were sad that I would never give them grandchildren and they must have talked and argued and comforted each other privately, but – after a long discussion one Sunday afternoon – they saw that I was serious and never questioned me on the subject again. They swallowed their doubts and disappointment and, much later, came to love and respect Julian. They were surprised and almost overwhelmed with delight when I told them they were to be grandparents. No-one prepares you for the falling in love that you have with your grandchild and I saw tears in my mother's eyes as Jamie folded his tiny fingers round hers; I know he held a special place in their hearts always.

Jamie's primary school was round the corner from us and when the time came for him to go to secondary school, we faced a problem. The one in our catchment area had a terrible reputation and so we sent him to King's College, Wimbledon, a very good school indeed, but not right for Jamie and he was wretched there. Of course, we took him away. We visited various schools and the one Jamie liked best – and we were equally impressed, mostly by the headmaster – was a co-educational, so–called "progressive" school near Farnham called Frensham Heights. But it would be impossible to do a daily commute to it and the thought of Jamie boarding was unthinkable to me. Admittedly it was only weekly boarding and weekends would be spent at home. Even so, the thought of being parted from him and him possibly being homesick or lonely was unbearable as, unlike me, he wouldn't even have a Fiona to be his companion and protector.

Jamie, however, longed to go there and Julian and I chatted it out over several days that ran into weeks. Eventually Julian said, "Who is this decision for, Isla? For Jamie or for you?"

I felt as if I had been slapped. I was being utterly selfish. What was important was to find a school where Jamie would not only follow the curriculum but would grow in confidence, would find other interests, sport and music, and would learn to respect himself and his colleagues and also learn about self-discipline

Jamie aged 3

and understand how to work for exams, where he would gain friends and have some fun. Frensham Heights was perfect.

He started in the autumn when he was eleven and I felt sick with grief as I waved him goodbye, handing my beloved boy into the hands of people I didn't know, just as my parents had done all those years ago.

As chance would have it, I was touring in a terrible production of a Keith Waterhouse play when Jamie was delivered to his new school. Julian was in Corfu, being the villain in a James Bond film, "For Your Eyes Only". It was my parents who took Jamie there and saw him into his dormitory shared with five other boys. It must have been a painful déjà vu for them, unpacking the trunks with the name-taped towels and sheets and his school clothes all neatly folded, and waving him goodbye as their car sped away down the rhododendron-ed drive (rhododendrons again, as there had been at Kilbryde castle), the blue Surrey hills in the distance the backdrop for his small blonde figure, standing erect, not letting his apprehension show. But, of course, they had seen his wide, round, dark-pupiled eyes, his slightly wobbly chin, as my mother kissed him and my father shook his hand and patted him gently on the shoulder. Jamie, at that age had a marked resemblance to me. Perhaps their little stab of pain was as much for their conker-haired daughter as it was for their vulnerable, strong but sensitive grandson.

I made sure that I was at his school early on each Saturday morning to pick him up and to take him back on Sunday evenings. Weekends became sacrosanct, a time when it was just the three of us, with visits occasionally from Jamie's friends, but a time when we would be together. He was never left at school and there was no play or concert, no cricket or football match that Julian or I did not attend. Being able to support and

277

encourage Jamie became a matter of huge importance and there were jobs I turned down because it meant being away during the holidays or not being able to get back for his weekends. Not different from many working actors really. But I wonder if my need of Julian and Jamie, my need of our family unit, was not coloured by the absence of one when I was a child. I was aware that a protective love of Jamie could be stifling, so when he was accepted for drama school, aged only just eighteen, I remembered my parents allowing me to share a room in London aged only seventeen. They let me go and that was what I would have to do with Jamie. It felt right, it was time, it was his turn to "walk away" and discover the world for himself.

* * * * *

Fiona and I spent our early adulthood apart. I had been used to phoning her with a triumph, with a disappointment, with a rejection, with news of a new boyfriend or a new role. I enjoyed her tales of the hospital ward – pranks and jokes as well as the inevitable sadness that being a nurse brings, however hard you try to stay objective. It seemed strange at first phoning my parents with life's daily occurrences. For so long they had not been party to joys or woes, but it took me less time than I could have imagined for it to become a daily routine and this persisted until each of their deaths 24 years apart.

Fiona married a dark haired "man-of-the-sea" (so I called him), Chris, who had piercing blue eyes and a remarkable resemblance to Paul Newman. The first years of their marriage were spent in Bermuda, where she nursed and he was an officer in the marine police.

When their first daughter, Joanna, was six weeks old, they

travelled to Virgin Gorda, part of the British Virgin Islands which, in 1970, was a "virgin island" – no electricity, no running water and certainly no shops and no doctor. Chris went to fill the post of Harbour Master in the newly opened Little Dix Bay marina. Fiona spent much of her time alone with her new daughter, sometimes literally isolated when the rain washed away the road. She occasionally had misgivings about her pioneer spirit, in the same way our grandmother Sara had trepidations as she stepped out of the dhooli onto the jungle floor that was soon to make way for tea.

I went to visit Fiona when Jamie was six and marvelled at her resilience as she batted away sand crabs and spiders the size of tea cups and steered her daughters (her second, Sara, was a small baby) away from poison apples and sea urchins. One day I had the misfortune to stand on one and the pain that shot up my leg took my breath away. Fiona came to find me and a distressed Jamie on the shore and bundled us into her little beach buggy and drove us to her house where she inquired if I needed a pee. She produced a bowl and urged me to try and I was in too much pain to argue. She placed my foot in the urine in the bowl – her nurse's nous had told her that the acid in the urine would remove the urchin's spines. It did. The strange things you learned as a nurse on an almost desert island. As her children grew, she and Chris decided it was time to return to England for their education. There was never any question of boarding school, sending the girls "home", or any separation. She was central to their lives as their friend, confidante and very much their mother.

When the girls were on the point of leaving school, she returned to nursing. She had various exams to take to bring her up to speed with all the new techniques and approaches

Fiona

and worked in a hospital in Maldon near her home and spent several years on the geriatric wing. She became a ward sister and I know enriched the lives of those she helped and the nurses she encouraged. But as a ward sister she wasn't doing much nursing – just long hours filling in forms or on the computer, responsible for her team, her patients and the ward. She loved her work, was fond of her colleagues and felt more than a little sad when she retired at 60. She now works as a volunteer in a hospice and derives as much pleasure from her grandchildren as I do from mine. She has remained my friend, my heroine really; what older sisters cannot know is that, in their younger sister, they have a fan for life. So it is with us.

TWENTY—ONE

Letting Go

It was poignant for me that I should be playing Kate and singing "I Hate Men" at the Bristol Old Vic when my father became ill. The diagnosis did not take long – lung cancer. All those years of cigarette and pipe smoking in the Men's Bar had finally caught up with him. He had given up the cigarettes years before in India, but he kept up the pipe on his return to England; he enjoyed the ritual of the cleaning, tobacco pouches, endless matches and finally the long, "cool" puff. I am sure it was far from cool and my mother complained that the smoke clung to the curtains in the drawing room. He was taken into hospital to have an operation to remove the offending cancer and one of his lungs. Once he was opened up, however, it was found that the tumour had spread and the removal of the lung was pointless. It was decided he should come home once he had recovered from the operation, have a short course of radiotherapy, but really to pray for a remission and to spend the summer months with us – my mother, Fiona and me.

He was taken into hospital in May 1981. He was seventy-two, I was thirty-six and Jamie was eleven, soon to be twelve. Jamie was close to his grandfather; they shared the same sense of humour and even now he has many of my father's mannerisms. Daddy decided, along with my mother and Fiona (although she asked questions as to the appropriateness of the decision), that the full facts of his illness were not to be revealed to me as it could upset me when I was rehearsing and performing. It was a wrong decision, as it deemed me not strong enough to weather the information and thus excluded me from doctors' opinions and hospital procedures. Of course I knew that my father was gravely ill and likely to die, how could I not? But no one confided in me. It was hurtful to be treated with kid gloves, but it was done from love and concern. Dad had always wanted to help and protect me in my work, finding the concept of going on stage in front of people each evening too terrifying to contemplate – and therefore deciding I must be shielded from upsetting information, supported in every way.

My father's remission lasted a mere three months before his cancer returned, making it hard for him to breath. The last time I saw him, I took hold of his hand and saw that the ring with "Ballo" on it was too big for his finger. I thought of that day long ago when we sat together in the heather looking for golf balls. He died on 27th September 1981, two days before my birthday. My mother's long journey into widowhood had begun and was to last for twenty-four years. She never got used to being without him and although she sometimes had company, she was always alone.

Losing a partner after forty years is a bitter blow and it takes courage to walk into the future with only memories by your side. My mother was never short of courage. She was sustained, I hope, by Fiona and me and our children. She met up every week with her friends, The Girls, and she went on outings to the theatre, to country houses and gardens, but she had no-one to return home to, no-one to tell about her day, no-one to laugh with or complain to. The house, which for a long time held my father's clothes and belongings (she wound his watch ritually every day), was redolent with his memory; sometimes she said she even felt his presence, but she must have been lonely without him. She never complained – why is it loneliness is something shameful to admit to, as if it is somehow your fault? She wasn't good at joining clubs, so the WI was out. She tended her garden in summer and read and listened to the radio in winter, she went shopping most days, just for the trip. On her death, Fiona and I found hoards of shampoo, soap, face powder and tights in her cupboard – a throw-back to the Indian days of stocking up when she was "Home".

We visited her often with Jamie, and Fiona, home from the Caribbean with Chris and their two daughters, Jo and Sara, did the same. She looked forward to these visits and planned the meals with specially chosen wine. I can imagine the melancholy of the clearing up on our departure, emptying the tea cups, plumping the cushions, discarding half eaten biscuits and cake, reminding her of her aloneness after the buzz of activity the day had brought.

However, I remember being surprised when, one evening, having just seen a documentary on TV about a young boy of Army parents being left at boarding school, she expressed sympathy and sadness, "Poor wee boy, he looked so small, so vulnerable, so lonely as he settled into his dormitory trying not to cry."

The little boy was eight and it was indeed moving to watch him, to observe all the little interns coming to terms with their surroundings. I am not sure if she was putting away the similarity of our situations because she didn't want to resurrect her own pain, or if she was acknowledging how lonely and frightening it had been for Fiona and me. I did not ask her. Whatever the reason, it would have been pointless and cruel to chastise her for a decision made long ago in a different political climate and made because it was deemed to be the right one.

We spoke on the telephone daily, sometimes several times a day, and I saw her not as often she would have liked, but she was only an hour's drive away, so I'd drop in for a couple of hours whenever I could. She was becoming more and more immobile and in the last year of her life she had carers twice a day who helped her to dress and undress, got her meals, helped her to the loo and washed her. Her world became smaller and the last few months of her life were not happy and that sits like a weight on my heart; she hated being dependent, she was lonely and, at eighty-eight, wondered why she had lived so long – she had been twenty-four years without my father and she often expressed how she longed to join him. She kept falling out of bed and couldn't get up and it soon became evident to her carers, to Fiona and me and to her, that she could no longer go on living alone. She was fiercely adamant that she would not live with Fiona or with me, however persuasive we might try to be and so she went into a residential home on a temporary basis until a long term decision could be decided upon. She hated it, missed her birds and the foxes in her garden, she found it hard to make friends and, I think when she concluded that this was what her life was to be (she wouldn't hear the brighter alternatives we presented), she turned her face to the wall.

She died in the early hours of April 8th with Fiona and me by her bedside. We spent her last day with her; she was not conscious, but Fiona, who had many years' experience nursing the elderly and being with them when they died, said that hearing was usually the last sense to go. We talked to her and to each other, we reminisced, we laughed over shared family memories and sang to her quietly; "The Road to Mandalay", "The girl that I Marry", "Lovely" and of course, "Love

Walked In", songs we had all sung together when Dad was alive. Her breathing altered and then stopped.

So Fiona and I were orphans. But we had each other. Besides, our Mum and Dad are never too far away – Jamie will scratch his head in the very same manner that my father did when he was puzzled or anxious, his hair grows in the same way and when he walks towards me from a distance. it could be Ian as a young man again. My second little granddaughter, Ava, has my mother's bright blue eyes and her drawn together, quizzical blonde brows and her alabaster pale skin. I answer the phone and as Fiona speaks to me it is my mother's voice I hear, her laugh – and I only have to look at my hands to remember her hands using the same gesture. In the mirror some mornings I see her looking back at me.

No, they are not very far away.

TWENTY–TWO

Looking Back and Forward

Looking back at my life, I ponder on what decisions I've made that were informed by my Indian/Scottish background; if my focus on family is more pronounced because mine was separated during my early growing up. I know that my childhood had many blessings – Ayah and my early Indian influences, Miss Evans enabling me to read, my self-reliance, my close bond with my sister and my parents – loving, even when absent.

I have followed my dream of an acting career that has enabled me to do good, stimulating, challenging work without the manacles of extreme fame to keep me a prisoner and away from the very people I am trying to portray (so many famous actors are unable to travel on a tube, shop in a supermarket). I have journeyed to interesting places all round the world in my work and have met fascinating, generous-hearted people. I have been fortunate to be healthy, with a strong constitution; I've had days I didn't know how I was going to afford Jamie's school meals, let alone pay the mortgage or my income tax, but on the whole I have had money to feed and clothe my family and give us all small treats, if not huge amounts of wealth. (People assume all actors earn vast sums and are astonished when I tell them of the Equity minimum paid to most actors in the West End or the provinces).

As for wisdom, I am still waiting for that. But I feel more

confident in myself, I have learnt to trust my instincts and I hope that I have an open mind, although I have many of the prejudices of late middle age against certain things: body piercing, atonal music, tattoos, the smell of unwashed hair, bad manners, bullying and unkindness, drunken people on Friday nights, CCTV cameras and too many requests to join Facebook. And I prefer to be called an actress rather than an actor – I find no shame in the word actress. All these quibbles are a generational thing, I have no doubt.

I have tried to take rejection on the chin. I've been cut to the quick by clever-dick critics and wounded to the heart by faithless friends and Julian and I have both done things to hurt each other in our long marriage. I've worked with some truly talented actors and some who couldn't really act at all. I've met fascinating people who are stars because of their personalities, unconnected to their work. I've got used to the pejorative term "Lovey" (I've never known anyone use that term in my profession) and kept my lips sealed when even friends say that I can feign any emotion – "She's an actress you know, she can act anything," that because I'm an actress none of my emotions can be real. This irritates more than hurts, an assumption that I must be shallow because I show the emotions of characters outside myself. And I've learnt to tolerate the rudeness of strangers. On a tube train on my way to perform in a matinee of "The History Boys", I was sitting opposite two elderly women who were murmuring to each other about the fact that I had been on TV in a repeat of something the night before. One nudged the other who looked up and said, in the sort of tones that would shatter glasses in Harrods, "Oh, I don't like her." I got off the tube to be met by a greasy haired man in an anorak who said, "Isla, Isla, may I take your photograph? I've got to use up my film." On such occasions, laughter acts as arnica on the bruises of the heart.

On the upside, I have had letters of such kindness from strangers, some telling me that I have made a small difference to their lives by a certain performance; I've even been told that someone wanted a life in the theatre because of something they had seen me in. Such letters are warming and humbling and I feel lucky, because I dare say had they seen the part played by someone else, they would have been just as uplifted, just as moved, but they have taken the time and trouble to thank me. These are rewards not taken lightly.

Being in a theatre company is a very close and bonding experience; you get to know each other fast. People expect it to be a bitchy back-stabbing place, but in truth the bitching usually springs from insecurity or disappointment turned to bitterness and more often there is generosity, kindness, warmth and support amongst colleagues. There needs to be, because we all have to trust each other as we are all inter-dependent.

Anthony Quayle once said to me, "Never envy anybody anything, Isla. You never know what they have to pay for it." It took me a long time to puzzle out what he meant, but I noticed that the person with the brilliant career had a severely autistic child, or an abusive husband, the happy marriage often held a deep sorrow by being childless, the person with genius intelligence was often lonely, the earth mother surrounded by a brood of babes might long for the spotlight she had given up for their sake. We all of us have disappointments and blessings – it's a question of balance. For nothing stays the same, all things change and although one hopes one is ready for the change, it's often a shock when it comes – the up or the down.

Getting to know my parents as a young adult brought

surprises – and comforts, too. All through my growing up, I observed their love and respect for each other. I don't know how much of that rubbed off on me, but my greatest blessing of all was meeting Julian when I did. I admire and respect him as an actor and as a man. I value my friendship with him and cherish his love. We laugh together, share many opinions and always seem to have a lot to say to each other.

Julian is very romantic. He observes hints put out for Christmas and birthdays – indeed, on my 50th birthday he did something so touching it still brings tears to my eyes. In the early autumn of 1994 I would go each day to our local picture gallery and look at a painting by Sue Campion that spoke to me, in the way that paintings sometimes do, and made me smile. Five girls in green dresses and jaunty berets dancing with such joy and unselfconscious abandon, it couldn't help but lift your spirits. I loved it. On September 29th Julian had arranged a dinner party to be held in a private room at our local restaurant, Sonnys, and about twenty really close chums came. The birthday menu had been chosen by Julian from all the things I enjoyed – so, of course, no fish. Halfway through the meal, one of my friends pointed to a painting on the wall of the private room and there were "my girls" in their jaunty berets dancing. "Oh," I said, "that is my favourite painting!" Julian looked at me and said smiling, "I think you had better take it home." It hangs on the wall of our stairs and each day continues to make me smile.

I remember chatting to Jamie about Julian's signet ring with the Glover crest on it. "When you are eighteen, you will get a ring like this – all the men in the Glover family get a ring like this when they come of age," said Julian.

"What if Jamie had been a girl – would she have got the Glover ring?"

"Oh no," came the reply, "only the men in the family wear this ring."

My feminist feathers were ruffled and a pretty hot row ensued.

A year later, on our ninth wedding anniversary, Julian and I decided we would have a blessing on our marriage at St Mary le Bow church – just us, Jamie, my parents and Julian's mother (Fiona and Chris were still in the Virgin Islands). As we entered the church, to my astonishment, I found it full of our friends and decorated with an abundance of white and cream flowers.

When the moment arrived that the vicar spoke the words, "With this ring I thee wed..." Julian placed the Glover signet ring with its crest and motto *"Surgite Lumen Adest* on my finger. I wear it always, even on stage.

What I hadn't expected was my grand-daughters. Through the nine years of Jamie's former marriage there was no hint or sign of children. It would have been impertinent and heartless to make any enquiries; it just didn't happen and I hugged to myself the disappointment in what appeared to be a grandchild-less future. I was overwhelmed on occasion with sadness, almost grief – sometimes to the point of tears, which I spilled in shameful secret – looking at families with children shopping at the local farmer's market on Saturday mornings. I'd peer through the window of the crèche at my gym and watch with full and heavy heart the children laughing and playing, when I knew I'd never have that, I'd never have loving hugs or sticky kisses from little people who would be mine to cherish and protect and love with no conditions at all.

Then Jamie met the love of his life in Sasha, one of the most artlessly beautiful women I have ever met. She is also fiercely intelligent and warm and generous of spirit. He went through anguish at the break-up of his marriage, but knew that Sasha was the person he had to be with. It wasn't long before Edie, my first granddaughter, was born, who swept my heart up with a blink of her very long eyelashes and held it fast in the grip of her tiny fist. We spent much time together, chatting amiably, in her local park (the chat was rather one-sided), as I pointed out squirrels and birds and flowers and occasionally a miraculous red sunset, a black storm cloud or a rainbow. I would weave stories about everything and became a rabbit (with my voice), a mole, a fox, a dog. We went on journeys with our imaginations and had many adventures and a great deal of fun. Two and a half years later Ava-Rose came quietly and with little fuss into the world. She was pale and fair with eyes that held the beauty of summer skies. People kept on saying her blue eyes would fade, but they have remained bright, piercing; she looks as if she holds the mystery of the universe in her round blonde head and will impart its secret to us, her chosen few, when she chooses to bestow it upon us. She has a smile that will melt hearts, and she wakes each morning laughing.

With both children to delight and absorb me, I find their presence brings me more joy than most theatrical roles. I have a twinge of regret that I never played some of the great roles, Juliet, Lady Macbeth, Hedda Gabler, Cleopatra – but then, I did get to play many others – Viola, Miss Julie, Nora, both Vivie and Mrs Warren and countless others and I felt a sense of propriety about them all. It's balance again – things even out.

My real regret is that my parents never met my grand-girls, especially my mother, who was witness to my tearful congratulations to Fiona on receiving the news that her eldest daughter, Joanna, was pregnant. I was so glad for her, properly, joyously glad, but that grandchild-less part of me was envious and stricken. My mother knew this – how glad she would be to know that I have not one granddaughter, but two.

Being without my parents as a little girl didn't scar or wound me, not in any depth. It made me glad of them when they came home, when we became reacquainted, and it has made me consciously pleased and fiercely protective and grateful for my own family. I treasure each day with them, sometimes turning down work in order to spend time with them; and it is not a sacrifice, it is just something I need to do.

It is hardly novel to say that I can't believe that I have an old ladies' bus pass, for most people of my age feel the same – we feel young in spirit and, if we are lucky, we are not too stiff and doddery of body. But now my conker-coloured hair owes more to the skill of my hairdresser than to any pigment bestowed by nature. The Missy Baba Isla of India has gone and the young girl who shared a dressing room and a two-day film shoot with Paul McCartney has gone, as has the ambitious actress and the young mother, proud, fierce and doting; all have shed their seven-year skins and I'm left with me, made up of little fragments and pieces of all the Islas that have breathed since September 1944.

I can't imagine leaving this world, but leave it I will, bequeathing, I hope, memories and smiles for Julian, Jamie and Sasha, Edie and Ava and, of course, Fiona, and echoes of me – a tune, a smell, a sight – that will nudge them into thinking of me. And who can ask more than that?

Isla

Postscript

Edie and I climbed the rickety loft ladder that led to our dusty attic. She was only three, so Julian stood beneath her holding the ladder as she clambered up, ready to catch her if she fell. We were to seek out the Beatrix Potter books my mother had kept in her attic for fifty years. We opened the black steel trunk together which still had "Blair-Hill Not Wanted on Voyage" painted on the top in white letters. Inside was my mother's wedding veil and the pearl and lily of the valley headdress she had worn at her marriage and the lavender blue bonnet and Edwardian style dress I had worn at mine. Edie tried on the bonnet and we laughed as it fell over her eyes. We found the silver horseshoe that had been tied to our car as Julian and I sped away after our reception. And there were the books in a shoe box, little scuffed, scratched books, some scribbled on by my five year old self, and on the cover of them my mother had written "This book belongs to Isla Blair-Hill."

Inside "Jemima Puddle Duck", my favourite, on my favourite page – the one with foxgloves and the fox looking cunning and Jemima looking sweet and foolish – was a flat little bulge wrapped in yellowing, Bronco lavatory paper. I unpeeled the fragile tissue-y covering and there inside, was a flattened, dry, almost grey, marigold – Ayah's farewell marigold. I imagined its pungent, tangy sweetness and Ayah's coconut hair oil – but there was no scent at all, just a strange mouldy dustiness.

"What is it, Raderah?" asked Edie.

"It was once an orange flower, a marigold that was given to me in India by someone I loved very much."

I unpeeled it from its fifty-seven-year-old wrapping and it crumbled between my fingers, stiff dark brown shards of petals disintegrating into powder. I rolled the remaining fragments between my fingers and settled them into the little groove of the wispy paper and then Edie and I blew it into the rafters of the attic and watched the thin veil of powder settle on the cobwebs on the eaves and on the pink insulation foam of the roof: a tiny piece of India resting here in my house in Barnes.

We carefully climbed down the ladder, Edie still in my blue bonnet. I closed the door to the loft and followed her into the golden autumn light to pick up the windfall apples and pears in my English garden.

Glossary

The spelling of these words is my own,
as I have only heard them spoken.

arni – elephant
ayah – nanny
bandicoot – large rat
beedee – type of Indian
  cigarette.
betel nut – chewed like
  tobacco, producing
  red liquid
burra–peg – large measure
  of alcohol
chokra – butler
chota–peg – small measure
  of alcohol
chupplis – sandals,
  flip–flops
cumbli – blanket
cutcha – haphazard
dhobi – laundry man
dhooli – chairs carried
  between two poles
dhoti – man's sarong
goosle – bath
goosle kawasti – bath time
krait – small poisonous
  snake
lili – bed
juldi juldi – quickly, quickly

Malayalam – Indian
  language, ethnic group.
maradadi – over the top,
  glitzy
matey – kitchen help
meen – fish
nimbu–pani – lime juice
  and soda
peri–dori – Manager
perria pamba – big snake
perria pulli – tiger
poochi – insect
pow – tiny, mean measure
  of alcohol
pulli – panther
pyti – mad
salaam – greeting
sari – woman's dress
sena–dori – Assistant
  Manager
shikaar – shooting, hunting
syce – stable boy
Tamil – language spoken
  in Kerala, ethnic group
tapal – post
tiffin – lunch
topee – pith helmet

COIMBATORE DISTRICT

UDUMALPET TALUK

Perottu Malai △ 2252

Kumarikkal

Anamallai Reserved Forest

National Park

2552

Iravikulam

Malayattur Reserved Forest

2695 △ Anaimudi

VAGAVI

TAL

RAJAMALLAY DIVN

NYAMAKAD

KADALAAR

KANNIAMALLAY

TH

PERIAVURRAI

MAD

o Mankulam

Instant Tea Factory

NULLATANNI
Munnar Town

GRAHAMSL

KALAAR

Mannankandam
Village

LETCHMI

SEVENMALLAY

CHOKANAD

Ottaparai Ridge △ 1856

PULLIVASAL

Pallivasal Village

To Cochin, Kottayam etc.

To Idukki

216